Autodesk® InfraWorks® 2020 Engineering Design

Learning Guide

Imperial Units - 1st Edition

ASCENT - Center for Technical Knowledge®
Autodesk® InfraWorks® 2020
Engineering Design
Imperial Units - 1st Edition

Prepared and produced by:

ASCENT Center for Technical Knowledge
630 Peter Jefferson Parkway, Suite 175
Charlottesville, VA 22911

866-527-2368
www.ASCENTed.com

Lead Contributor: Jeff Morris

ASCENT - Center for Technical Knowledge is a division of Rand Worldwide, Inc., providing custom developed knowledge products and services for leading engineering software applications. ASCENT is focused on specializing in the creation of education programs that incorporate the best of classroom learning and technology-based training offerings.

We welcome any comments you may have regarding this guide, or any of our products. To contact us please email: feedback@ASCENTed.com.

© ASCENT - Center for Technical Knowledge, 2019

All rights reserved. No part of this guide may be reproduced in any form by any photographic, electronic, mechanical or other means or used in any information storage and retrieval system without the written permission of ASCENT, a division of Rand Worldwide, Inc.

The following are registered trademarks or trademarks of Autodesk, Inc., and/or its subsidiaries and/or affiliates in the USA and other countries: 123D, 3ds Max, Alias, ATC, AutoCAD LT, AutoCAD, Autodesk, the Autodesk logo, Autodesk 123D, Autodesk Homestyler, Autodesk Inventor, Autodesk MapGuide, Autodesk Streamline, AutoLISP, AutoSketch, AutoSnap, AutoTrack, Backburner, Backdraft, Beast, BIM 360, Burn, Buzzsaw, CADmep, CAiCE, CAMduct, Civil 3D, Combustion, Communication Specification, Configurator 360, Constructware, Content Explorer, Creative Bridge, Dancing Baby (image), DesignCenter, DesignKids, DesignStudio, Discreet, DWF, DWG, DWG (design/logo), DWG Extreme, DWG TrueConvert, DWG TrueView, DWGX, DXF, Ecotect, Ember, ESTmep, FABmep, Face Robot, FBX, Fempro, Fire, Flame, Flare, Flint, ForceEffect, FormIt 360, Freewheel, Fusion 360, Glue, Green Building Studio, Heidi, Homestyler, HumanIK, i-drop, ImageModeler, Incinerator, Inferno, InfraWorks, Instructables, Instructables (stylized robot design/logo), Inventor, Inventor HSM, Inventor LT, Lustre, Maya, Maya LT, MIMI, Mockup 360, Moldflow Plastics Advisers, Moldflow Plastics Insight, Moldflow, Moondust, MotionBuilder, Movimento, MPA (design/logo), MPA, MPI (design/logo), MPX (design/logo), MPX, Mudbox, Navisworks, ObjectARX, ObjectDBX, Opticore, P9, Pier 9, Pixlr, Pixlr-o-matic, Productstream, Publisher 360, RasterDWG, RealDWG, ReCap, ReCap 360, Remote, Revit LT, Revit, RiverCAD, Robot, Scaleform, Showcase, Showcase 360, SketchBook, Smoke, Socialcam, Softimage, Spark & Design, Spark Logo, Sparks, SteeringWheels, Stitcher, Stone, StormNET, TinkerBox, Tinkercad, Tinkerplay, ToolClip, Topobase, Toxik, TrustedDWG, T-Splines, ViewCube, Visual LISP, Visual, VRED, Wire, Wiretap, WiretapCentral, XSI.

NASTRAN is a registered trademark of the National Aeronautics Space Administration.

All other brand names, product names, or trademarks belong to their respective holders.

General Disclaimer:

Notwithstanding any language to the contrary, nothing contained herein constitutes nor is intended to constitute an offer, inducement, promise, or contract of any kind. The data contained herein is for informational purposes only and is not represented to be error free. ASCENT, its agents and employees, expressly disclaim any liability for any damages, losses or other expenses arising in connection with the use of its materials or in connection with any failure of performance, error, omission even if ASCENT, or its representatives, are advised of the possibility of such damages, losses or other expenses. No consequential damages can be sought against ASCENT or Rand Worldwide, Inc. for the use of these materials by any third parties or for any direct or indirect result of that use.

The information contained herein is intended to be of general interest to you and is provided "as is", and it does not address the circumstances of any particular individual or entity. Nothing herein constitutes professional advice, nor does it constitute a comprehensive or complete statement of the issues discussed thereto. ASCENT does not warrant that the document or information will be error free or will meet any particular criteria of performance or quality. In particular (but without limitation) information may be rendered inaccurate by changes made to the subject of the materials (i.e. applicable software). Rand Worldwide, Inc. specifically disclaims any warranty, either expressed or implied, including the warranty of fitness for a particular purpose.

AS-IFW2001-END1IM-SG // IS-IFW2001-END1IM-SG

Contents

 © 2019, ASCENT - Center for Technical Knowledge®

© 2019, ASCENT - Center for Technical Knowledge®

© 2019, ASCENT - Center for Technical Knowledge®

Preface

The *Autodesk® InfraWorks® 2020: Engineering Design* guide is designed for people using any of the following software packages:

- Autodesk® InfraWorks®
- Autodesk® Architecture, Engineering and Construction Collection

The guide provides you with a fundamental knowledge of the accelerated design process that uses data-rich 3D models with high-end visualizations. This enables you to create, evaluate, and better communicate 3D site plan proposals for faster approvals.

Topics Covered

- Roadway Design:
  - Create property boundaries for parcels, easements, and right-of-ways
  - Create and modify design roads with precise parameters
  - Add components and decorations to roads
  - Adjust roadside grading
  - Apply and review superelevations in component roads
  - Modify how design roads intersect using a standard intersection or roundabout
  - Optimize the vertical design of a roadway
  - Create gradient maps based on selected feature sets to identify areas with low impact for site or corridor optimization
  - Find an optimal horizontal design of the roadway which yields a cost effective and environmentally-friendly solution
  - Run traffic simulation to analyze and animate design traffic
- Bridge Design:
  - Add bridges to a design roadway
  - Work with bridge deck and girder cross sections
  - Perform analysis and design checks on all the pre-stressed girders of your bridge

- Drainage Design:
  - Run a watershed analysis
  - Create or modify culverts
  - Create a pavement drainage network
  - Analyze the pavement drainage network
- Point Cloud Modeling:
  - Preparing the point cloud
  - Create a terrain from a point cloud
  - Create features from a point cloud

Prerequisites

- Access to the 2020.0 version of the software, to ensure compatibility with this guide. Future software updates that are released by Autodesk may include changes that are not reflected in this guide. The practices and files included with this guide might not be compatible with prior versions (i.e., 2019).

Note on Software Setup

This guide assumes a standard installation of the software using the default preferences during installation. Lectures and practices use the standard software templates and default options for the Content Libraries.

Students and Educators can Access Free Autodesk Software and Resources

Autodesk challenges you to get started with free educational licenses for professional software and creativity apps used by millions of architects, engineers, designers, and hobbyists today. Bring Autodesk software into your classroom, studio, or workshop to learn, teach, and explore real-world design challenges the way professionals do.

Get started today - register at the Autodesk Education Community and download one of the many Autodesk software applications available.

Visit www.autodesk.com/education/home/

Note: Free products are subject to the terms and conditions of the end-user license and services agreement that accompanies the software. The software is for personal use for education purposes and is not intended for classroom or lab use.

© 2019, ASCENT - Center for Technical Knowledge®

Lead Contributor: Jeff Morris

Specializing in the civil engineering industry, Jeff authors training guides and provides instruction, support, and implementation on all Autodesk infrastructure solutions.

Jeff brings to bear over 20 years of diverse work experience in the civil engineering industry. He has played multiple roles, including Sales, Trainer, Application Specialist, Implementation and Customization Consultant, CAD Coordinator, and CAD/BIM Manager, in civil engineering and architecture firms, and Autodesk reseller organizations. He has worked for government organizations and private firms, small companies and large multinational corporations and in multiple geographies across the globe. Through his extensive experience in Building and Infrastructure design, Jeff has acquired a thorough understanding of CAD Standards and Procedures and an in-depth knowledge of CAD and BIM.

Jeff studied Architecture and a diploma in Systems Analysis and Programming. He is an Autodesk Certified Instructor (ACI) and holds the Autodesk Certified Professional certification for Civil 3D and Revit.

Jeff Morris has been the Lead Contributor for *Autodesk InfraWorks: Engineering Design* since 2019.

© 2019, ASCENT - Center for Technical Knowledge®

In this Guide

The following images highlight some of the features that can be found in this guide.

Link to the practice files

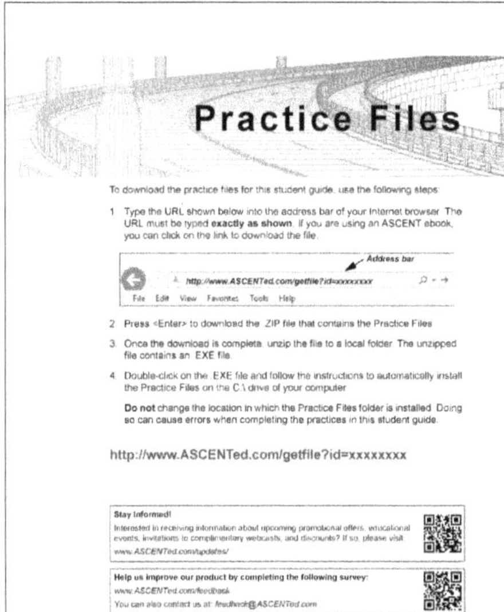

Practice Files

To download the practice files for this student guide, use the following steps:

1. Type the URL shown below into the address bar of your Internet browser. The URL must be typed **exactly as shown**. If you are using an ASCENT ebook, you can click on the link to download the file.

2. Press <Enter> to download the .ZIP file that contains the Practice Files.
3. Once the download is complete, unzip the file to a local folder. The unzipped file contains an .EXE file.
4. Double-click on the .EXE file and follow the instructions to automatically install the Practice Files on the C:\ drive of your computer.

   Do not change the location in which the Practice Files folder is installed. Doing so can cause errors when completing the practices in this student guide.

http://www.ASCENTed.com/getfile?id=xxxxxxxx

Stay Informed!
Interested in receiving information about upcoming promotional offers, educational events, invitations to complimentary webcasts, and discounts? If so, please visit:
www.ASCENTed.com/updates/

Help us improve our product by completing the following survey:
www.ASCENTed.com/feedback
You can also contact us at: *feedback@ASCENTed.com*

Practice Files

The Practice Files page tells you how to download and install the practice files that are provided with this guide.

Chapter 1

Getting Started

In this chapter you learn how to start the AutoCAD® software, become familiar with the basic layout of the AutoCAD screen, how to access commands, use your pointing device, and understand the AutoCAD Cartesian workspace. You also learn how to open an existing drawing, view a drawing by zooming and panning, and save your work in the AutoCAD software.

Learning Objectives in this Chapter

- Launch the AutoCAD software and complete a basic initial setup of the drawing environment.
- Identify the basic layout and features of AutoCAD interface including the Ribbon, Drawing Window, and Application Menu.
- Locate commands and launch them using the Ribbon, shortcut menus, Application Menu, and Quick Access Toolbar.
- Locate points in the AutoCAD Cartesian workspace.
- Open and close existing drawings and navigate to file locations.
- Move around a drawing using the mouse, the **Zoom** and **Pan** commands, and the Navigation Bar.
- Save drawings in various formats and set the automatic save options using the **Save** commands.

Learning Objectives for the chapter

Chapters

Each chapter begins with a brief introduction and a list of the chapter's Learning Objectives.

Side notes

Side notes are hints or additional information for the current topic.

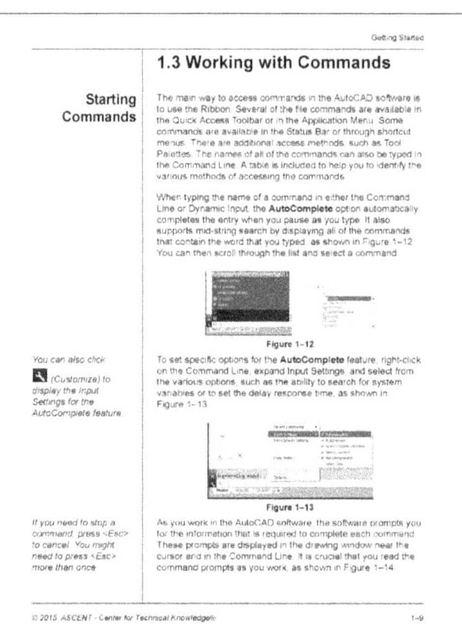

Getting Started

1.3 Working with Commands

Starting Commands

The main way to access commands in the AutoCAD software is to use the Ribbon. Several of the file commands are available in the Quick Access Toolbar or in the Application Menu. Some commands are available in the Status Bar or through shortcut menus. There are additional access methods, such as Tool Palettes. The names of all of the commands can also be typed in the Command Line. A table is included to help you to identify the various methods of accessing the commands.

When typing the name of a command in either the Command Line or Dynamic Input, the **AutoComplete** option automatically completes the entry when you pause as you type. It also supports mid-string search by displaying all of the commands that contain the word that you typed, as shown in Figure 1–12. You can then scroll through the list and select a command.

Figure 1–12

You can also click (Customize) to display the Input Settings for the AutoComplete feature.

To set specific options for the **AutoComplete** feature, right-click on the Command Line, expand Input Settings, and select from the various options, such as the ability to search for system variables or to set the delay response time, as shown in Figure 1–13.

Figure 1–13

If you need to stop a command, press <Esc> to cancel. You might need to press <Esc> more than once.

As you work in the AutoCAD software, the software prompts you for the information that is required to complete each command. These prompts are displayed in the drawing window near the cursor and in the Command Line. It is crucial that you read the command prompts as you work, as shown in Figure 1–14.

© 2015, ASCENT - Center for Technical Knowledge® 1–9

Instructional Content

Each chapter is split into a series of sections of instructional content on specific topics. These lectures include the descriptions, step-by-step procedures, figures, hints, and information you need to achieve the chapter's Learning Objectives.

Practice Objectives

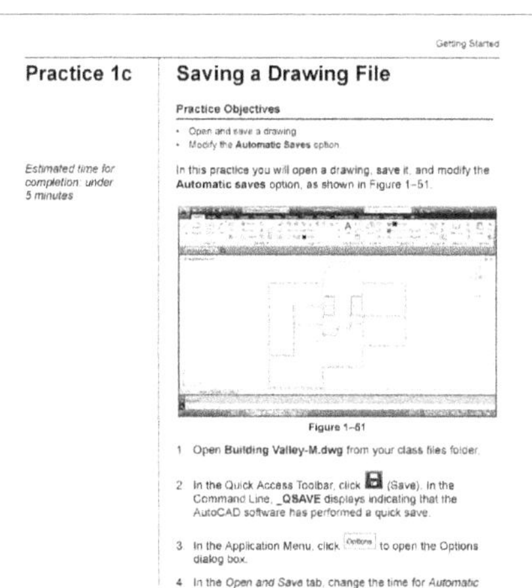

Getting Started

Practice 1c **Saving a Drawing File**

Practice Objectives

- Open and save a drawing
- Modify the **Automatic Saves** option

Estimated time for completion: under 5 minutes

In this practice you will open a drawing, save it, and modify the **Automatic saves** option, as shown in Figure 1–51.

Figure 1–51

1. Open **Building Valley-M.dwg** from your class files folder.
2. In the Quick Access Toolbar, click (Save). In the Command Line, **_QSAVE** displays indicating that the AutoCAD software has performed a quick save.
3. In the Application Menu, click Options to open the Options dialog box.
4. In the *Open and Save* tab, change the time for *Automatic save* to **15** minutes.

Practices

Practices enable you to use the software to perform a hands-on review of a topic.

Some practices require you to use prepared practice files, which can be downloaded from the link found on the Practice Files page.

Getting Started

Chapter Review Questions

1. How do you switch from the drawing window to the text window?
   a. Use the icons in the Status Bar.
   b. Press <Tab>.
   c. Press <F2>.
   d. Press the <Spacebar>.
2. How can you cancel a command using the keyboard?
   a. Press <F2>.
   b. Press <Esc>.
   c. Press <Ctrl>.
   d. Press <Delete>.
3. What is the quickest way to repeat a command?
   a. Press <Esc>.
   b. Press <F2>.
   c. Press <Enter>.
   d. Press <Ctrl>.
4. To display a specific Ribbon panel, you can right-click on the Ribbon and select the required panel in the shortcut menu.
   a. True
   b. False
5. How are points specified in the AutoCAD Cartesian workspace?
   a. X value x Y value

Chapter Review Questions

Chapter review questions, located at the end of each chapter, enable you to review the key concepts and learning objectives of the chapter.

© 2019, ASCENT - Center for Technical Knowledge®

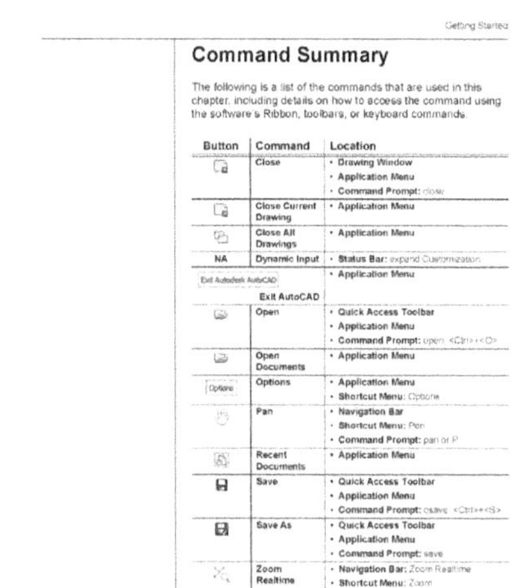

Getting Started

Command Summary

The following is a list of the commands that are used in this chapter, including details on how to access the command using the software's Ribbon, toolbars, or keyboard commands.

Button	Command	Location
	Close	• **Drawing Window** • **Application Menu** • **Command Prompt:** close
	Close Current Drawing	• **Application Menu**
	Close All Drawings	• **Application Menu**
NA	Dynamic Input	• **Status Bar:** expand Customization
Exit Autodesk AutoCAD	Exit AutoCAD	• **Application Menu**
	Open	• **Quick Access Toolbar** • **Application Menu** • **Command Prompt:** open, <Ctrl>+<O>
	Open Documents	• **Application Menu**
Options	Options	• **Application Menu** • **Shortcut Menu:** Options
	Pan	• **Navigation Bar** • **Shortcut Menu:** Pan • **Command Prompt:** pan or P
	Recent Documents	• **Application Menu**
	Save	• **Quick Access Toolbar** • **Application Menu** • **Command Prompt:** qsave, <Ctrl>+<S>
	Save As	• **Quick Access Toolbar** • **Application Menu** • **Command Prompt:** save
	Zoom Realtime	• **Navigation Bar:** Zoom Realtime • **Shortcut Menu:** Zoom

Command Summary

The Command Summary is located at the end of each chapter. It contains a list of the software commands that are used throughout the chapter, and provides information on where the command is found in the software.

© 2019, ASCENT - Center for Technical Knowledge®

Practice Files

To download the practice files for this guide, use the following steps:

1. Type the URL shown below into the address bar of your Internet browser. The URL must be typed **exactly as shown**. If you are using an ASCENT ebook, you can click on the link to download the file.

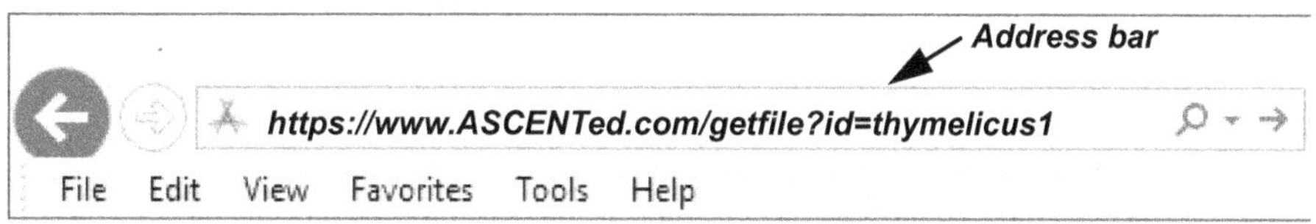

2. Press <Enter> to download the .ZIP file that contains the practice files.
3. Once the download is complete, unzip the file to a local folder. The unzipped file contains an .EXE file.
4. Double-click on the .EXE file and follow the instructions to automatically install the practice files on the C:\ drive of your computer.

   Do not change the location in which the practice files folder is installed. Doing so can cause errors when completing the practices.

   The default practice files folder location is:
   C:\InfraWorks Design Practice Files

https://www.ASCENTed.com/getfile?id=thymelicus1
https://www.ASCENTed.com/getfile?id=thymelicus2
https://www.ASCENTed.com/getfile?id=thymelicus3

Stay Informed!

Interested in receiving information about upcoming promotional offers, educational events, invitations to complimentary webcasts, and discounts? If so, please visit:

www.ASCENTed.com/updates/

Help us improve our product by completing the following survey:

www.ASCENTed.com/feedback

You can also contact us at: *feedback@ASCENTed.com*

 © 2019, ASCENT - Center for Technical Knowledge®

Creating Component Roads

There are two types of roads that can be created in the Autodesk® InfraWorks® software: conceptual roads (existing roads) and component roads (proposed design roads). You can use the component roads to add engineering parameters to road designs and the rule-based tool sets to lay out a preliminary roadway design. During the creation process, you can instantly visualize the designed road in context with its surroundings. In this chapter, you learn how to set design speeds, adjust curve radii, and improve traffic flows through detailed interchanges and roundabouts.

Learning Objectives in this Chapter

- Create right of ways and easements for road corridors.
- Design an engineered road with precise design parameters (such as design speed, tangent length, and specific curve radii).
- Modify the horizontal layout of a component road.
- Modify the vertical layout of a component road.
- Add superelevations to a component road.
- Modify how two component roads intersect using the Intersection asset card or stack.

1.1 Parcels, Right of Ways, and Easements

Before a road can be built, it is important to ensure that the proper permissions are legally granted to anyone planning on using the road. This is done by will, by deed, or by contract. An easement grants the right to use property that is owned by another. Easements are most often used to deliver utilities (e.g., water, sewer, electrical, etc.) to parcels. Right of ways are easements that permit a person to travel or pass through a parcel of land that is not owned by the traveler. Easements on a deed generally remain with the land in perpetuity, while a right of way is often granted with an explicit expiration (25 years).

Information about existing right of ways, easements, and parcel boundaries can be obtained from the local recorders office or other government entities. Several government agencies provide electronic files representing parcel boundaries (in the form of Geographic Information data) either for free or for a small fee.

Import Property Boundaries

Some right of ways have been put aside by government agencies for road development for years. In cases like this, it is necessary to import existing property boundaries to ensure that your road proposals stay within the designated corridors. Importing parcel, easement, and right of way data is no different than importing any other GIS data. Once imported and configured, parcels, easements, and right of ways are listed in the Model Explorer under Area of Interest. Once imported, you can view existing and proposed surface contours within the property boundaries and control the contour intervals.

How To: Import Existing Parcel Boundaries

1. In the In Canvas tools, click (Build, manage, and analyze your infrastructure model)> (Create and manage your model)> (Data Sources).
2. In the Data Sources panel, expand (Add file data source) and select the type of file required, as shown in Figure 1–1.

© 2019, ASCENT - Center for Technical Knowledge®

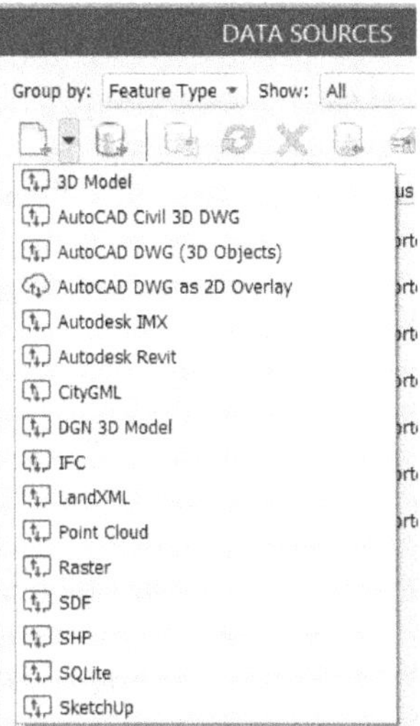

Figure 1–1

3. Select the file containing the property boundary data. Click **Open**.
4. In the Data Sources explorer, double-click on the property boundary layer to open the Data Source Configuration dialog box.
5. Set the *Type* to **Parcels**, **Easements**, or **Right of Ways**, as shown in Figure 1–2, then check the following:
   - On the *Geo Location* tab, confirm that the *Coordinate System* is set correctly.
   - On the *Source* tab, set the *Draping Options* and set *Clip to model extent*, as required.
   - On the *Table* tab, fill in as many table fields as you can.

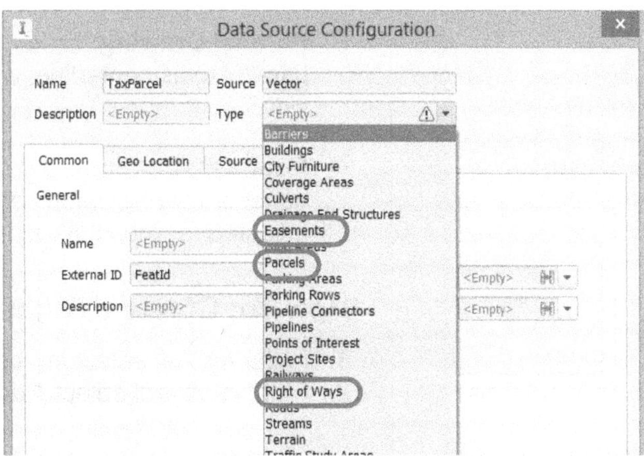

Figure 1–2

6. Click **Close & Refresh**.

Create Parcels and Easements

If electronic versions of the property boundaries are not available, you might need to manually create a parcel or easement. This can be done using the tools that are available in the (Design, review and engineer roads) tool.

How To: Manually Create Parcels or Easements

1. In the In Canvas tools, expand (Design, review and engineer roads)> (Design roadways), and click either (Parcels) or (Easements), as required.
2. In the model, click the first vertex for the starting point of the property boundary.
3. Move the cursor in the direction of the next vertex. If you know the required distance, type it and press <Enter> to lock in the distance. Click to set the vertex when the angle seems correct.
4. Repeat Step 3 for all but the last vertex.
5. Move the cursor in the direction for the last vertex. If you know the required distance, type it and press <Enter> to lock in the distance. Double-click to set the last vertex when the angle looks correct.

Create Right of Ways

You create right of ways (ROW) slightly different than parcels and easements. When drawing a ROW, there are three options:

- **Free-Form Shape:** Enables you to create free-form polygons.
- **Parallel Drawing:** Enables you to offset an existing feature parallel to its centerline, with equal or varying values on each side.
- **Road Offset:** Enables you to select a road to offset with equal or varying values on each side. The length can also be adjusted for the ROW as required.

How To: Create a Right of Way from a Road

1. In the model, select the component road.
2. Right-click and select **Add Right of Way**.

© 2019, ASCENT - Center for Technical Knowledge®

How To: Manually Create a Right of Way

1. In the In Canvas tools, expand (Design, review and engineer roads)> (Design roadways), and click  (Right of Ways).
2. In the model, click the starting point centerline for the ROW.
3. Move the cursor in the direction of the next centerline vertex. If you know the required distance, type it and press <Enter> to lock in the distance. Click to set the centerline vertex when the angle looks correct.
4. Repeat Step 3 for all but the last centerline vertex.
5. Move the cursor in the direction of the last centerline vertex. If you know the required distance, type it and press <Enter> to lock in the distance. Double-click to set the last vertex when the angle looks correct.

Display Contours

The advantage of adding parcels, easements, and right-of-ways to the model is that you can display the existing or proposed ground contours in them. This helps improve terrain visualization and better understand the drainage and slope on the site. Once a parcel is created or imported, select the boundary. In its asset card, toggle on the contours and set their interval, as shown in Figure 1–3.

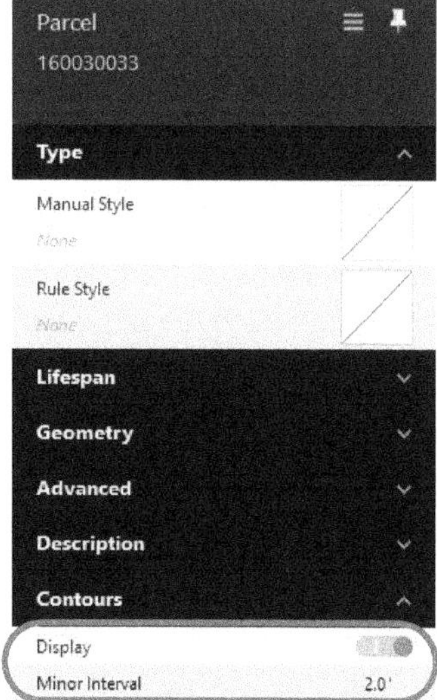

Figure 1–3

Practice 1a Work with Parcels

Practice Objectives

- Import existing parcel lines from GIS data.
- Create right of ways for the new roads.

In this practice, you will import GIS data provided by the city and configure it as parcels. You will then create new right of ways for proposed roads.

Task 1 - Import and configure existing parcel boundaries.

1. In the Home Screen, click **Open**.
2. In the *C:\InfraWorks Design Practice Files\RoadwayDesign* folder, select **DesignRoad.sqlite** and click **Open**.
3. In the Utility Bar, click (Bookmark) and select **ProjectArea**. Ensure that **A_Task1** is the current proposal.
4. In the In Canvas tools, click (Build, manage, and analyze your infrastructure model)> (Create and manage your model> (Data Sources).
5. In the Data Sources panel, expand (Add file data source) and select **SHP** for the type of file, as shown in Figure 1–4.

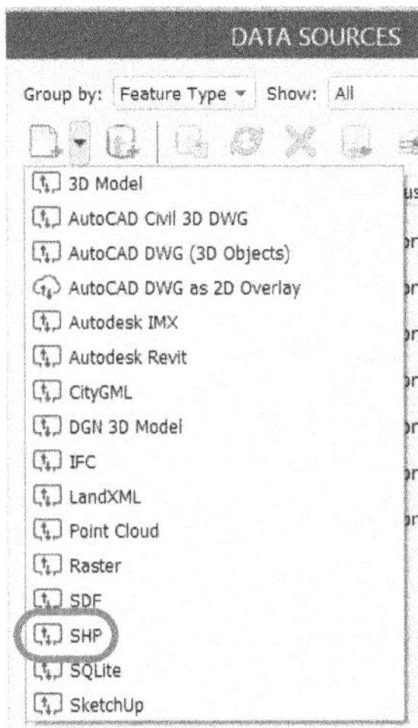

Figure 1–4

© 2019, ASCENT - Center for Technical Knowledge®

6. Browse to *C:\InfraWorks Design Practice Files\Shape Files*, select **TaxParcel.shp** and click **Open**.

7. In the Data Sources explorer, double-click on the **TaxParcel**[1] layer to open the Data Source Configuration dialog box. Set the following parameters, as shown in Figure 1–5:
   - *Type:* **Parcels**
   - *Geo Location* tab, *Coordinate System*: **UT83-CF**
   - *Source* tab, *Draping Options*: **Drape**
   - *Source* tab: **Clip to model extent**
   - *Table* tab, *Name*: **PARCEL_NO**
   - *Table* tab, *Description*: **ACREAGE**
   - *Table* tab, *Tag*: **OWNERNAME**
   - *Table* tab, *User Data*: **MKT_CNTVAL**

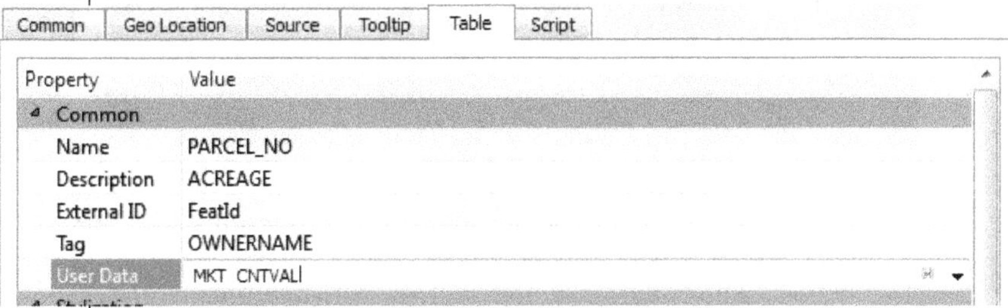

Figure 1–5

8. Click **Close & Refresh**.

9. In the Utility Bar, click (Control visibility, display, and selectability of features) to open the Model Explorer.

10. Make sure the Parcels layer under Area of Interest is turned on, as shown in Figure 1–6.

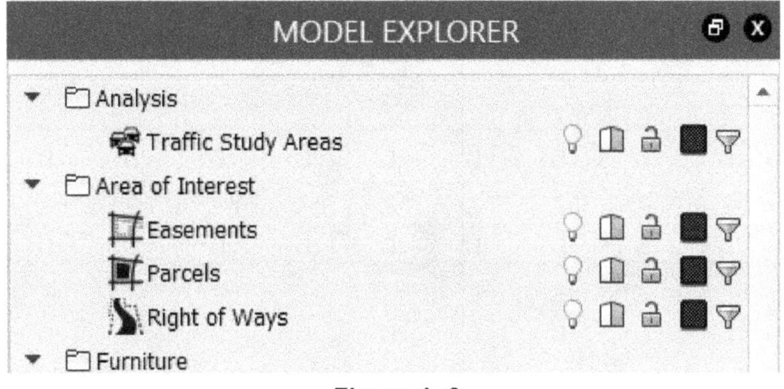

Figure 1–6

1. (Department, GIS Division of the Utah County Information Systems, 2013)

© 2019, ASCENT - Center for Technical Knowledge®

11. In the model, select the parcels shown in Figure 1–7, one at a time, by clicking on their border lines. In their asset cards, toggle on the contour display for each one.

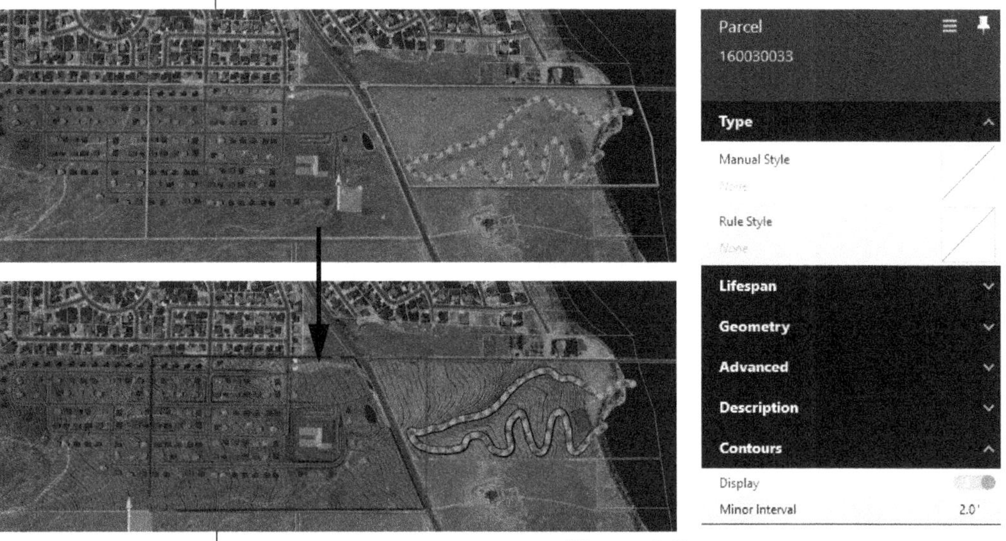

Figure 1–7

12. Press <Esc> to release the last parcel.

© 2019, ASCENT - Center for Technical Knowledge®

Task 2 - Create a right of way from a road.

1. In the model, select the component road shown in Figure 1–8.

Figure 1–8

2. Right-click and select **Add Right of Way**.
3. Press <Esc> to release the selection.
4. In the Utility Bar, click (Control visibility, display, and selectability of features).
5. In the Model Explorer, click (Layer Visible) to the right of Parcels to toggle them off. This causes both the parcel lines and the contours to be hidden.

1.2 Creating Component Roads

Component roads are used to create design roads in InfraWorks. Component roads follow two sets of standards: Road Design Standards, which are preprogrammed into the software, and Project Design Standards, which are manually input by you.

The Road Design Standards parameters are set when creating the model in the New Model dialog box, under the *Design Standards* section, as shown in Figure 1–9. The American Association of State Highway and Transportation Officials (AASHTO) design criteria is the most commonly used standard within the United States of America. In addition to setting the standards, you can set the driving direction for the road to be the left or right side of the road. Alternately, if the Design Standards were not set when creating the model, you can set them during the design process using the Model Properties dialog box, as shown in Figure 1–10. You can also set the driving direction for the road to be the left or right side of the road here.

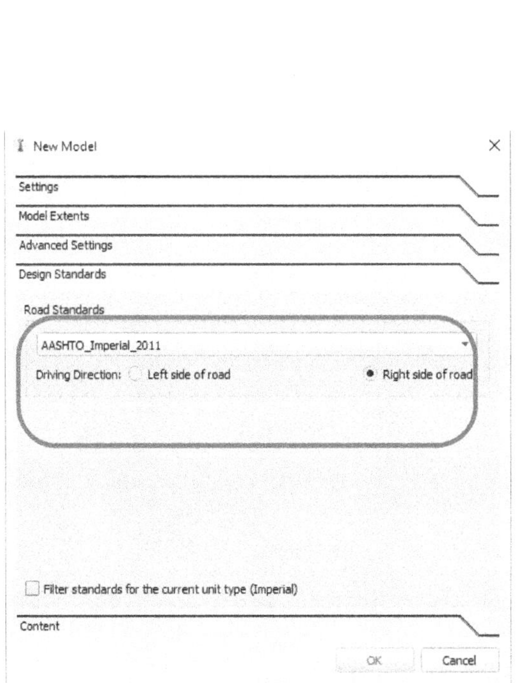

Figure 1–9

Figure 1–10

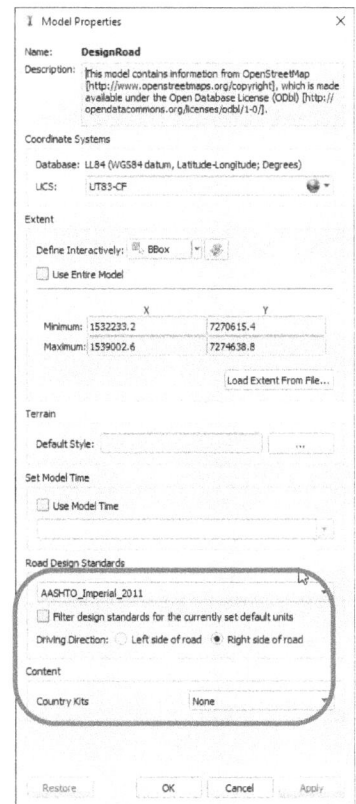

© 2019, ASCENT - Center for Technical Knowledge®

Component Roads provide much more flexibility and control when designing roads than conceptual roads. They enable you to add, delete, and modify each component of the road (lanes and curbs) separately, as shown in Figure 1–11.

This means that you do not have to create a new road style for every minor change to the road cross section. If conceptual roads already exist in the model, you can convert them into a component road. When a conceptual road is converted to a component road, the following occurs:

- The number of lanes and their track width are preserved.
- All component depths are set to the default 0.2 meters for lanes and sidewalks.
- The track top surface category material is applied to the entire component when converting from a conceptual road style.

Figure 1–11

Hint: Upgraded Models

Earlier versions of InfraWorks software contained both Design roads and Component roads. When opening a model that contains the earlier design roads, they are automatically converted to component roads. The original design road styles are matched to component road assemblies which makes the upgrade process seamless.

Road Function

Selecting the correct road function is a crucial part of setting the design parameters. Four road functions are available in the road asset card, as shown in Figure 1–12. The road function automatically sets the default design speed to be used for the roadway design.

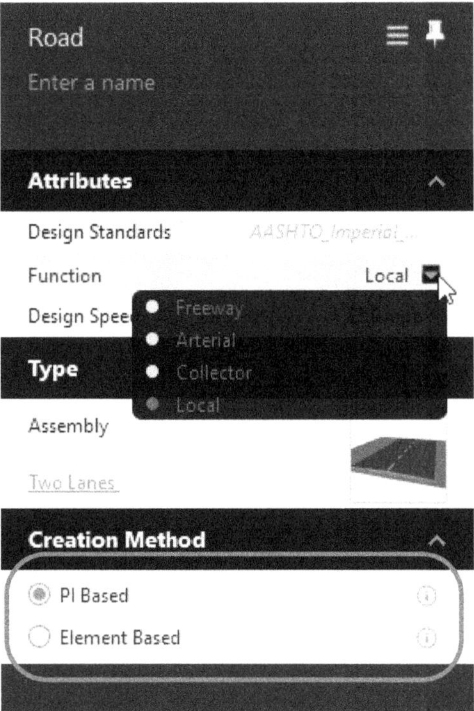

Figure 1–12

The Design speed is the maximum speed that the road is designed for, and should not be confused with the legally permitted travel speed. The default design speed for a roadway depends upon the function of the road being designed. A full list of the available options is shown in the table below.

Road Function	Maximum Design Speed
Highway Roads	70 mph
Arterial Roads	50 mph
Collector Roads	40 mph
Local Roads	30 mph

© 2019, ASCENT - Center for Technical Knowledge®

If a road's design speed changes, you can change it during the creation process by typing the new speed in the *Speed* field that displays next to the cursor, as shown in Figure 1–13. Or you can change it in the Design Road asset card, anytime the road is selected.

Figure 1–13

Horizontal Curves and Spirals

The design speed property of a roadway sets the minimum and maximum permitted curve radius and spiral lengths for a given point of intersection (PI) along a roadway. The default curve type is set to *Spiral Curve Spiral*. To change the curve type used at a PI, right-click on the curve to display a fly-out menu, shown in Figure 1–14. As you set the PI's, tangent lines (which project all of the way to the actual point of intersection) display in white, curves display in green, and spirals display in magenta. Geometry dimensions also appear, as shown in Figure 1–14.

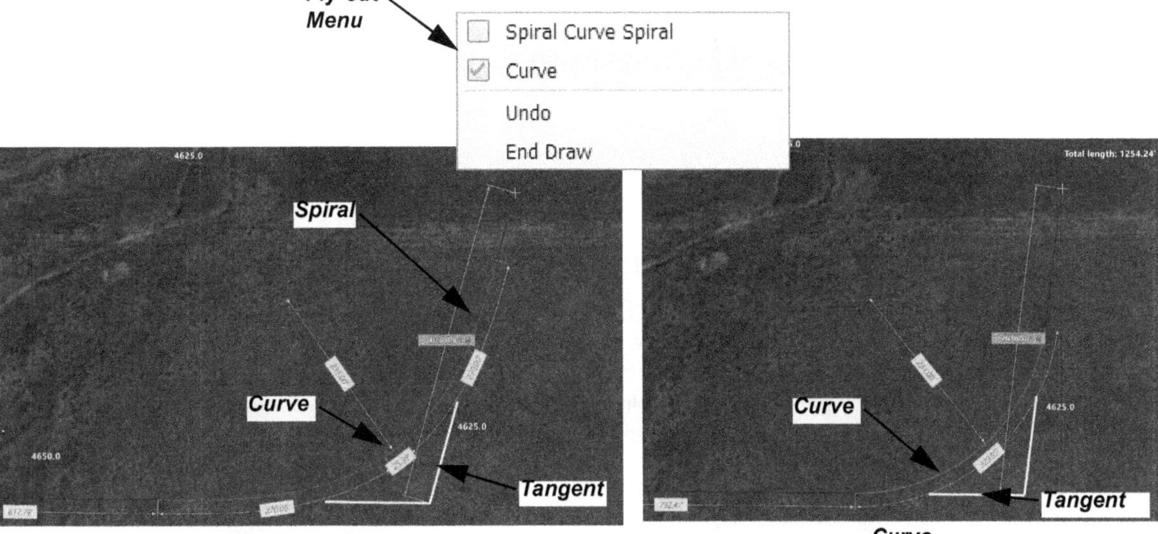

Spiral Curve Spiral ***Curve***

Figure 1–14

How To: Convert a Conceptual Road to a Component Road

1. In the model, select a conceptual road.
2. Right-click on the conceptual road and select **Convert to Component Road**, as shown in Figure 1–15.

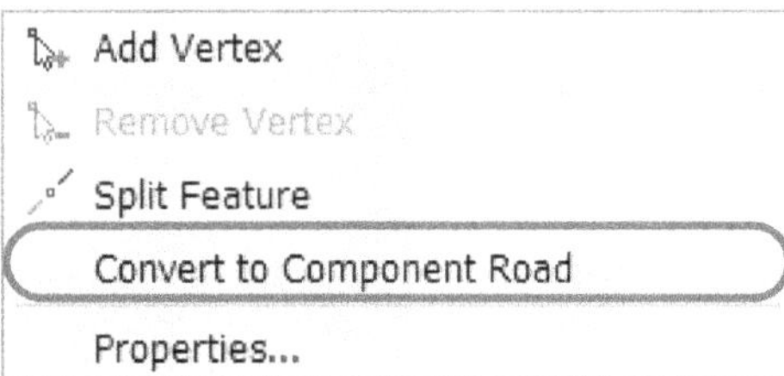

Figure 1–15

Hint: Interoperability with Autodesk Civil 3D Roads

Roads that you import from the Autodesk Civil 3D software or from an .IMX file automatically become component roads. When you open an InfraWorks model in Civil 3D which has component roads, the roads include surfaces and subassemblies. Roads with spiral curves in Civil 3D maintain their spiral types when brought into InfraWorks but cannot be changed.

How To: Create a Component Road from Scratch

1. In the In Canvas tools, click (Design, review and engineer roads)> (Design roadways)> (Component Roads).
2. In the Road asset card, select the following (as shown in Figure 1–18):

   Creation Method (two options to chose from):

   - PI Based: Pick points for the points of intersections along the centerline of the road, as shown in Figure 1–16. The InfraWorks software automatically places lines, curves or spirals for you according to the function and design speed.

 © 2019, ASCENT - Center for Technical Knowledge®

- Element Based: Click to place the endpoints of objects (tangents and curves) along the centerline of the road, as shown in Figure 1–17.

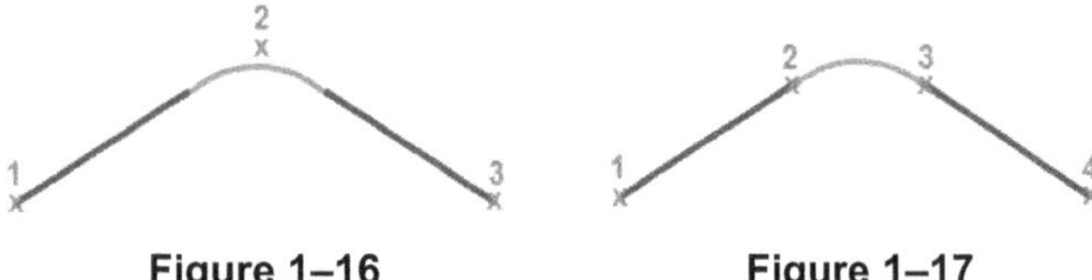

Figure 1–16 **Figure 1–17**

Type: Click on the assembly name to change which assembly the road uses.

Attributes:

- Select the appropriate function for the component road.
- Modify the Design Speed as necessary.

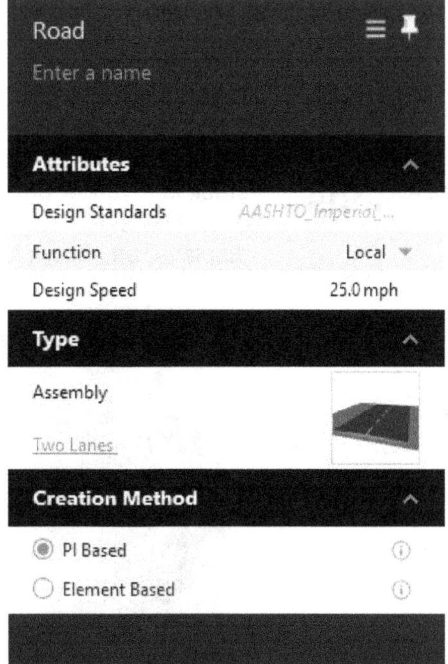

Figure 1–18

3. In the model, click to set the starting point of the new roadway.
4. In the model, move the cursor toward the next PI or Element. Type a design speed and distance in their respective fields, and then press <Enter> to set the values. Click to set the second PI or Element end-point when the angle looks correct.

5. In the model, move the cursor in the direction toward the next PI or Element and then right-click to display the curve options.
6. According to the project requirements, select **Curve** or **Spiral Curve Spiral** for the transition between tangents, as shown in Figure 1–19.

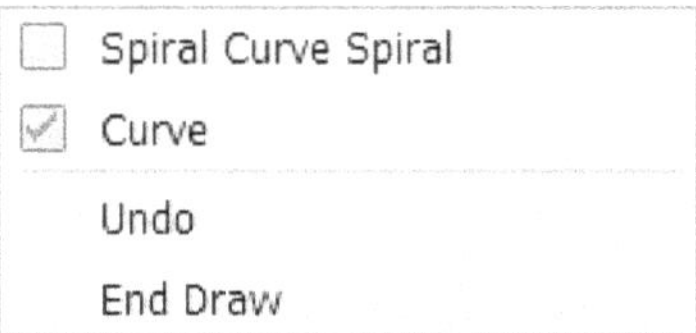

Figure 1–19

7. Repeat Steps 5 to 6 until all except the last horizontal PI is set for the roadway design.
8. Double-click to set the last point or right-click and select **End Draw**.

Design Standard Warnings

When a specific component of the road is selected, the road component stack displays a warning if the component violates the selected design standards. Initially, all that displays in the stack is a yellow bar next to the component. When you hover over the field in the stack, more information about the error displays, as shown in Figure 1–20.

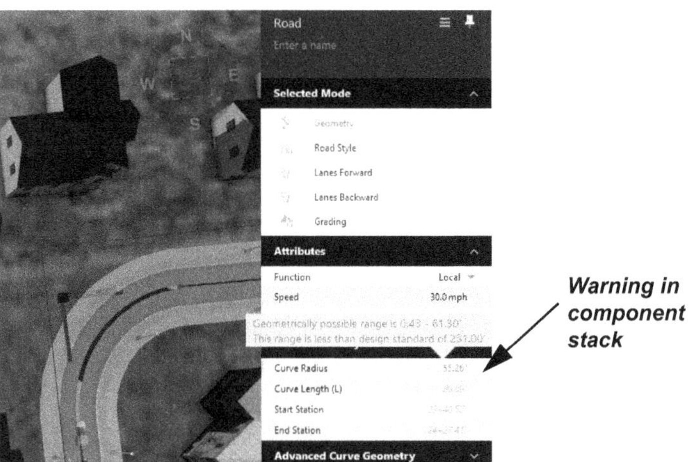

Figure 1–20

© 2019, ASCENT - Center for Technical Knowledge®

Add Detail to Component Roads

Not every road is created the same. Typical road cross sections vary according to their location and use. A freeway has a much different cross section than a local road. Even local road cross sections can vary as the road crosses into a new governing jurisdiction. Consider the following examples:

- One city might require a meandering sidewalk for pedestrians and bikes, while another might have bike lanes that are adjacent to vehicular traffic.
- One city might require a curb and gutter, while another might not, as shown in Figure 1–21.
- One area of a city might require a specific type of street light, while another area might require something different, as shown in Figure 1–21.
- One soil type may allow for a 2:1 slope for the daylight lines, while other soil types might require a more gradual slope.

Figure 1–21

When working with component roads, you can add new components (sub-assemblies) and decorations as required along specific stations. In addition, you can easily change entire assemblies along component roads and the grading of the daylight lines as the road crosses different soil types.

How To: Add Components to a Component Road

1. In the model, select the component road.
2. Right-click on the component road and select **Insert Road Component**.
3. In the Select Component asset card, select the assembly you want to insert.

© 2019, ASCENT - Center for Technical Knowledge®

4. In the model, proceed as follows:
   - Place the cursor so that the orange line is located where the new component belongs, as shown in Figure 1–22.
   - Double-click to place the component and end the command.
   - Alternatively, you can click once to place the component, and then adjust the length using the component's gizmo, as shown in Figure 1–23. Once you have adjusted the component's length, press <Esc> to end the command.

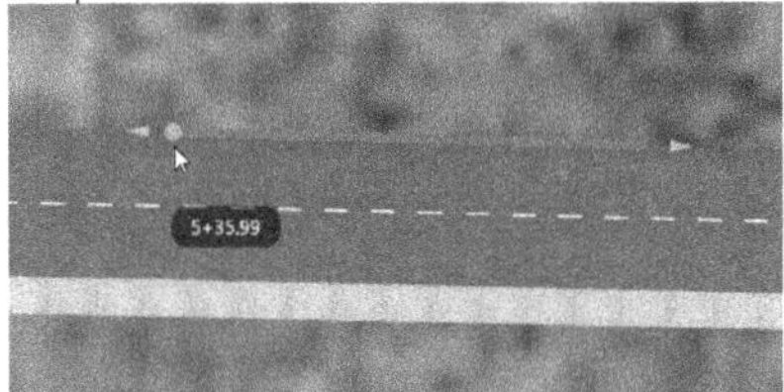

Figure 1–22

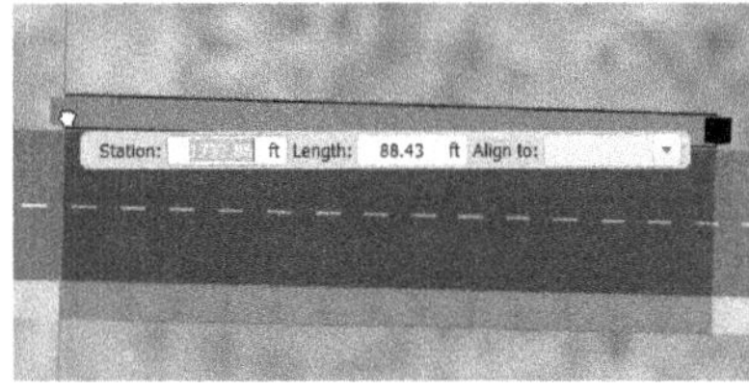

Figure 1–23

   - When adjusting a component's length, you can have it snap to the Start of road, as shown in Figure 1–24, or to the End of road.

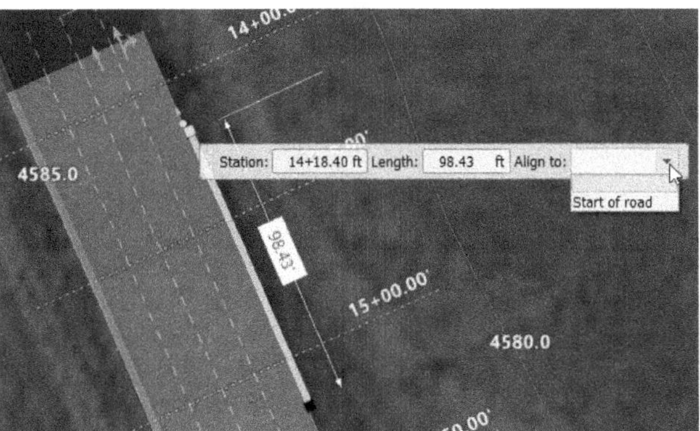

Figure 1–24

© 2019, ASCENT - Center for Technical Knowledge®

5. Select the new component and make any required changes to its length using the component's gizmo. Also make any required changes to its properties using its stack, as shown in Figure 1–25.

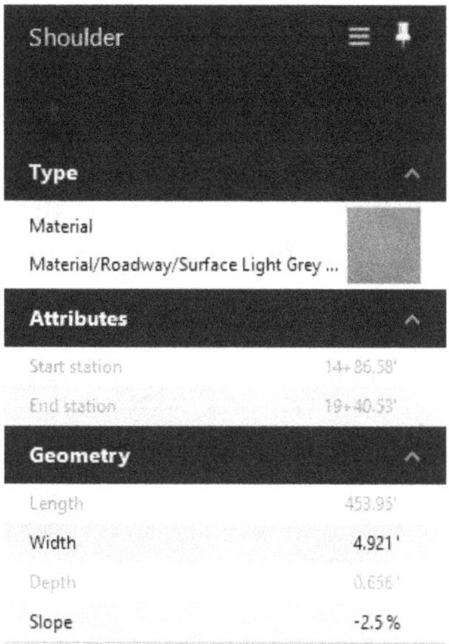

Figure 1–25

6. Press <Esc> to clear the selection of the component.

How To: Add Decorations to Component Roads

Hint: You can use the filter at the top to narrow your search for decorations.

1. In the model, select the component road.
2. Right-click on the component road and select **Place Decorations**.
3. In the Select Decoration asset card, select the city furniture you wish to insert.
4. In the model, place the cursor so the orange line is located where the new decoration belongs and then double-click to place the component.

© 2019, ASCENT - Center for Technical Knowledge®

5. Select the new component and make any required changes to its length using the component's gizmo. Also make any required changes to its properties using its stack, as shown in Figure 1–26.

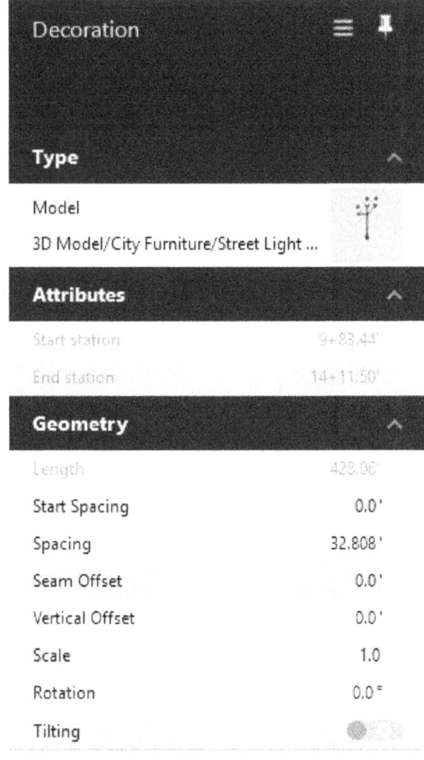

Figure 1–26

6. Press <Esc> to clear the selection of the component.

Reuse Assemblies

Once you create a component road assembly, you can save it for reuse on other roads.

How To: Save an Assembly for Reuse

1. In the model, select the component road you wish to reuse.
2. Right-click on the component road and select **Add to Library**.
3. In the model, click to select a cross section of the component road to add to the library.
4. In the Add To Library asset card, type a name and press <Enter>.

 © 2019, ASCENT - Center for Technical Knowledge®

Practice 1b Create a Component Road

Practice Objectives

- Replace a sketched road with a component road in order to apply design parameters to it.
- Create a component road from scratch.

In this practice, you will create a new proposal. You will then turn an existing sketched road into a component road in order to add engineering parameters. Finally, you will add a new component road to access the future parking lot for the white water park.

Task 1 - Convert a sketched road to a component road.

1. In the Home Screen, click **Open**.
2. In the *C:\InfraWorks Design Practice Files\RoadwayDesign* folder, select **DesignRoad.sqlite** and click **Open**.
3. In the Utility Bar, click (Bookmark) and select **ProjectArea**. Ensure that **B_Task1** is the current proposal.
4. In the Utility Bar, expand *Proposal* and select **Add**.
5. In the Add New Proposal dialog box, type **DesignRoad** for the name and click **OK**.
6. In the model, select the road shown in Figure 1–27.

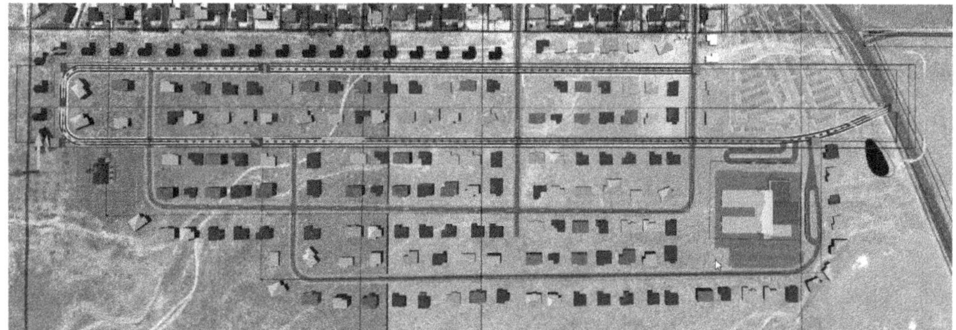

Figure 1–27

7. Right-click on the road and select **Convert to Component Road**, as shown in Figure 1–28.

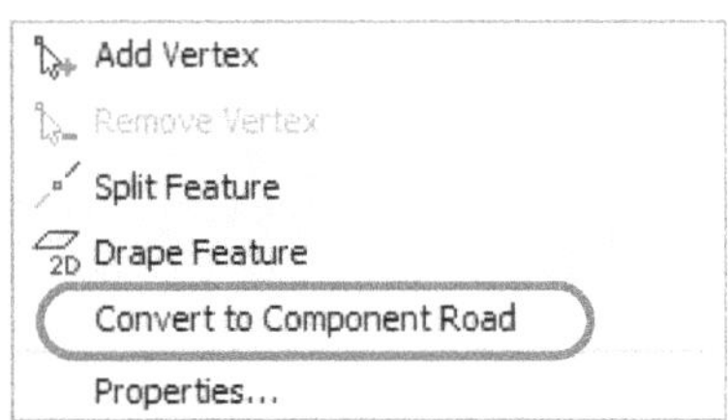

Figure 1–28

8. In the Road asset card that displays, expand the *Attributes* area and ensure that *Function* is set to **Local**, as shown in Figure 1–29.

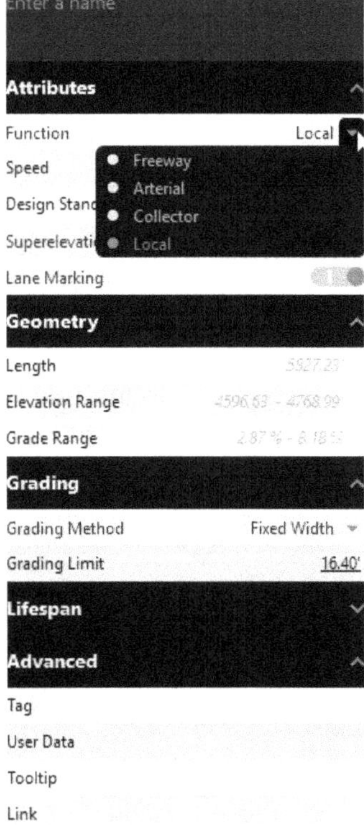

Figure 1–29

9. Press <Esc> to release the road selection.

10. In the Utility Bar, click (Bookmark) and select **School**.

11. In the model, select the carpool lane north of the school that was imported from the Autodesk Civil 3D software.

© 2019, ASCENT - Center for Technical Knowledge®

12. In the Road asset card, expand the *Attributes* area and set the *Function* to **Local**.

13. In the *Speed* field, type **25**.

14. Press <Esc> to clear the road selection.

15. In the Utility Bar, click (Bookmark) and then select **River**.

16. In the model, select **S Redwood Rd.** (shown in Figure 1–30).

Figure 1–30

17. Right-click on the road and select **Convert to Component Road**.

18. In the Road asset card that displays, expand the *Attributes* area and set the *Function* to **Collector**, as shown in Figure 1–31.

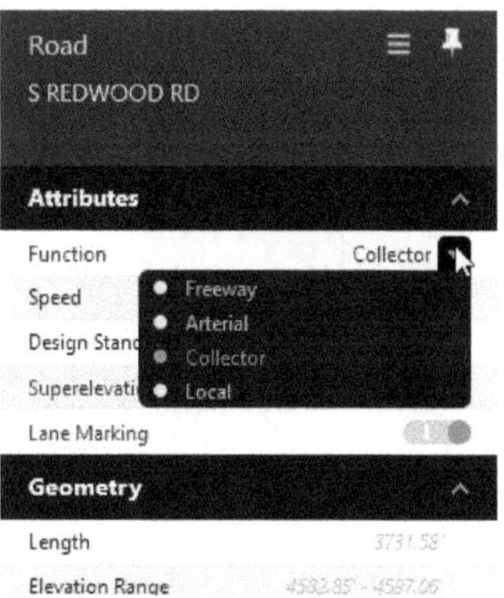

Figure 1–31

19. In the *Speed* field, type **45**.

20. Press <Esc> to clear the road selection.

Task 2 - Create a new component road.

In this task, you will create a new component road. POI (Point of Interest) tacks have been placed to help you pick the points of intersection (PIs).

1. Continue working in the same model as the last task. If you did not complete the last task, in the Utility Bar, expand *Proposal* and select **B_Task2** to make it current.
2. In the Utility Bar, click (Bookmark) and select **River**.
3. In the In Canvas tools, click (Design, review and engineer roads)> (Design roadways)> (Component Roads).
4. Under Creation Method, select **PI Based**. Under Type, click the Assembly name to select a different assembly.
5. In the Select Assembly asset card, select **Component>Assembly>Two Lanes**, as shown in Figure 1–32.

Figure 1–32

© 2019, ASCENT - Center for Technical Knowledge®

6. In the model, click to set the starting point of the new roadway at the **Point 1** POI tack shown in Figure 1–33.

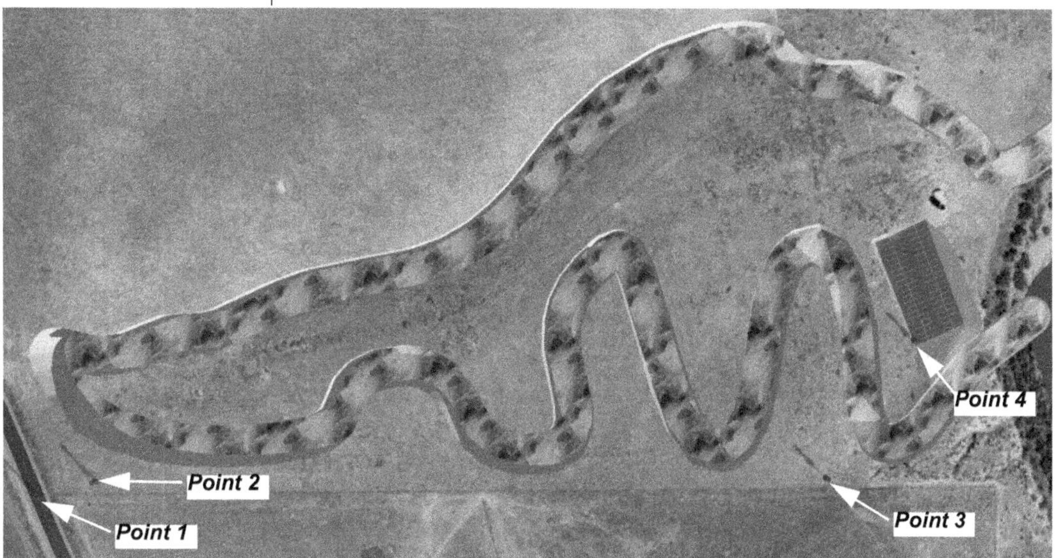

Figure 1–33

7. In the model, move the cursor to the east and click on the **Point 2** POI tack shown in Figure 1–33.

8. In the model, complete the following steps to place the third PI:
   - Move the cursor to the east near **Point 3**.
   - Right-click and select **Curve** from the menu.
   - Click on the **Point 3** POI tack shown in Figure 1–33.

9. Keeping the same curve type, double-click on the **Point 4** POI tack shown in Figure 1–33 to complete the road.

Task 3 - Add detail to a component road.

In this task, you will remove components, then add components and decorations to S Redwood Rd.

1. Continue working in the same model as the last task. If you did not complete the last task, in the Utility Bar, expand *Proposal* and select **B_Task3** to make it current.

2. In the Utility Bar, click (Bookmark) and select **3-WayIntersection**.

3. In the model, select **S Redwood Rd**. Click on one of the shoulders on the outside edges of the road. Right-click and select **Delete Component**. Repeat this for both sides of the road and the eastern center lane, as shown in Figure 1–34.

Be careful when deleting the extra lane at the center line. Ensure that you select the lane and not the road. You can tell by looking at the asset card that displays.

Remove Shoulders and eastern center lane

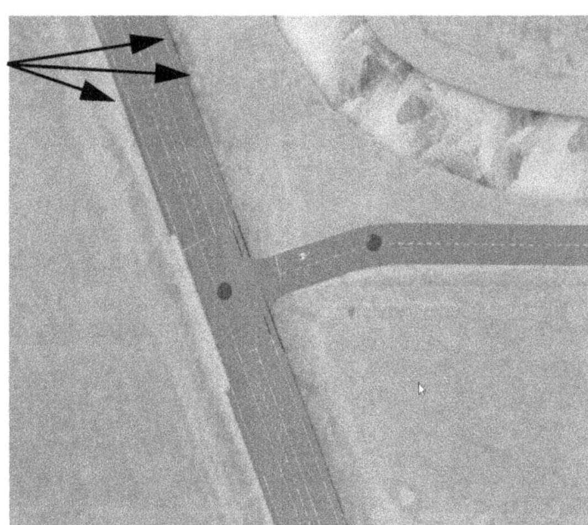

Figure 1–34

4. Select the remaining center lane. In the Lane stack, change the *Width* to **12**.

5. There are additional lanes with a width of 0.25' behind the stripes, as shown in Figure 1–35. These lanes must be removed to avoid issues, if you require a roundabout or add any lane beyond them. Click on one of the lanes found behind the stripes. Right-click and select **Delete Component**. Repeat this process to remove all lanes found behind the stripes.

© 2019, ASCENT - Center for Technical Knowledge®

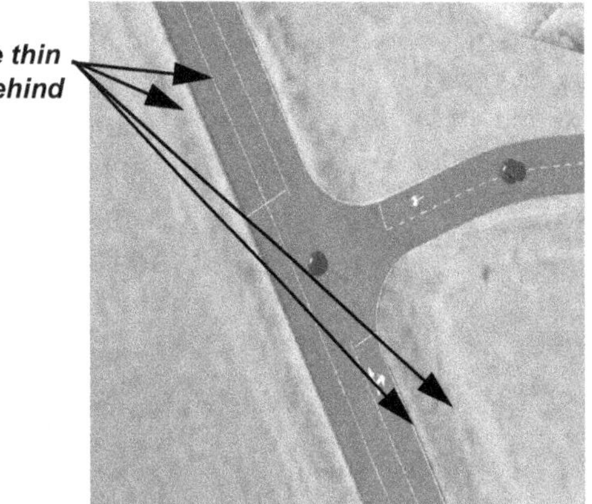

Figure 1–35

6. Right-click on S Redwood Rd. and select **Insert Road Component**.
7. In the Select Component asset card, select the **Lane** assembly.
8. In the model, do the following:
   - Place the cursor so the orange line is located on the far east side of the road, south of the intersection, as shown in Figure 1–36. Click once to place the lane.
   - Adjust the assembly length and transition lengths using the four gizmos, as shown in Figure 1–37.

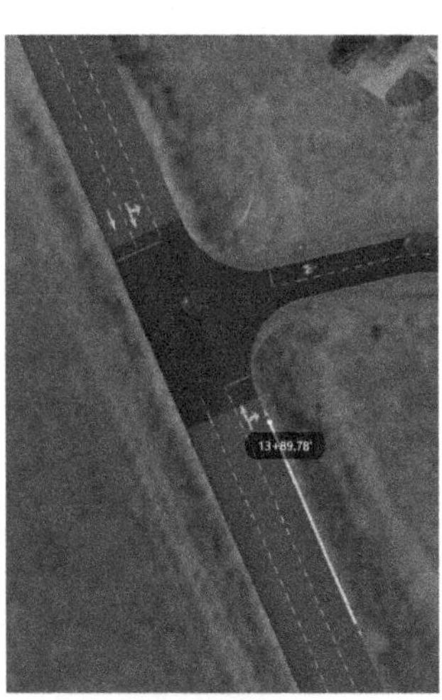

Figure 1–36

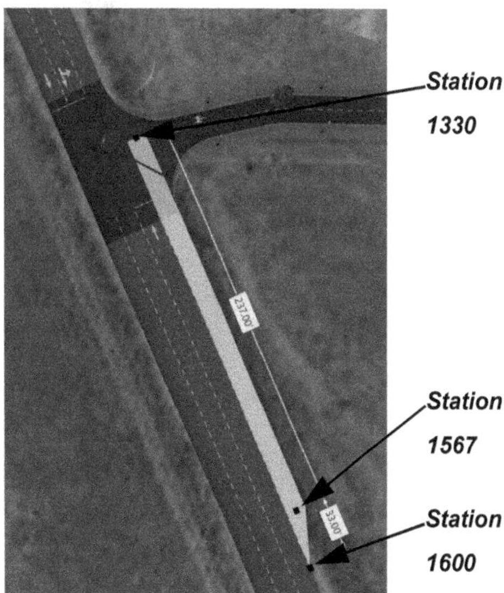

Figure 1–37

© 2019, ASCENT - Center for Technical Knowledge®

Hint: In between adding each component, you might need to press <Enter> to accept the station ranges, then <Esc> to deselect the component and select the road.

9. Repeat Steps 6 to 8 to add the following components, as shown in Figure 1–38.
   - Add the **Curb & Gutter** assembly to both edges of the road from **Start of road** to **End of road**.
   - Add the **Sloped Grass Median** to both sides of the road from **Start of road** to station **1650 with a 50' transition**.
   - Add the **Sidewalk** assembly to both sides of the road from **Start of road** to station **1600** with a **0'** transition.

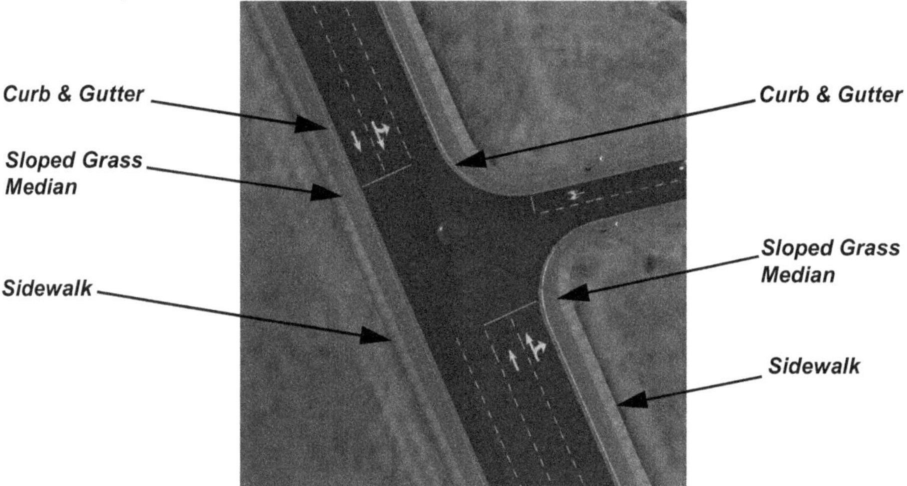

Figure 1–38

10. Right-click on S Redwood Rd. and select **Place Decorations**.

11. In the Select Decoration asset card, type **Light** in the search, and then select **Street Light w_3 Bulbs**.

© 2019, ASCENT - Center for Technical Knowledge®

Note that the lights only go to station 1650 since both components surrounding it only extend that far. To add lights to the end of the road, you would have to add another decoration.

12. In the model, place the cursor so that the insertion line follows the edge of the sidewalk and grass median on the east side of the road, as shown in Figure 1–39. Click to place the decoration.

Figure 1–39

The client wants to see what a less expensive light looks like. On the west side of the road, you add a different style of light to show them how it looks in contrast with the first light. Once they decide which light they like best, you can simply change the assembly on one side of the road.

13. Right-click on S Redwood Rd. and select **Place Decorations**.

14. In the Select Decoration asset card, type **Light** in the search, then select **Lightpole**.

15. In the model, place the cursor so the insertion line follows the edge of the sidewalk and grass median on the west side of the road, as shown in Figure 1–40. Orbit the model so that you can see the results.

Figure 1–40

16. In the Decoration stack, for the Rotation, type **180** and then press <Enter>, as shown in Figure 1–41.

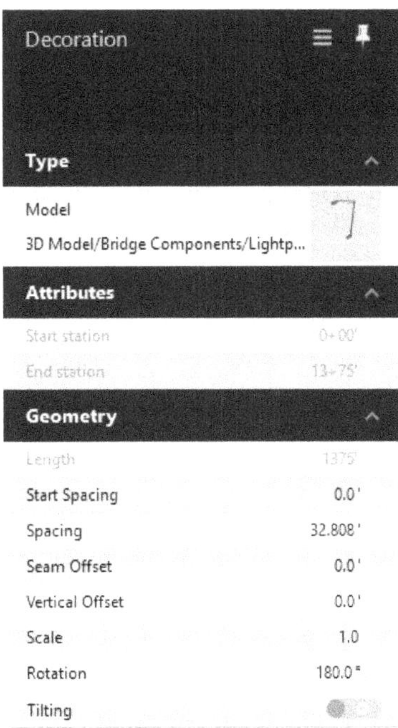

Figure 1–41

© 2019, ASCENT - Center for Technical Knowledge®

17. Press <Esc> to clear the selection of the decoration. Examine the model.

The client has decided that they prefer the more expensive three-bulb street light. Rather than remove the single light pole, you can simply change the decoration.

18. In the model, click on the light decoration on the west side of the road slowly twice to display the Decoration stack.
19. In the Decoration stack, click on the style name.
20. In the Select Component palette, select **3D Model/City Furniture/Street Light w_3 Bulbs**, as shown in Figure 1–42. Click **OK**.

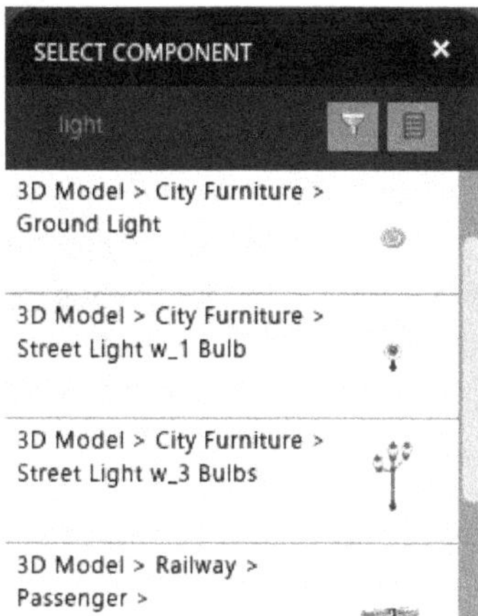

Figure 1–42

21. Press <Esc> twice to clear the selection of the decoration and component road.

Task 4 - Save a new assembly.

1. If you did not complete the last task, in the Utility Bar, expand *Proposal* and select **D_Task3** to make it current.
2. In the model, select **S Redwood Rd.**
3. Right-click on S Redwood Rd., hover over *Road Assembly* and select **Add to Library**.

4. In the model, click to select a cross section of S Redwood Rd., as shown in Figure 1–43.

Figure 1–43

5. In the Add To Library asset card, type **Collector** for the name and press <Enter>.

© 2019, ASCENT - Center for Technical Knowledge®

1.3 Modifying Horizontal Layouts

You can change the horizontal layout of a component road using gizmos or the Road asset card. When making a lot of changes, to the roadway, you may want to delay the model regeneration for component roads. This allows you to reduce how much time you spend waiting on the model to regenerate. By default, each time any road centerline modifications are made, it cause the entire model to regenerate.

How To: Delay Road Regeneration

1. In the Utility bar, expand (Autodesk 360 account options), and click (Application Options).
2. In the left column of the Application Options dialog box, select Model Generation.
3. Put a check in the box next to Delayed Road Regeneration, as shown in Figure 1–44.

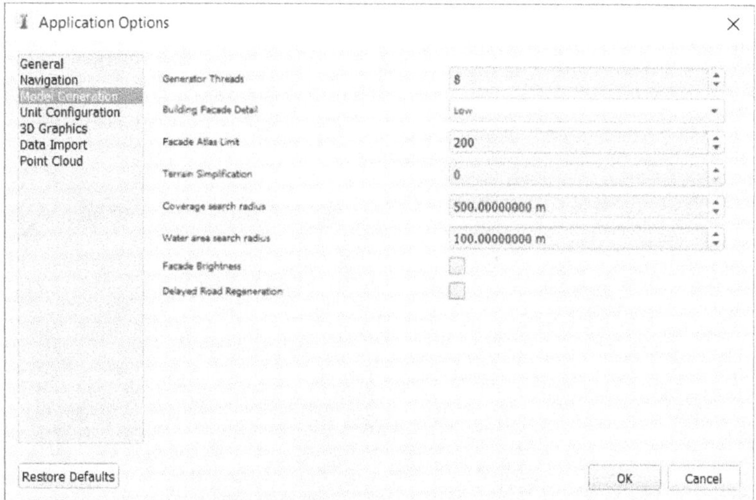

Figure 1–44

4. Click **OK**.

Horizontal Gizmos

When the component road is selected, gizmos display at various points along the road. Each gizmo is used to modify the roadway in specific ways, as described in the table below.

Gizmo	Location	Description
	Point of Intersection (PI)	Located at the endpoint of a road or at the horizontal point of an intersection. Changes the endpoint or PI location in the plan view, which changes the bearing and distance of the tangent.
	Curve Radius	Located at the midpoint of a curve. Changes the horizontal curve radius, affecting the curve's start/end points and length. Note that Spiral Curve Spiral curves do not contain this gizmo.
	Beginning of Curve or End of Curve	Located at the endpoint of a curve where it meets a tangent. Changes the horizontal curve radius, affecting the curve's start/end points and length. Note that Spiral Curve Spiral curves do not contain this gizmo.

When you right-click on different gizmos or segments of the road, different fly-out menus or fields display next to the cursor. Right-clicking on a Curve displays the menu shown in Figure 1–45. This menu enables you to change the curve into a spiral.

Figure 1–45

 © 2019, ASCENT - Center for Technical Knowledge®

Component Road Asset Card

The Component Road asset card has multiple edit modes (stacks). The current edit mode, or stack, is determined by what is selected on the road, as shown in Figure 1–46. Each stack provides options for editing different parts of the component road.

Centerline Selected

Curve Selected

Figure 1–46

- The top of the Road asset card lists the road name, which can be modified. At the bottom of the asset card, a description of the road can be added.

Centerline Edit (Road Asset Card)

The Centerline edit mode (shown in Figure 1–46) displays information about the road. Editable fields display in black text.

- The *Attributes* area displays the road Function, design Speed, Design Standards used, Superelevation and Lane Marking. Only the Design Standards cannot be changed in the *Attributes* area. Changing the **Function** should also change the design speed.

- The *Geometry* area displays the total length of the road, the range of elevations, and the range of grades along the road. Nothing in the *Geometry* area can be modified.

- The *Grading* area displays the Grading Method used and any Grading Limits you set.

- The *Lifespan* area enables you to enter a **Creation Date** and **Termination Date** for the road.

- The *Advanced* area enables you to add **Tags**, **User Data**, **Tooltips**, and **Links**.

How To: Replace Assemblies on Component Roads

1. In the model, select the component road.
2. Right-click on the component road, hover over *Road Assembly* and select **Replace Assembly**.
3. In the Select Draw Style asset card, select the required assembly.
4. In the model, either:
    - Hover over the component road and double-click to place the assembly over a selected section

    OR

    - Single-click to begin drawing the assembly at a specific station. Click again to indicate at which station the assembly should end.
5. Press <Esc> to clear the selection of the component.

© 2019, ASCENT - Center for Technical Knowledge®

Road Annotation

When a component road is selected in the model, station annotations display at set intervals and at certain geometry points, as shown in Figure 1–47. Clicking on a geometry label allows you to modify the geometry.

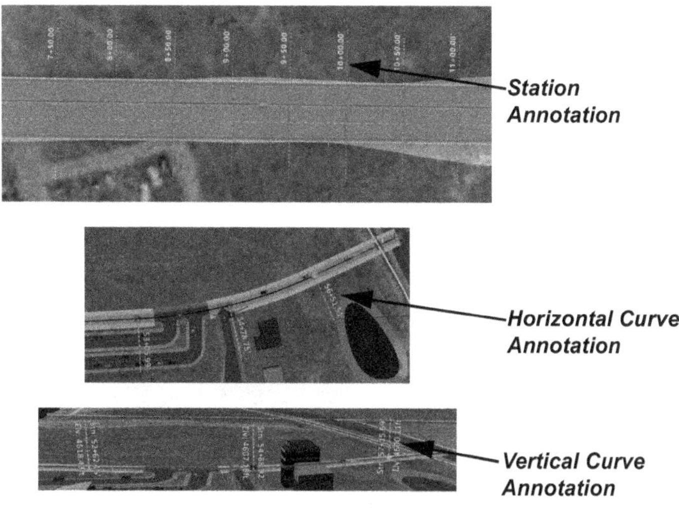

Figure 1–47

If specific geometry, such as a curve, is selected, the geometry annotation displays and adjusts in real-time as you drag gizmos during the modification process, as shown in Figure 1–48.

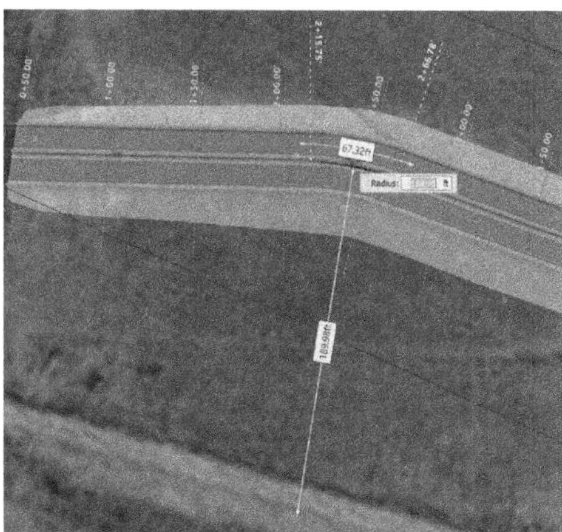

Figure 1–48

Roadside Grading

Grading components enable you to set the daylight slopes from the edge of the assembly to the existing ground surface. Roadside grading for component roads can be controlled in its asset card. You can set the material, slope, and width.

You can chose between a fixed width or fixed slope grading method. When the *Fixed Width* option is selected, you can only set the **Grading Limit** parameter for the road, as shown in Figure 1–49. However, selecting the *Fixed Slope* option enables you to change the **Material**, **Cut Slope**, **Fill Slope**, and the **Grading Limit**, as shown in Figure 1–50.

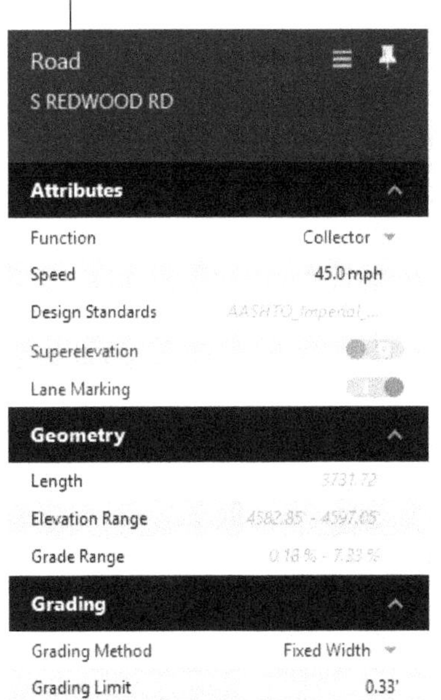

Figure 1–49

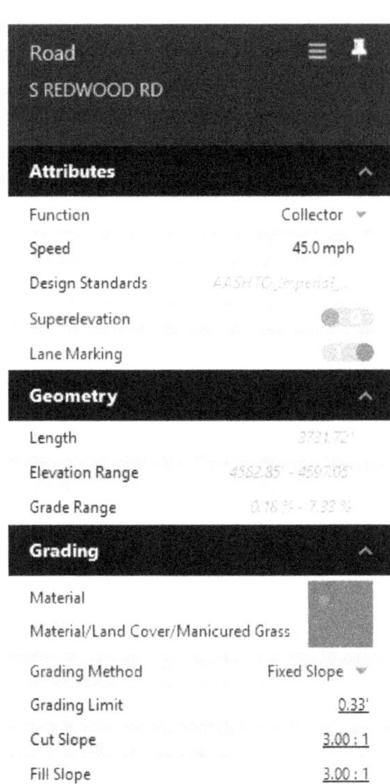

Figure 1–50

Altering the grading using the Road asset card applies the grading parameters for the entire road, as well as both sides of the road. Selecting one grading component on one side of the road enables you to modify the grading on each side of the road separately. You can also split grading slopes as required to transition from one slope (2:1) to another (3:1) and change the material on each, as shown in Figure 1–51.

© 2019, ASCENT - Center for Technical Knowledge®

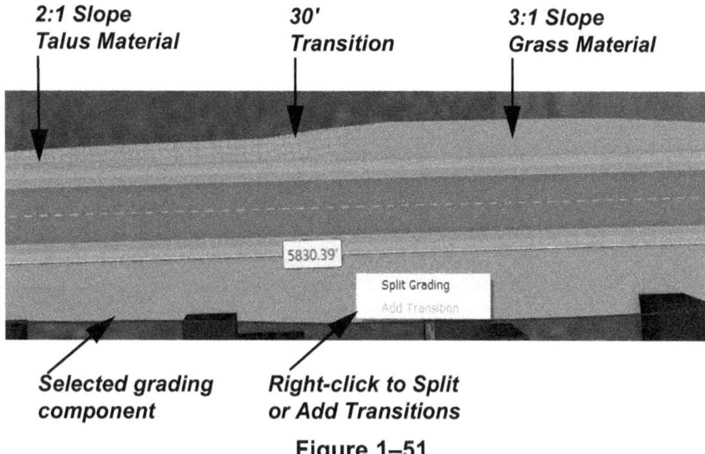

Figure 1–51

How To: Modify Roadside Grading Sections

1. In the model, select the component road.
2. In the Road asset card, under Grading, set the required material, grading method, grading limit, and cut/fill slopes, as shown in Figure 1–52.

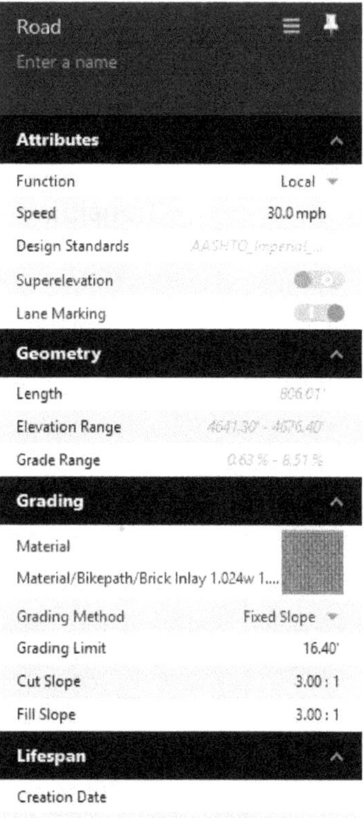

Figure 1–52

3. In the model, select a grading component on one side of the road to modify.
4. Right-click and select **Split Grading**, as shown in Figure 1–53.

Figure 1–53

5. In the model, double-click to set the split point at the required station or type the station and hit <Enter>, as shown in Figure 1–54.

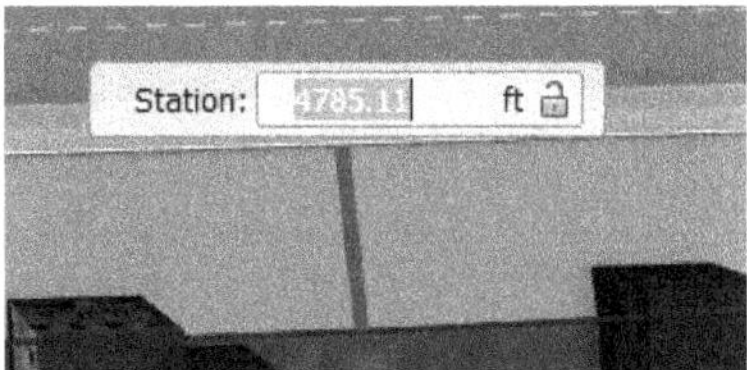

Figure 1–54

6. In the model, click to select the grading slope on the side of the spit that requires a different slope or material.
7. In the Grading stack, set the material and slope.
8. In the model, select the grading material on the side of the split that you wish to transition. Right-click and select **Add Transition**.

© 2019, ASCENT - Center for Technical Knowledge®

1.4 Modifying Vertical Layouts

Vertical Gizmos

When the model view is rotated more than 45 degrees from plan view, a different set of gizmos display that enable you to change the vertical design of a component road. A full list of the available gizmos is shown in the table below.

Gizmos	Location	Description
	Point of Vertical Intersection (PVI)	Located at the endpoint of roads or at the vertical point of intersection (PVI). Changes the PVI station or elevation, but not both at the same time.
	High/Low Point of Curve	Located at the highest point of a crest curve, or the lowest point of a sag curve. Changes cannot be made with this gizmo: it is for reference only.
	Point of Vertical Tangency	Located at the endpoint of a vertical curve where it meets the tangent. Changes the curve length, affecting the curve's start/end points and radius.
	Maintain Tangent Grade	Located at the point of vertical intersection when the PVI is selected. Changes the PVI location while keeping the grade of one tangent.

Additional tools display when you right-click. Depending on where you right-click, a different fly-out menu displays. Right-clicking on a tangent line displays the tools shown in Figure 1–55. Right-clicking (PVI Gizmo) displays the tools shown in Figure 1–56.

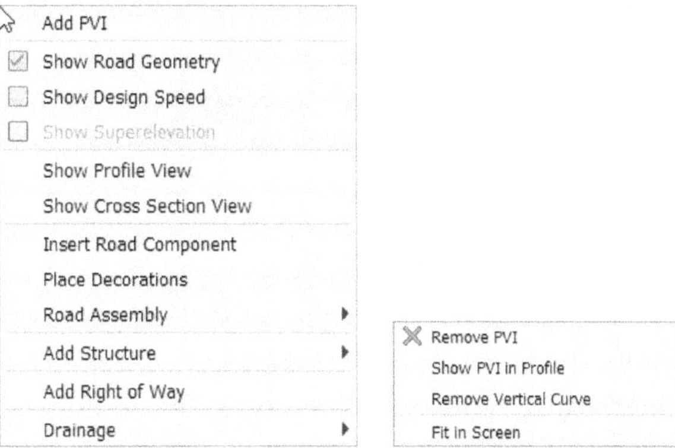

Figure 1–55 **Figure 1–56**

How To: Add and Adjust Points of Vertical Intersection in the Model View

1. In the model, select the component road.
2. Rotate the view more than 45 degrees past plan view to display the vertical gizmos.
3. Right-click on the component road where you need to add a PVI. Select **Add PVI** from the fly-out menu.
4. In the model view, click (PVI Gizmo). In the *Elevation* field, type a new elevation or type the station field to change its location, as shown in Figure 1–57. Alternatively, you can click and drag (PVI Gizmo) up and down to change the elevation, or drag it left and right to change its station.

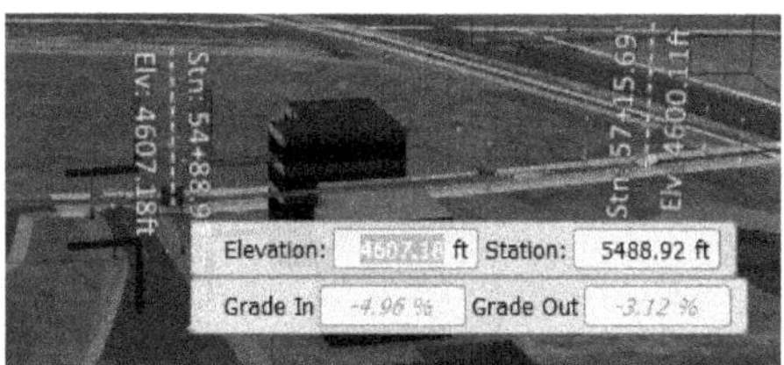

Figure 1–57

Profile View

When you right-click anywhere on the component road, the *Show in Profile* option displays in the fly-out menu. This opens a panel that shows the stations and elevations at the road centerline, as shown in Figure 1–58.

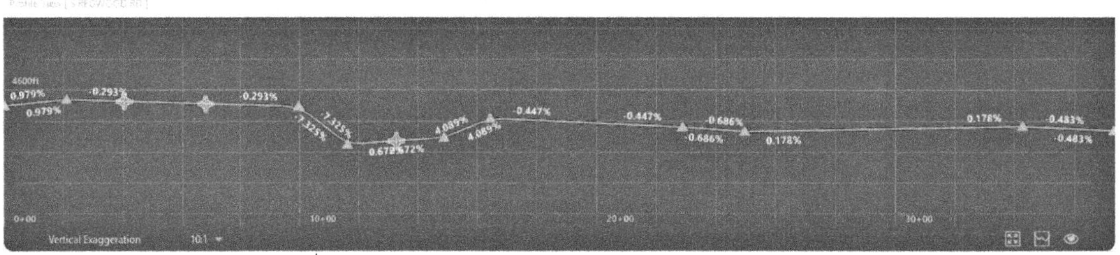

Figure 1–58

© 2019, ASCENT - Center for Technical Knowledge®

- You can control the vertical exaggeration and select which items display in the profile view in the top left corner of the panel. Items that can be displayed include:
  - Horizontal geometry
  - Existing ground
  - Culverts
  - Finished ground
- The mouse wheel can be used to zoom in/out of the profile view.
- Holding the left mouse button enables you to pan in the profile view.
- Only two gizmos display in the profile view, which are described as follows:

Gizmos	Location	Description
	Point of Vertical Intersection (PVI)	Located at the endpoint of a road or at the vertical point of an intersection. Changes the endpoint or PVI station and elevation.
	Point of Vertical Tangency	Located at the endpoint of a vertical curve where it meets the tangent. This gizmo is for display purposes only and does not modify the profile.

Additional tools display when you right-click inside the profile view. Depending on where you right-click, a different fly-out menu displays. Right-clicking on a tangent line provides the tools shown in Figure 1–59. Right-clicking on either of the profile view gizmos provides the tools shown in Figure 1–60.

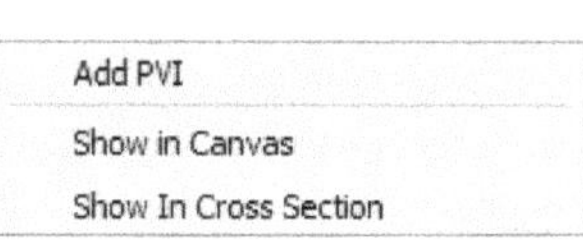

Figure 1–59

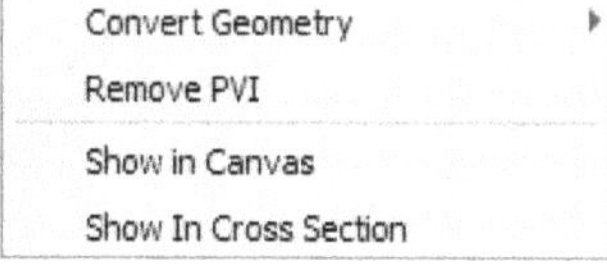

Figure 1–60

Curve Properties

When right-clicking on a vertical curve, you can select Curve Properties to see specific curve values, as shown in Figure 1–61. Changes can be made to any value not grayed out.

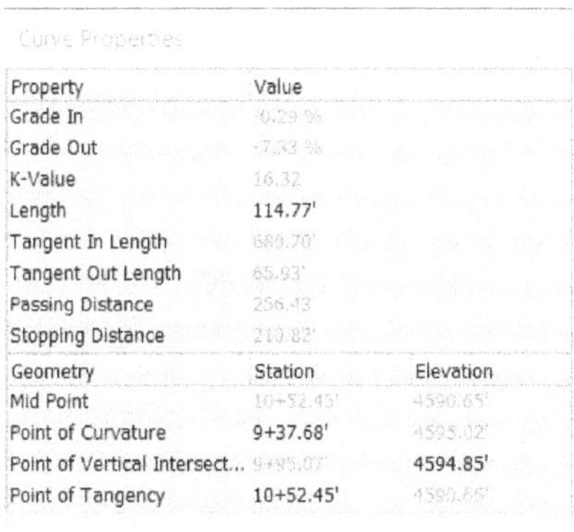

Curve Properties

Property	Value	
Grade In	-0.29 %	
Grade Out	-7.33 %	
K-Value	16.32	
Length	114.77'	
Tangent In Length	680.70'	
Tangent Out Length	65.93'	
Passing Distance	256.43'	
Stopping Distance	210.82'	
Geometry	**Station**	**Elevation**
Mid Point	10+52.45'	4590.65'
Point of Curvature	9+37.68'	4595.02'
Point of Vertical Intersect...	9+95.07'	4594.85'
Point of Tangency	10+52.45'	4590.65'

Figure 1–61

How To: Adjust Points of Vertical Intersection (PVI) in the Profile View

1. In the model, select the component road.
2. Ensure that the Road asset card is set to **Geometry** mode.
3. Right-click anywhere on the component road and select **Show in Profile** from the fly-out menu.
4. In the Profile View, click (PVI Gizmo) and drag the PVI to its new station and elevation, as shown in Figure 1–62.
   - If the **Auto update model** option is checked in the Profile View palette, the change happens simultaneously in the model. If this option is not checked, the model updates as soon as you move the cursor into the model.

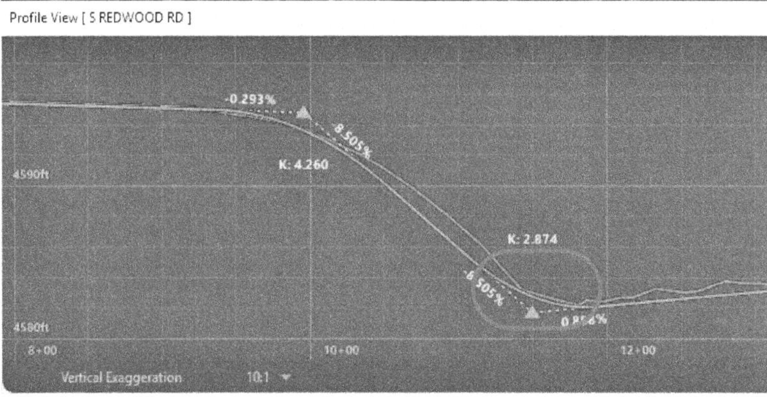

Figure 1–62

© 2019, ASCENT - Center for Technical Knowledge®

Practice 1c Modify Component Roads

Practice Objective

- Modify the component road using the asset card and gizmos.

In this practice, you will modify the alignment by adjusting the horizontal curve radii and splitting the road into two different styles (typical cross sections). You will then set the daylight slopes for the road and adjust the vertical design by inserting PVI's and moving gizmos as required, as shown in Figure 1–63.

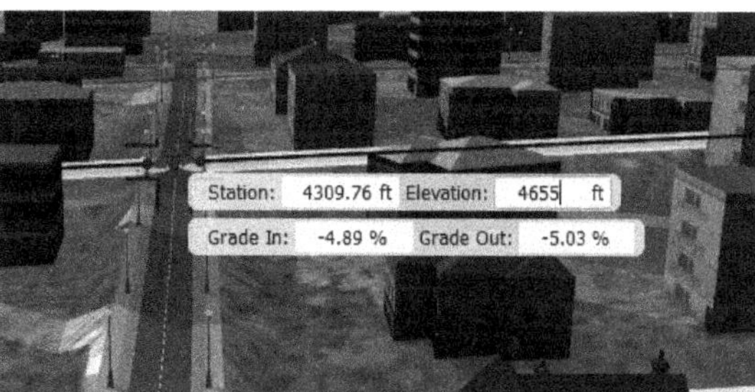

Figure 1–63

Task 1 - Modify the horizontal design.

In this task, you will modify the horizontal layout of the component road by modifying the curve radius, adding another style to a portion of the road, and adding daylight slopes.

1. Continue working in the same model as the last practice. If you did not complete the last practice, in the Utility Bar, expand *Proposal* and select **C_Task1** to make it current.
2. In the Utility Bar, click (Bookmark) and select **New Neighborhood**.

Gizmos display in the model on the component road.

3. In the model, select the road shown in Figure 1–64.

Figure 1–64

4. Zoom in on the west end of the road (near the church), as shown in Figure 1–65.

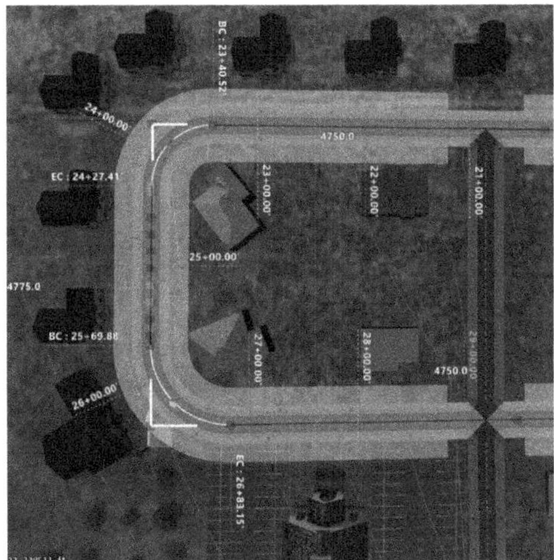

Figure 1–65

5. In the model, click on (Curve Radius Gizmo) in the south-west corner, as shown in Figure 1–65, above. In the *Radius* measurement, type **60**. Press <Enter> to accept the radius.

6. Repeat Step 7 for the curve in the north-west corner. Press <Enter> to release the curve radius gizmo.

7. In the Utility Bar, click (Bookmark) and select **Change Style**.

8. With the road still selected, right click and hover over *Road Assembly* and select **Replace Assembly**.

© 2019, ASCENT - Center for Technical Knowledge®

9. In the Select Draw Style dialog box, select the **Component>Custom>RedwoodRd** road assembly, as shown in Figure 1–66.

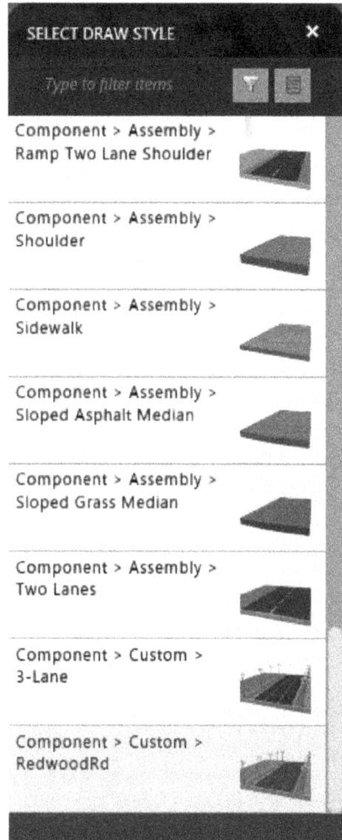

Figure 1–66

10. In the model, click a point near station **50+00** for the beginning of the assembly zone, as shown in Figure 1–67. Stretch the assembly zone to the end of the road where it meets S Redwood Rd., as shown in Figure 1–67. Press <Enter> to accept the change.

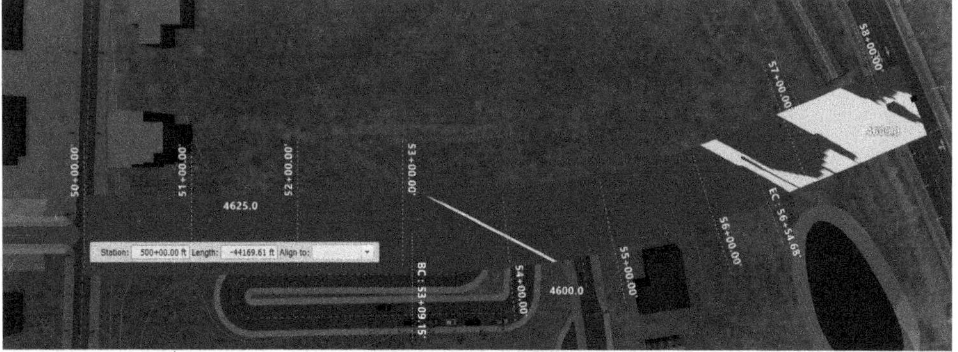

Figure 1–67

11. In the Road asset card, set the following options, as shown in Figure 1–68:
    - *Grading Method*: **Fixed Slope**
    - *Material*: **Manicured Grass**
    - *Grading Limit*: **33'**
    - Ensure that *Cut Slope* and *Fill Slope* are set to **3.0:1**.

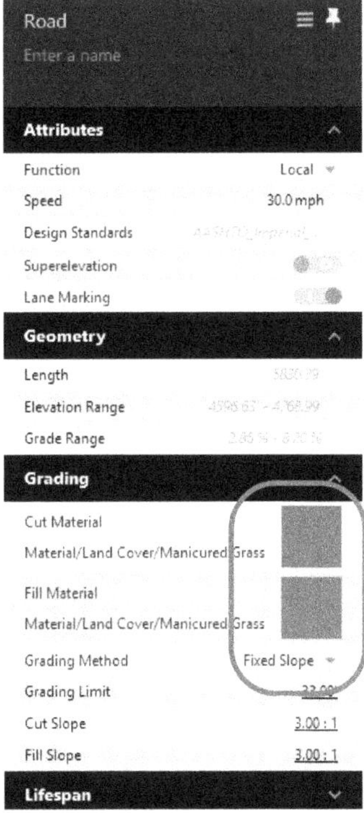

Figure 1–68

12. Press <Esc> to release the selected road.

Task 2 - Adjust the vertical profile of the component road.

1. Continue working in the same model as the last task. If you did not complete the last task, in the Utility Bar, expand *Proposal* and select **C_Task2**.
2. Click (Bookmark), and then select **DesignElevations**.

   Note that there are several locations where there is a lot of fill required along the new component road, as shown in Figure 1–69. This could cause flooding issues for the proposed homes. In this task, you will modify the vertical design of the new road to prevent flooding in the neighborhood.

© 2019, ASCENT - Center for Technical Knowledge®

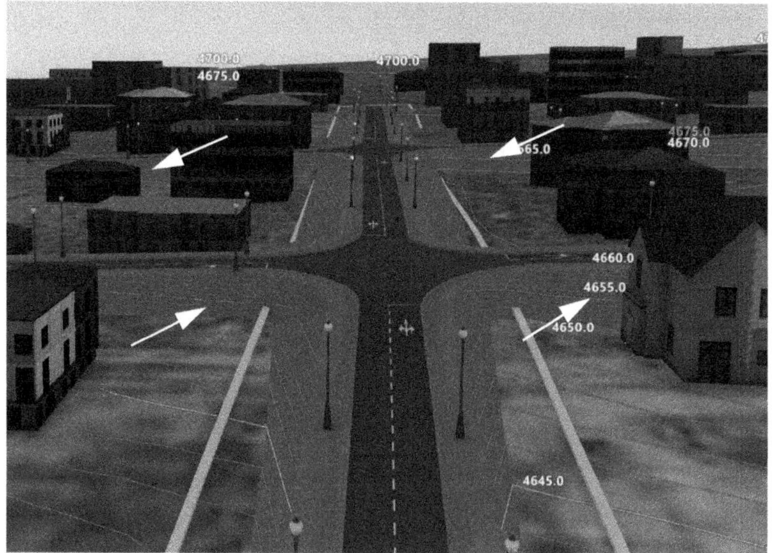

Figure 1–69

3. In the model, select the component road.

Since the DesignElevations bookmark is rotated more than 45 degrees from a plan view, anything you do, effects the vertical design.

4. In the model, right-click on the intersection labeled **Point 1** in Figure 1–70. Select **Add PVI** from the fly-out menu. Do the same for **Point 2** in Figure 1–70.

Figure 1–70

5. In the model, right-click on the (PVI Gizmo) for Point 1. Select **Show PVI in Profile** from the fly-out menu.

Pan and zoom as required to see the PVI.

6. In the Profile View, click (PVI Gizmo) to move the PVI you just inserted closer to the Station **7+00** and elevation **4650**, as shown in Figure 1–71.

Note that all Profile View changes regenerate simultaneously in the model as soon as you move the cursor into the model window.

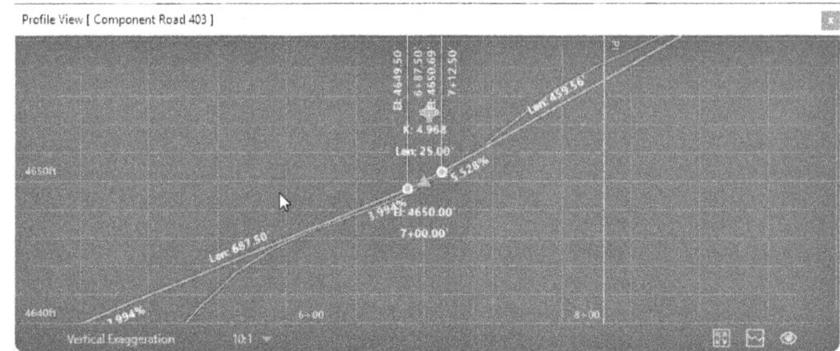

Figure 1–71

If the Point 2 PVI disappears, right-click and re-add it.

7. In the model view, left-click on (PVI Gizmo) at Point 2. In the *Elevation* field, type **4655**, as shown in Figure 1–72. The sketch road becomes an overpass at the intersection.

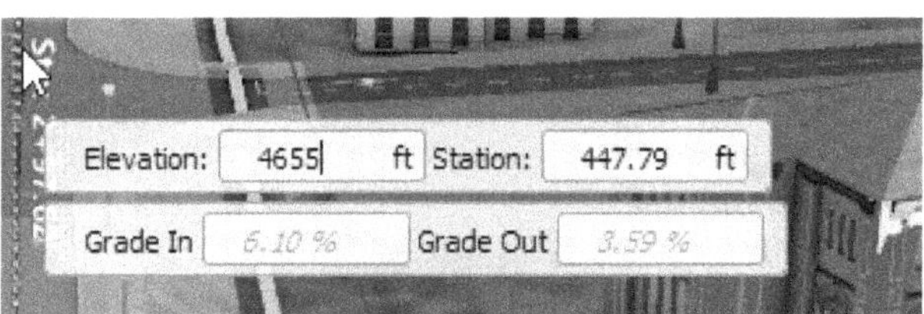

Figure 1–72

8. Select the component road running north to south. Right-click at the point 2 intersection and select **Add PVI**.

9. Click the new (PVI Gizmo). In the *Elevation* field, type **4655**, as shown in Figure 1–73.

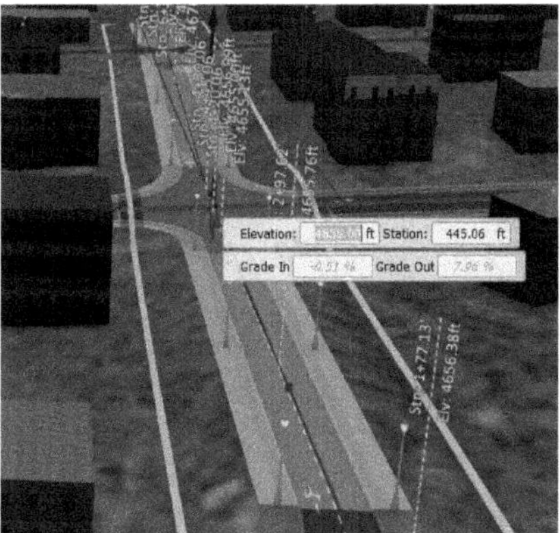

Figure 1–73

 © 2019, ASCENT - Center for Technical Knowledge®

Task 3 - Set roadside grading.

1. If you did not complete the last task, in the Utility Bar, expand *Proposal* and select **C_Task3** to make it current.

2. In the Utility Bar, click (Bookmark) and select **3-WayIntersection**.

3. In the model, select **S Redwood Rd.**

4. In the Road asset card, under Grading, set the *Grading Method* to **Fixed Slope** and the *Material* to **Manicured Grass**, as shown in Figure 1–74.

Note that you might not notice a difference in the side slopes because the Grading Limit is so small.

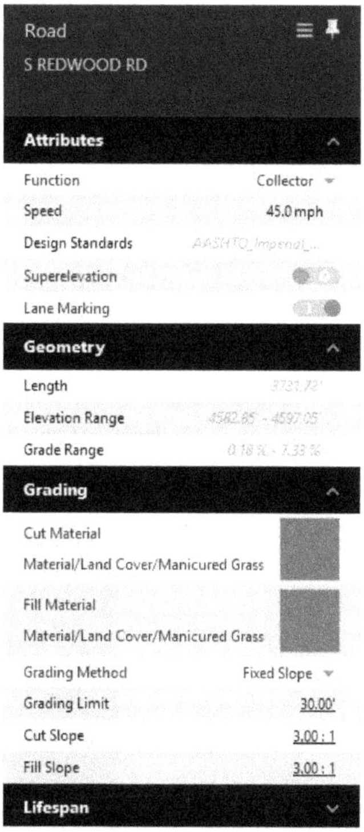

Road
S REDWOOD RD
Attributes
Function Collector
Speed 45.0 mph
Design Standards AASHTO_Imperial_...
Superelevation
Lane Marking
Geometry
Length 3731.72'
Elevation Range 4582.85 - 4597.05
Grade Range 0.18 % - 7.33 %
Grading
Cut Material
Material/Land Cover/Manicured Grass
Fill Material
Material/Land Cover/Manicured Grass
Grading Method Fixed Slope
Grading Limit 30.00'
Cut Slope 3.00 : 1
Fill Slope 3.00 : 1
Lifespan

Figure 1–74

5. Set the *Grading Limit* to **30**.

6. Select the grading slope on the west side of S Redwood Rd.

7. Right-click and select **Split Grading**, as shown in Figure 1–75.

Figure 1–75

8. For the stations, type **1400** + <Enter> and **1700** + <Enter>. Then press <Enter> again to complete the command.

9. In the model, select the section of grading between stations 1400 and 1700.

10. In the Grading stack, change the *Cut Slope* and *Fill Slope* to **5:1**. The results are shown in Figure 1–76.

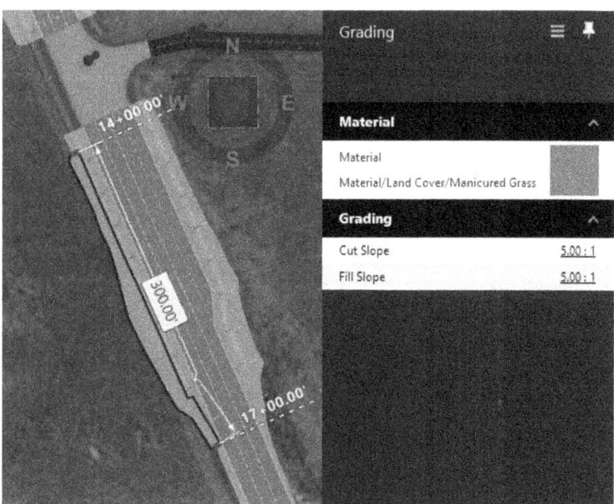

Figure 1–76

11. Press <Esc> twice to release the component and road selection.

© 2019, ASCENT - Center for Technical Knowledge®

1.5 Component Road Superelevation

You can apply superelevations to component roads. Once applied, you can inspect cross sections through critical stations of the road. Superelevation critical station gizmos display as blue slices along the road, as shown in Figure 1–77. In addition, yellow and red tracks display beside the roadway, representing runoff and runout areas, which are also shown in Figure 1–77.

Figure 1–77

How To: Apply Superelevations to Component Roads

1. In the model, select a component road.
2. In the Road asset card, under *Attributes*, toggle on the **Superelevation** option, as shown in Figure 1–78.
3. Adjust the *Superelevation Input* values, as shown in Figure 1–78.

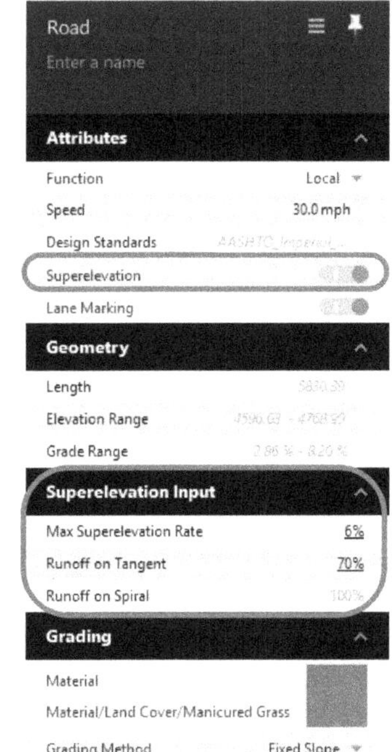

Figure 1–78

4. Press <Esc> to clear the selection of the road.

© 2019, ASCENT - Center for Technical Knowledge®

How To: View Road Cross Section Attributes in the Cross Section Viewer

1. Once superelevations are applied to a road, select the road in the model.
2. Click on a superelevation critical station gizmo. The Cross Section Viewer should display, as shown in Figure 1–79.

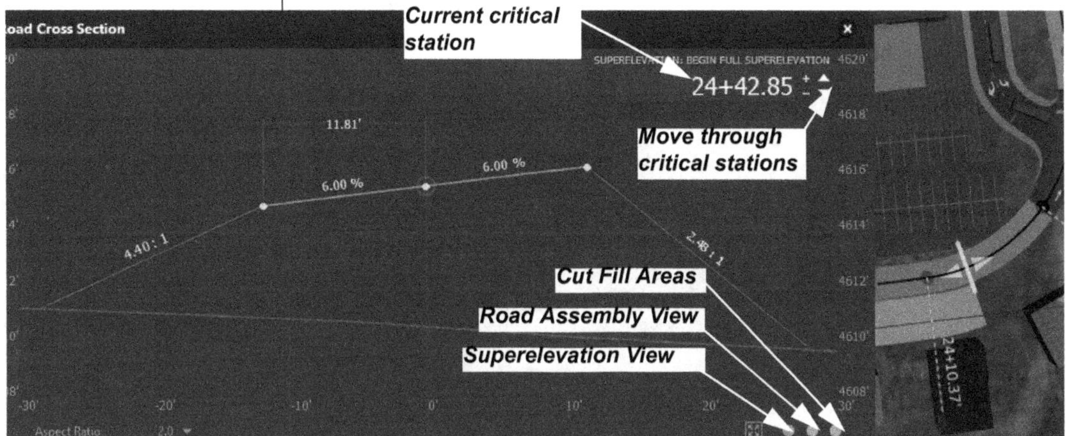

Figure 1–79

3. Click ▲/▼ (Next/Previous Critical Section) in the viewer to view other critical stations.

Practice 1d Review Superelevations

Practice Objective

- Toggle on superelevations for review.

In this practice, you will display the superelevation data for a component road, and then review the superelevation critical stations, as shown in Figure 1–80.

Figure 1–80

Task 1 - Display the superelevations for review.

1. Continue working in the same model as the last practice. If you did not complete the last practice, in the Utility Bar, expand *Proposal* and select **D_Task1** to make it current.
2. In the Utility Bar, click (Bookmark), and then select **RoundAbout**.
3. In the model, select **S Redwood Rd.** (road running north to south).

© 2019, ASCENT - Center for Technical Knowledge®

4. In the Road asset card, under *Attributes,* toggle on the *Superelevation* option, and then adjust the *Superelevation Input* values, as shown in Figure 1–81.

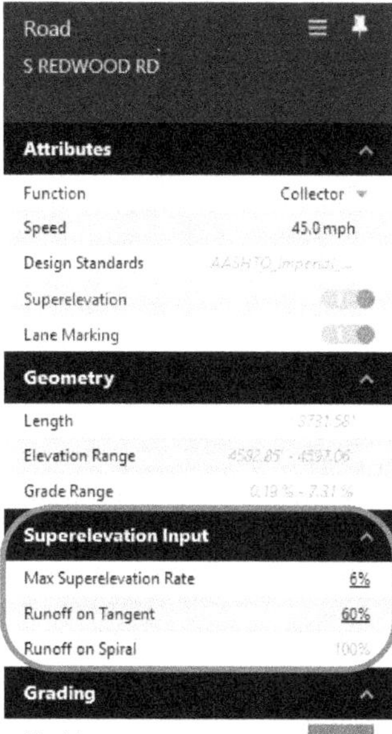

Figure 1–81

5. Click on a superelevation critical station gizmo, as shown in Figure 1–82. Review the superelevation data in the Cross Section Viewer.

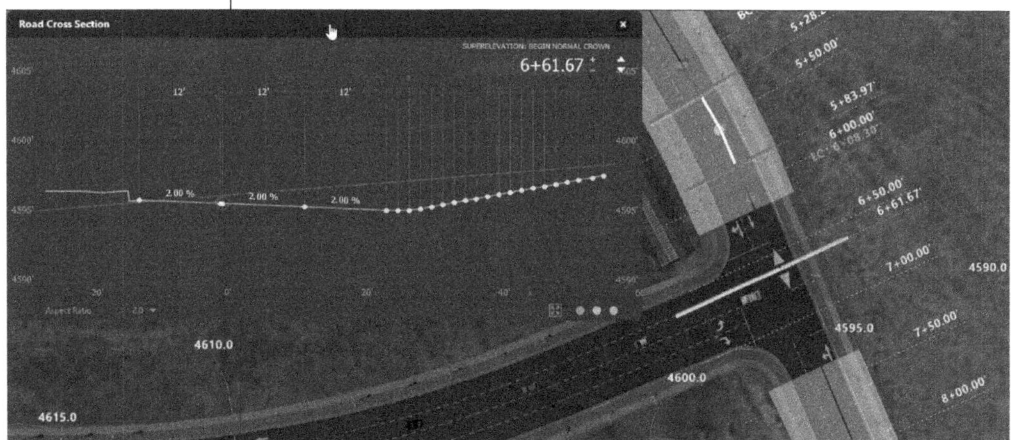

Figure 1–82

6. Click (Next Critical Section) in the viewer to view other critical stations in the current view.

7. Press <Esc> twice to clear the selection of the road.

1.6 Working with Intersections

When two component roads intersect each other, an intersection object is automatically created. Selecting an intersection in the model causes an Intersection asset card to display, as shown in Figure 1–83.

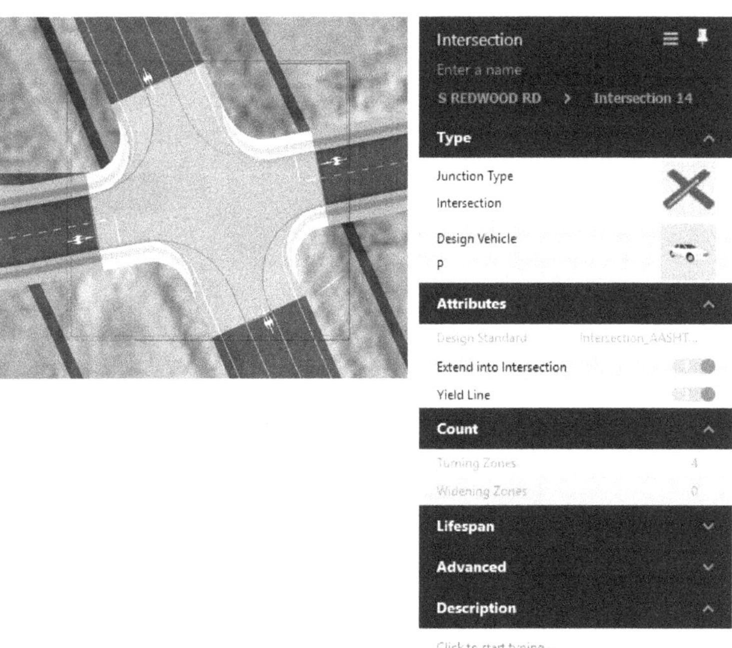

Figure 1–83

Similar to component roads, there are multiple Edit Modes for Intersections. The edit modes that are available depends on what you have selected in the model. Clicking once on the intersection enables you to set the Junction Type and other settings in the Intersection stack. Clicking twice on the intersection enables you to edit specific parts of the intersection. Depending on where you click the second time, you can edit the Lane Markings or Turning Zones, as shown in Figure 1–84.

© 2019, ASCENT - Center for Technical Knowledge®

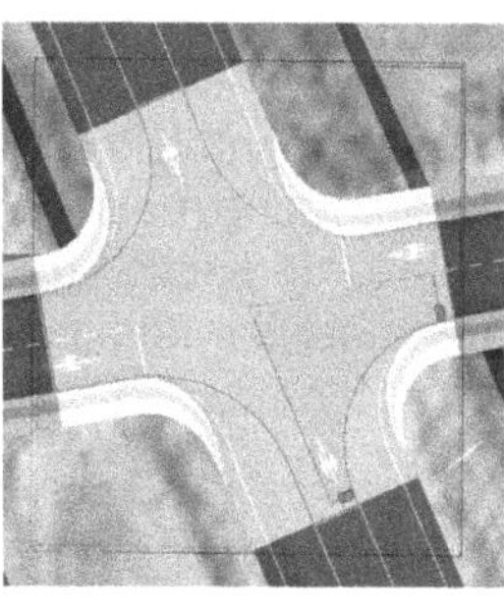

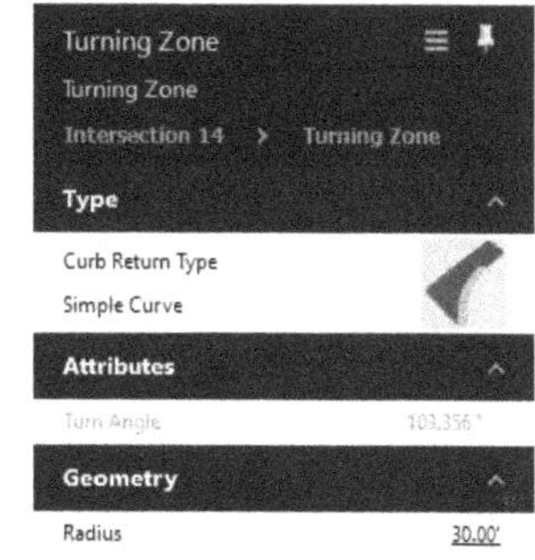

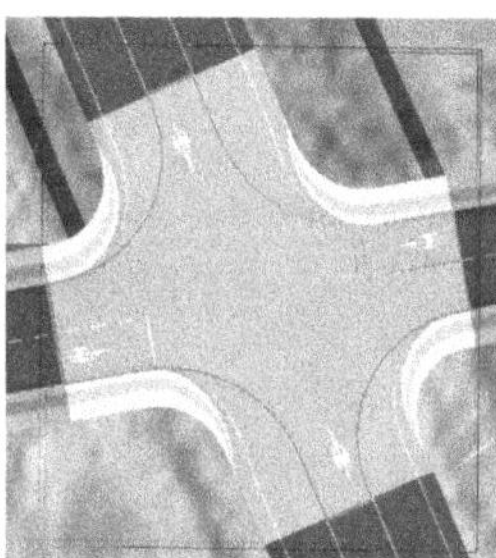

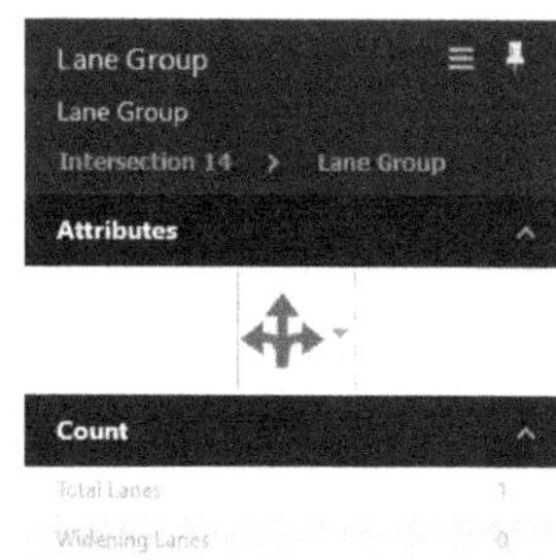

Figure 1–84

Junction Type

When an intersection is selected, the Type area displays in the Intersection asset card. Two Junction Types are currently available, as shown in Figure 1–85.

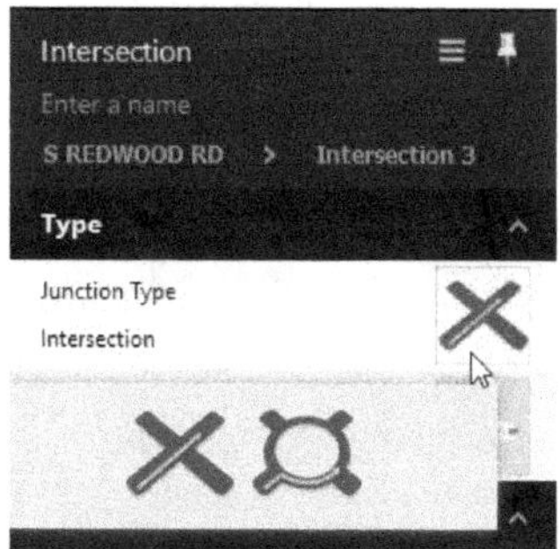

Figure 1–85

Standard Intersection

The standard intersection junction type is for three-way and four-way intersections. When a standard intersection junction type is selected, you can modify the vehicle class and turning zones. You can also create a traffic simulation.

Vehicle Class

Various design vehicle classes are available to set for the intersection rating, as shown in Figure 1–86. Changing the rating causes the intersection geometry to adjust in order to accommodate the design vehicle class.

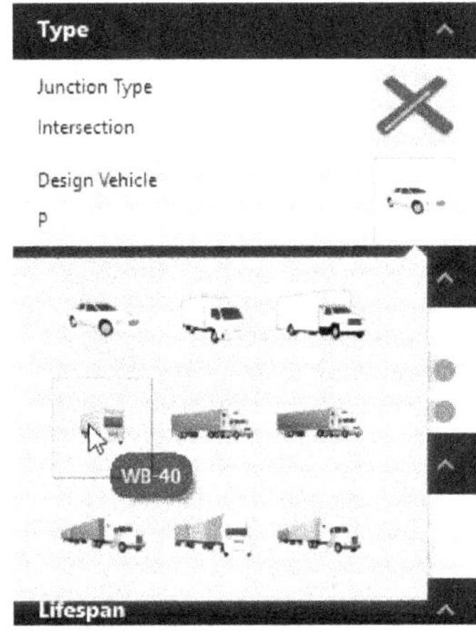

Figure 1–86

Turning Zone

Once an intersection is selected, you can select any of the turning zones within the intersection. This causes the Turning Zone stack to display, as shown in Figure 1–87. The curve type and curve radius for the curb return can be modified using the Turning Zone stack. If the **Simple Curve with Taper** option is selected, the radius, offset and taper parameters can all be set, as shown on the far right in Figure 1–87.

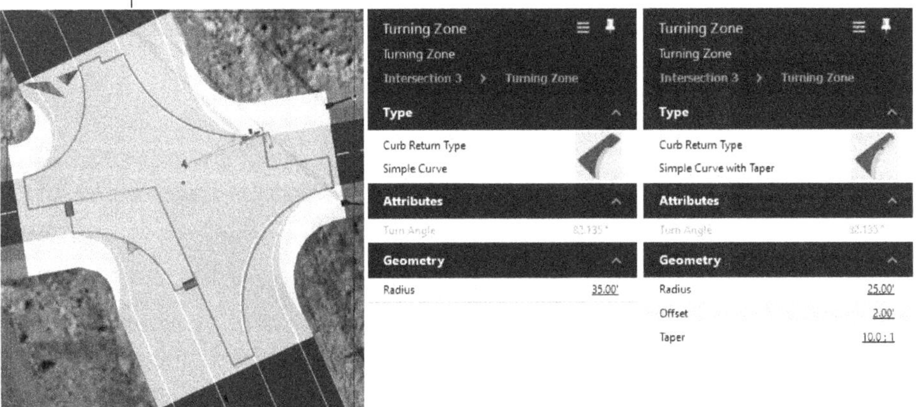

Figure 1–87

 © 2019, ASCENT - Center for Technical Knowledge®

Lane Markings

In the Intersection stack, under *Attributes,* you can modify how lanes are painted through the intersection. Lane markings can extend into intersections and create a yield line, as shown in Figure 1–88.

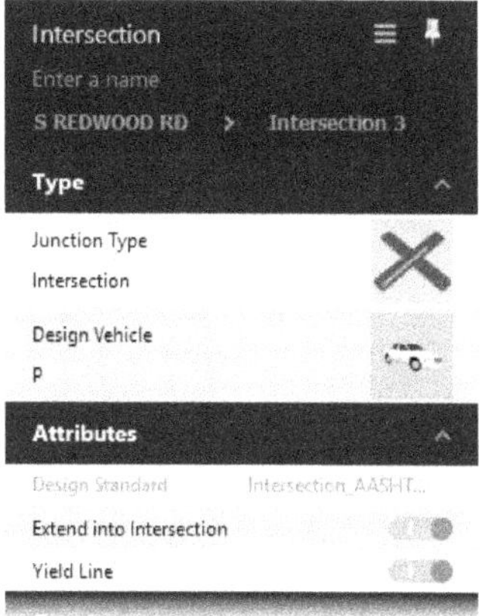

Figure 1–88

In order to set the directional arrows that indicate which way traffic can flow, you must select the Lane Group in the model. In the Lane Group stack, you can set the turn arrows under *Attributes*, as shown in Figure 1–89.

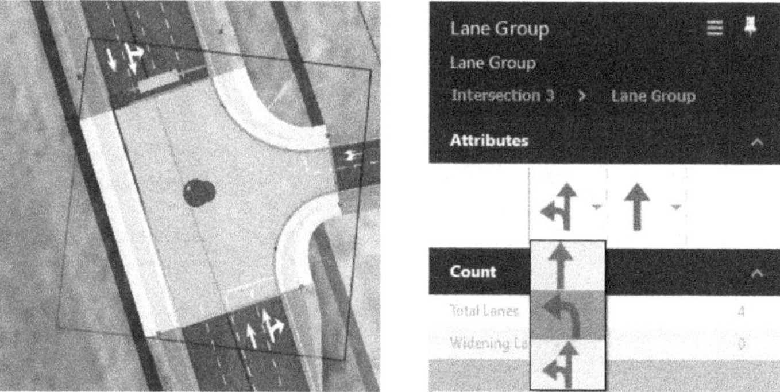

Figure 1–89

1.7 Roundabouts

The Roundabout junction type replaces the intersection geometry with a circular intersection for almost continuous traffic flow in one direction around a central island. There are several roundabout options to select from, as shown in Figure 1–90.

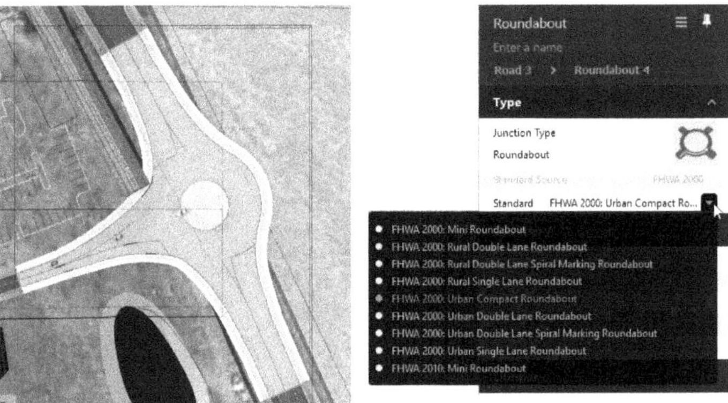

Figure 1–90

Once a roundabout is placed, you can use gizmos to modify it in both the horizontal and vertical directions, as shown in Figure 1–91. To see the vertical gizmos, the model must be orbited more than 45 degrees from a plan view.

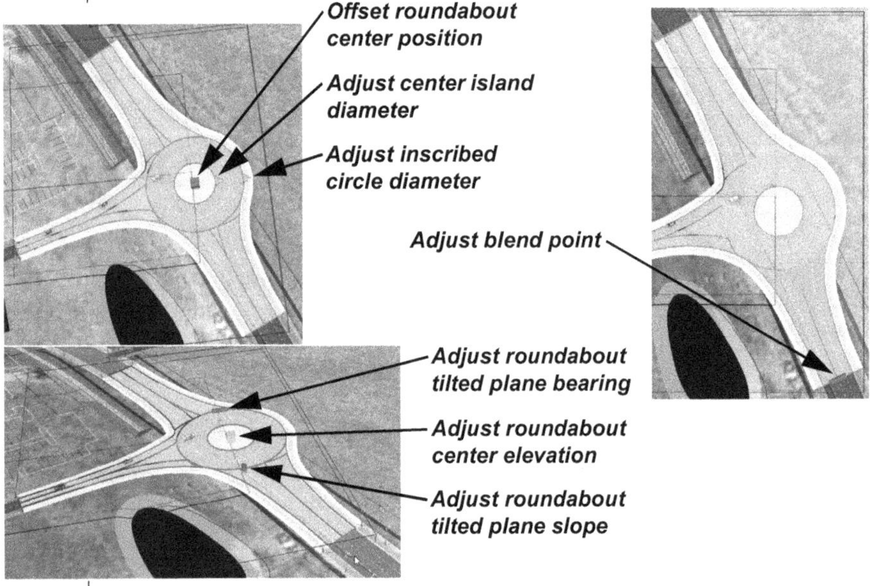

Figure 1–91

© 2019, ASCENT - Center for Technical Knowledge®

Practice 1e Modify Intersections

Practice Objectives

- Modify a standard intersection.
- Create a roundabout where two component roads intersect.

In this practice, you will modify a standard intersection to increase the curb radius. You will then turn another standard intersection into a roundabout to create a more continuous traffic flow.

Task 1 - Modify a standard intersection.

1. Continue working in the same model as the previous practice. If you did not complete the previous practice, in the Utility Bar, expand *Proposal* and select **E_Task1** to make it current.In the Utility Bar, click

   (Bookmark) and select **Lake Rd Intersection**.

2. Select the intersection. In the Intersection stack, in the *Design Vehicle* area, select **WB-40**, as shown in Figure 1–92.

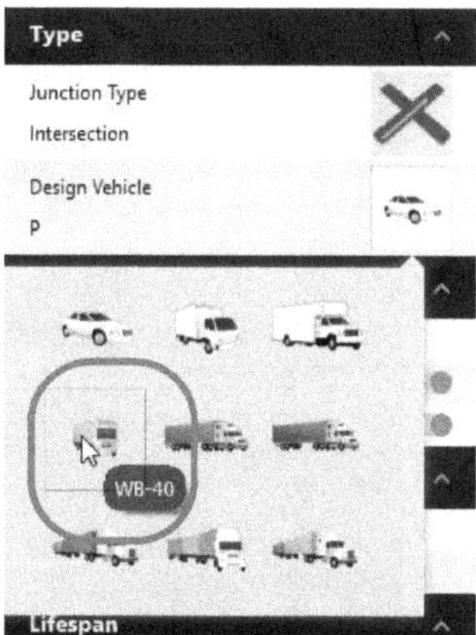

Figure 1–92

3. In the model, select the northeast turning zone of the intersection.

4. In the Turning Zone stack, change *Taper* to **20:1**, as shown in Figure 1–93.

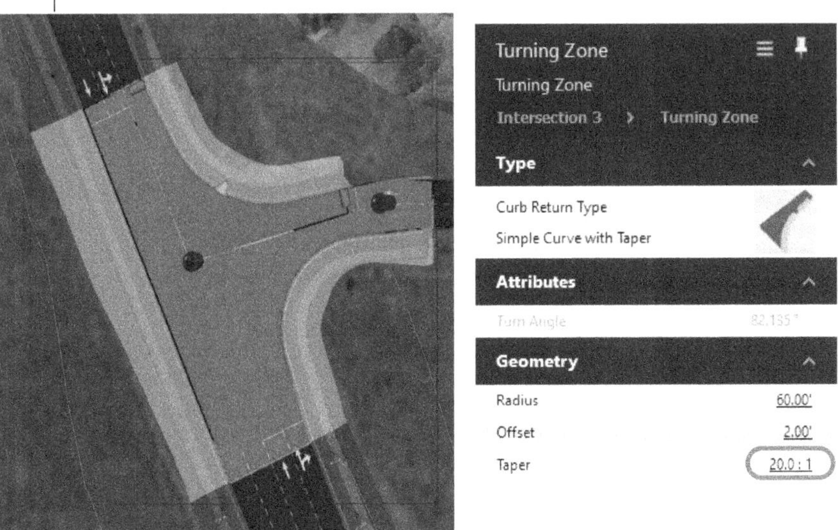

Figure 1–93

5. In the model, select the north lane group of the intersection. In the Lane Group stack, change the center lane to a left only, as shown in Figure 1–94.

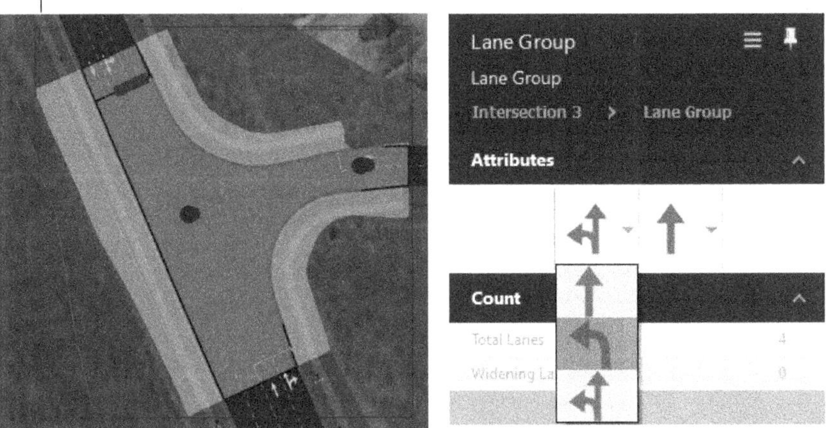

Figure 1–94

© 2019, ASCENT - Center for Technical Knowledge®

6. In the model, select the south lane group of the intersection. In the Lane Group stack, change the right lane to a right only, as shown in Figure 1–95.

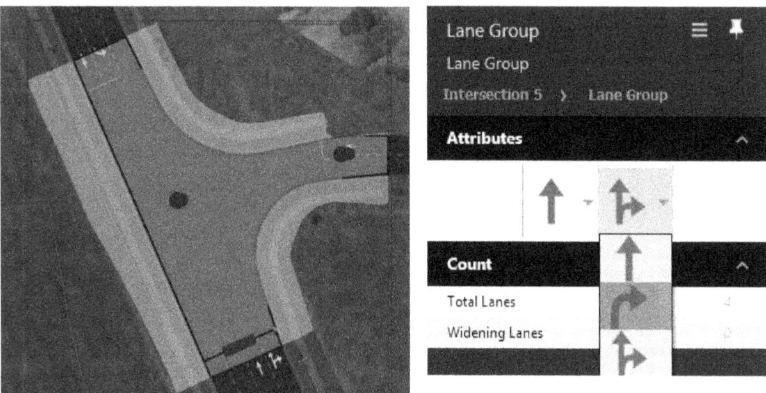

Figure 1–95

7. Press <Esc> to clear the selection of the intersection.

Task 2 - Turn a standard intersection into a roundabout.

In order to make sure traffic does not stop in this intersection, the design team has decided to replace the three-way intersection with a roundabout.

1. Continue working in the same model as the previous task. If you did not complete the previous task, in the Utility Bar, expand *Proposal* and select **E_Task2** to make it current.
2. In the Utility Bar, click (Bookmark) and select **Roundabout**.

© 2019, ASCENT - Center for Technical Knowledge®

3. Select the intersection shown in Figure 1–96.

Figure 1–96

4. In the Intersection asset card, in the *Type* area, for the Junction Type, select **Roundabout**.

5. In the Roundabout drop-down list, select **FHWA 2000-Urban Compact Roundabout**, as shown in Figure 1–97.

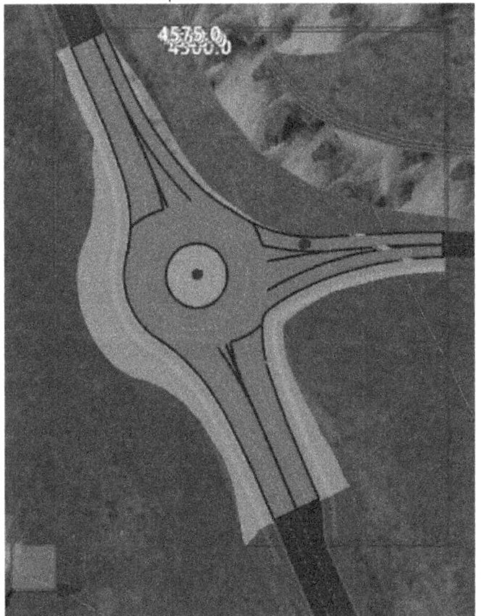

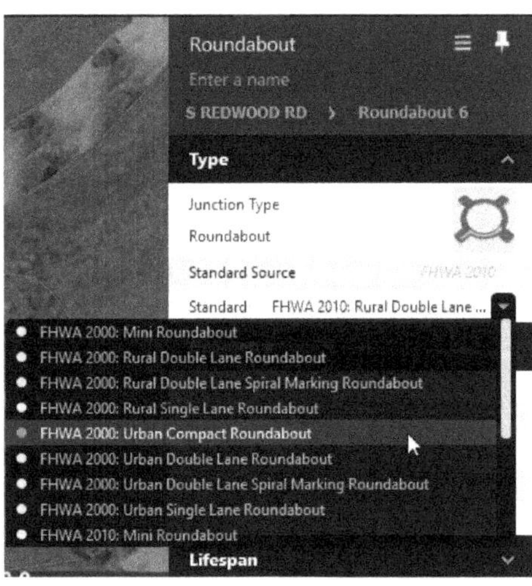

Figure 1–97

© 2019, ASCENT - Center for Technical Knowledge®

6. In the model, select the center island of the roundabout. Click (Offset roundabout center position gizmo) and move the center close **40** feet to the east and **20** feet to the south, as shown in Figure 1–98.

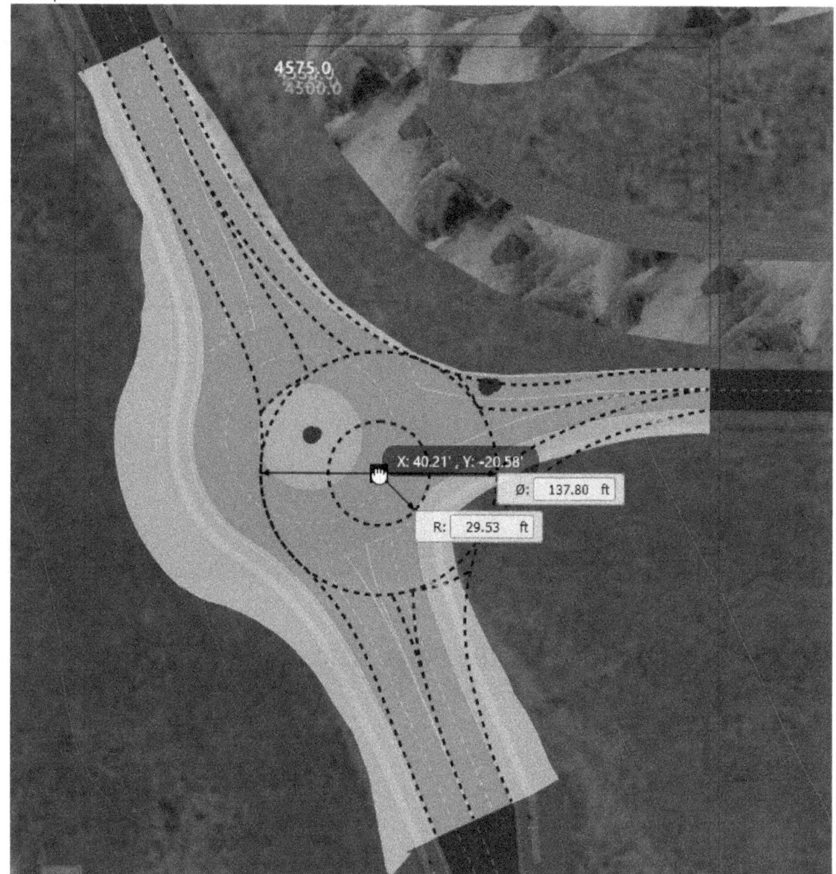

Figure 1–98

7. Orbit the model more than 45 degrees from plan view. Click (Adjust roundabout tilted plane slope gizmo) and move it up **4**%, as shown in Figure 1–99.

Figure 1–99

8. Press <Esc> to clear the selection of the roundabout.

© 2019, ASCENT - Center for Technical Knowledge®

Chapter Review Questions

1. How does a Right of Way differ from a Parcel or Easement?
    a. There is no difference.
    b. A Right of Way enables you to offset an existing feature parallel to its centerline, while Parcels or Easements must have each segment drawn in.
    c. Parcels or Easements enable you to offset an existing feature parallel to its centerline, while a Right of Way must have each segment drawn in.
2. Which of the following road functions would be used to set a maximum design speed of 50 mph?
    a. Freeway
    b. Arterial
    c. Collector
    d. Local
3. Which of the following dialog boxes can be used to set the component road standards? (Select all that apply.)
    a. New Model
    b. Application Options
    c. Model Properties
    d. Model Explorer
4. You can modify road geometry annotations that display in the model window when the road is selected.
    a. True
    b. False
5. You can click on a specific grading on one side of the road to edit its parameters independent of the rest of the road.
    a. True
    b. False
6. Intersection Objects are created automatically when two component roads cross each other.
    a. True
    b. False

7. Intersections can be any of the following. (Select all that apply).
    a. Single Point Urban Interchange (SPUI)
    b. 3-way Intersection
    c. 4-way Intersection
    d. Roundabout

© 2019, ASCENT - Center for Technical Knowledge®

Command Summary

Button	Command	Location
	Component Roads	• **In Canvas Tools:** Design, review, and engineer road>Design roads
	Easements	• **In Canvas Tools:** Design, review, and engineer roads>Design roads
	Parcels	• **In Canvas Tools:** Design, review, and engineer roads>Design roads
	Profile View	• **In Canvas Tools:** Design, review, and engineer roads>Review and modify roadway designs
	**Right of Ways**	• **In Canvas Tools:** Design, review, and engineer roads>Design roads

© 2019, ASCENT - Center for Technical Knowledge®

© 2019, ASCENT - Center for Technical Knowledge®

Analyzing Component Roads

Once you have created a component road, it is important to analyze it to ensure that it meets the design criteria. In this chapter, you learn how to analyze sight distances and improve traffic flows through detailed interchanges. Then, you learn how to calculate quantities and eventually balance cut and fill quantities for the design using cloud-based optimization tools.

Learning Objectives in this Chapter

- Add traffic movement to your project by running a traffic simulation.
- Identify the best horizontal location for a new roadway by running a corridor optimization.
- Calculate earthwork and material quantities for a roadway.
- Balance a component road's cut and fill values by running a vertical optimization.
- Analyze a roadway and intersection for sight distance obstructions.

2.1 Traffic Simulation

To use this feature, access to the Internet is required.

The Traffic Simulation module provides a way to run a traffic study of the project using a cloud-based traffic engine. Since it is cloud based, the model must be published to the cloud before a simulation can be run.

Once a model is published, the Traffic Simulation module can generate an animation file based on traffic demand. Traffic can include all modes of transportation, not just private vehicles. During the traffic study, the following can be defined:

- Demand matrices
- Profiles
- Vehicle types
- Driver types

The animation files that are created can be played in the model, adding traffic movement to your project. Additionally, traffic analysis results can be displayed as info-graphics in the model, as shown in Figure 2–1. Color coded queue lengths which are based on demand, display in the traffic study area for each component road intersection.

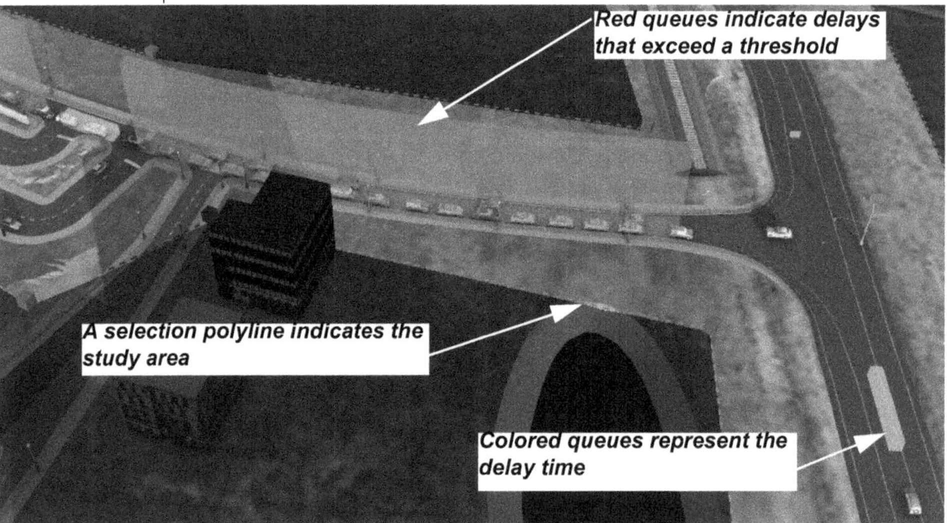

Figure 2–1

© 2019, ASCENT - Center for Technical Knowledge®

General Steps

The modeling process:

1. Define the traffic study area.
2. Add zones for traffic origin/destination/parking.
3. Define traffic demand.
4. Generate trips from demand.
5. Run simulation, collecting the results.
6. Analyze the results.

How To: Define a Traffic Study Area

The Component Roads are highlighted to indicate which roads can be analyzed using a traffic study.

1. In the In Canvas tools, expand (Design, review and engineer roads)> (Perform analysis in preparation for road design), and click (Traffic Simulation).
2. In the model, define a polyline to indicate the Traffic Study Area boundary.
3. If planning roads are included in the boundary, a message displays indicating that you have the option to turn them into component roads so that they can be analyzed during the traffic simulation, as shown in Figure 2–2. Click **Yes** or **No**, as required.

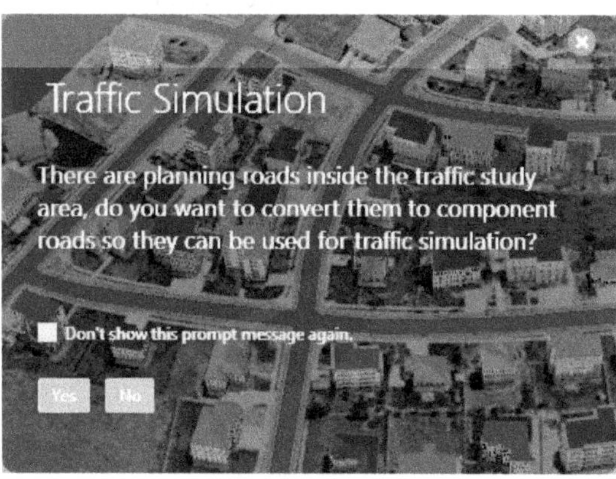

Figure 2–2

© 2019, ASCENT - Center for Technical Knowledge®

4. In the Traffic Study Area asset card, select the *Result Volumes* that suite your needs, as shown in Figure 2–3.

Figure 2–3

5. In the Simulation drop-down list, select the simulation length you wish to run, as shown in Figure 2–4.
   - **Quick Simulation:** Runs for 10 minutes.
   - The other simulations require more time to process.

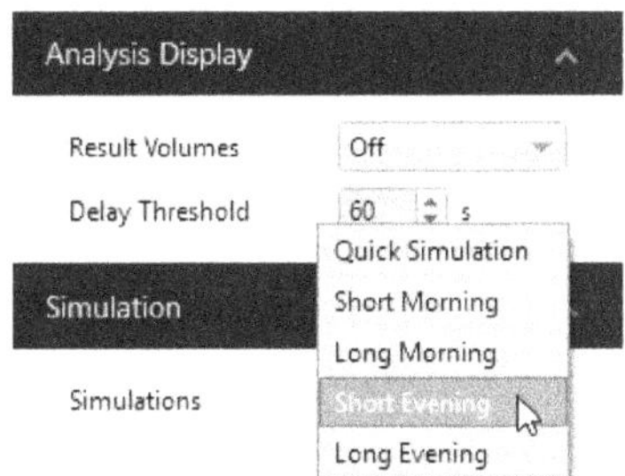

Figure 2–4

Note: Running a simulation costs cloud credits.

6. Click **Run Simulation**.

© 2019, ASCENT - Center for Technical Knowledge®

Traffic Analyst Panel

The Traffic Analyst Panel is where advanced parameters and multiple simulation variants are added to the traffic analysis. Figure 2–5 shows the Traffic Analyst Panel with the Intersection control panel open. Changing parameters and variables helps you to better predict traffic flow. For the best results, run the simulation a few times and analyze the distribution of results.

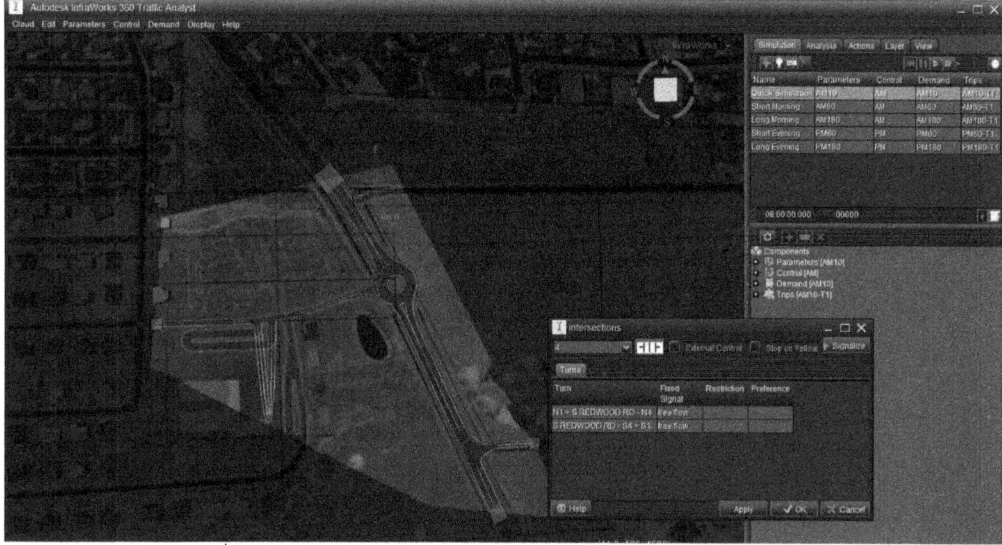

Figure 2–5

Parameters

Several parameters can be set during a traffic analysis, including:

- **Terms**: Windows of time during the day, specified as HH:MM. An unlimited number of terms can be defined for a network. Terms can overlap or be sequential, and can also specify the day of the week (weekday or weekend or a specific day).

You can access the MOBs window by using a button at the bottom of the Behaviors window.

- **Behaviors and Mobs**: Behaviors are assigned to either person types or vehicle types. They control decisions made by each person. A group of behaviors is a MOB (Mix of Behaviors).

A MOB must be created before restrictions can be added.

- **Restrictions and Speed Controls**: Restrictions are applied to surfaces to control the types of people or vehicles that can move on the surface.

Behaviors are applied to vehicle types.

- **Vehicle Types**: Controls the size, movement, and display of a vehicle in the model. A group of vehicle types is called a fleet.

© 2019, ASCENT - Center for Technical Knowledge®

Controllers

The Intersection Controller enables you to control conflicts between different streams of traffic. Each lane of an intersection can have a different control signal or no signal at all. When a lane is selected in the controller, an arrow displays in the Traffic Analyst Panel indicating the direction of traffic, as shown in Figure 2–6.

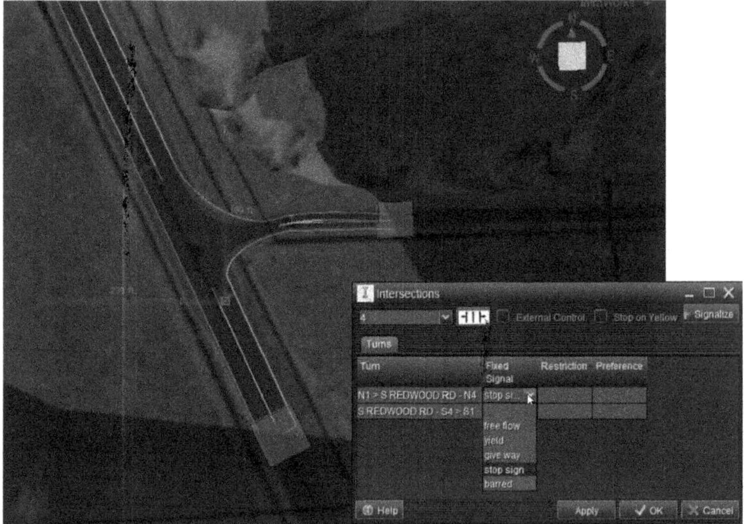

Figure 2–6

The Fixed Signal options below are listed in order of increasing priority:

- **Barred:** The turn is closed to all traffic.
- **Stop Sign:** The approaching traffic has a stop sign and must stop before proceeding through the intersection.
- **Give Way:** Approaching traffic has a Give Way sign and slows down accordingly.
- **Yield:** Approaching traffic is on the main road, but must cross an opposing stream, and must slow down on approach.
- **Free Flow:** Approaching traffic is on the main road, has priority, and does not need to check for conflicting traffic.

© 2019, ASCENT - Center for Technical Knowledge®

Demand

The Demand Editor enables you to modify the traffic counts for various times of day and origin points. Three tabs exist in the Demand Editor:

- **Directed Demand:** Uses origin-destination matrices where demand between all origin-destination pairs is known. When an origin point is selected in the Demand Editor, arrows display in the Traffic Analyst Panel indicating the destination of traffic, as shown in Figure 2–7.

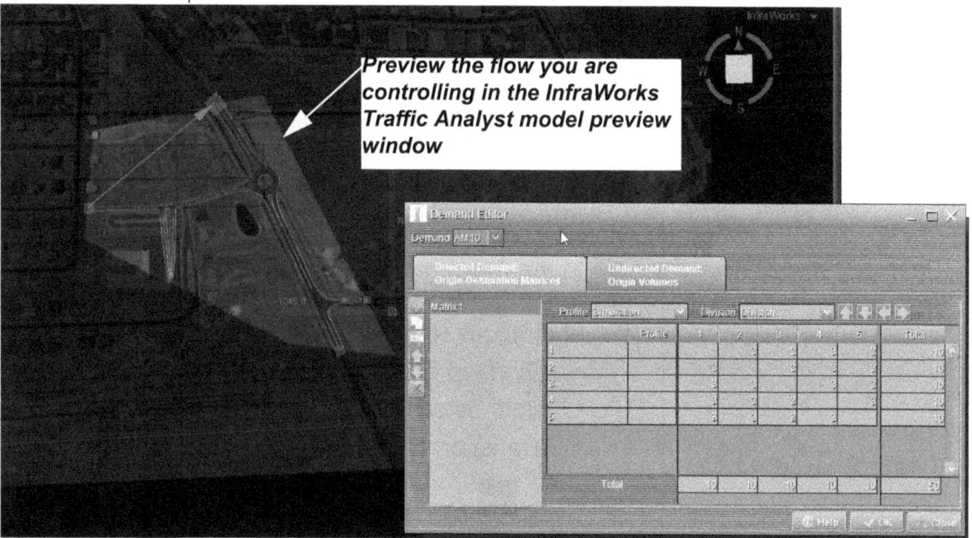

Preview the flow you are controlling in the InfraWorks Traffic Analyst model preview window

Figure 2–7

- **Undirected Demand:** Uses traffic volumes from an origin zone along with turning counts.

- **Transport Demand:** Lists all public transport services, departure times, and associated vehicle types.

How To: Control Traffic Flow per Intersection

1. Create a Traffic Simulation.
2. In the model, select the Traffic Study area boundary.
3. Right-click and select **Traffic Analyst Panel**.
4. Click **OK** in the two Traffic Simulation dialog boxes that display.
5. In the **Control** menu, select **Intersections**.
6. In the Intersections panel, select the intersection or roundabout to work with from the Intersection drop-down list.

7. Select a control in the *Fixed Signal* column for each turn, as shown in Figure 2–8.

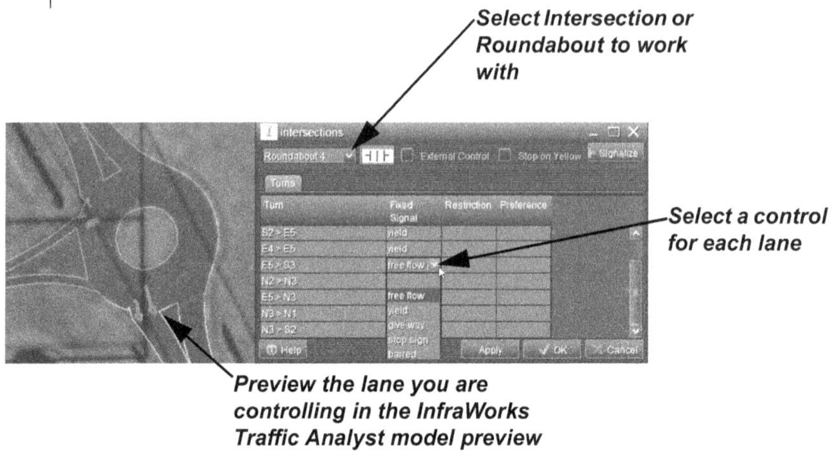
Select Intersection or Roundabout to work with
Select a control for each lane
Preview the lane you are controlling in the InfraWorks Traffic Analyst model preview window

Figure 2–8

8. Click **OK**,
9. In the **Demand** menu, select **Demand**.
10. In the Demand Editor, select the appropriate tab for the type of matrices required for the project:
    - Directed Demand
    - Undirected Demand
    - Transport Demand
11. Click (Add) to add an additional matrix, origin, or destination.
12. Input the traffic count for each profile.
13. Click **OK**.

© 2019, ASCENT - Center for Technical Knowledge®

Practice 2a Run a Traffic Study

Practice Objective

- Generate an animation file based on the default traffic demand.

In this practice, you will create a traffic study to analyze traffic flow along the component roads using default traffic counts. You will also set control signals for each lane at the signalized intersection.

Task 1 - Run a traffic study.

To complete this practice, access to the Internet is required.

1. In the Home Screen, click **Open**.
2. In the *C:\InfraWorks Design Practice Files\RoadAnalysis* folder, select **DesignRoadAnalysis.sqlite** and click **Open**.
3. In the Utility Bar, expand *Proposal* and select **A_Task1** to make it current.
4. In the Utility Bar, click (Bookmark) and select **ProjectArea**.
5. In the In Canvas tools, expand (Design, review and engineer roads)> (Perform analysis in preparation for road design), and click (Traffic Simulation).
6. A message should display noting that the model must be published. In the message's dialog box, click **Publish Model**.

If you receive a message indicating that you do not have rights to upload the model to the cloud, duplicate the model and try again.

7. In the Publish Model dialog box, set a publish location and select the resource **A_Task1**. Click **Publish**.
8. In the Publish Model message, click **Close**.
9. After publishing the model, the view reverts back to the Home view. In the Utility Bar, click (Bookmark) and select **ProjectArea** again.

10. In the In Canvas tools, expand (Design, review and engineer roads)> (Perform analysis in preparation for road design), and click (Traffic Simulation). The Component Roads are highlighted to indicate which roads can be analyzed using a traffic study.

11. In the model, define a polyline to indicate the Traffic Study Area boundary, as shown in Figure 2–9. Ensure that you double-click on the last point to finish the boundary.

Figure 2–9

12. In the message box that displays, click **Yes**, as shown in Figure 2–10.

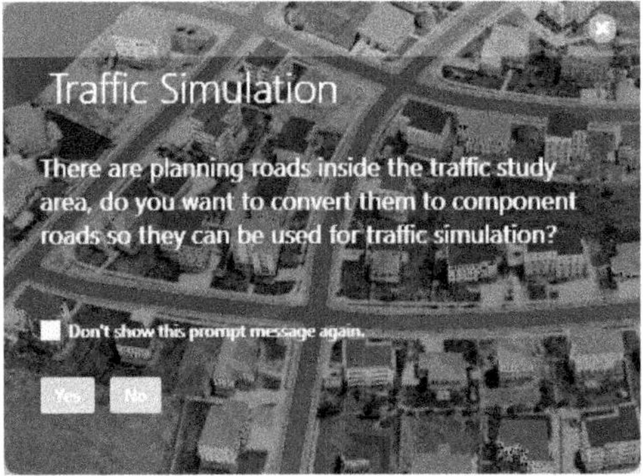

Figure 2–10

© 2019, ASCENT - Center for Technical Knowledge®

13. In the Traffic Study Area asset card, set the following options, as shown in Figure 2–11:
    - *Results Volume*: **Per Lane**.
    - *Simulations*: **Quick Simulation**.

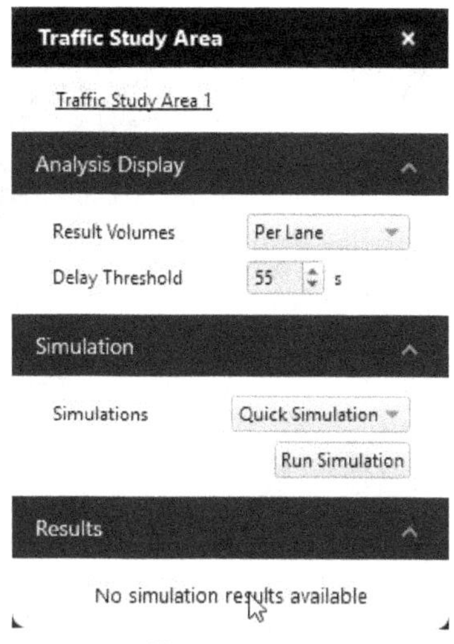

Figure 2–11

Running this simulation costs 1 cloud credit.

14. Click **Run Simulation**.

15. Click **OK** in the Traffic Simulation dialog box that displays.

16. With the Traffic Study area boundary still selected, right-click and select **Traffic Analyst Panel**.

17. Click **OK** in the two Traffic Simulation dialog boxes that display.

18. In the **Control** menu, select **Intersections**.

19. In the Intersections panel:
    - In the Intersection drop-down list, select **Roundabout 6**.
    - Select the *Fixed Signals* for each lane, matching those shown in Figure 2–12. Click **Apply**.

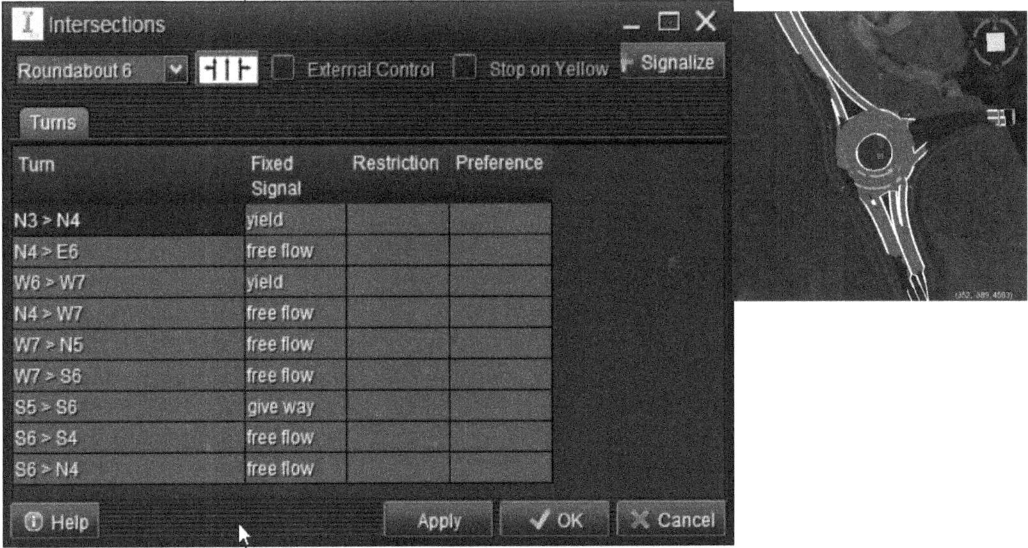

Figure 2–12

Hint: Arrows display for the currently selected lane in the InfraWorks Traffic Analyst model preview window, as shown in Figure 2–12.

20. In the Intersections panel:
    - In the Intersection drop-down list, select **Intersection 5**.
    - Select *Fixed Signals* for each lane, matching those shown in Figure 2–13.

© 2019, ASCENT - Center for Technical Knowledge®

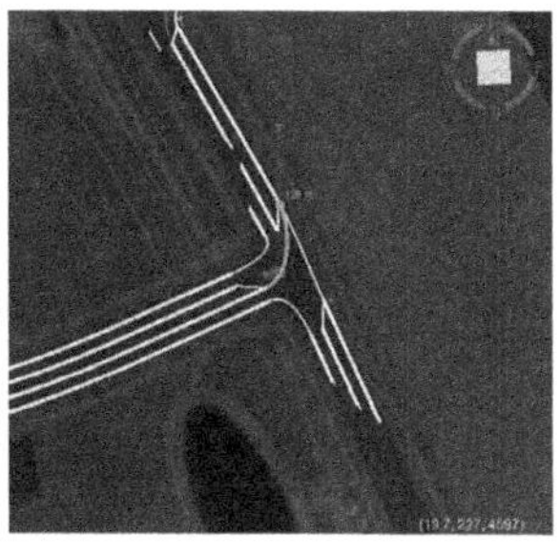

Figure 2–13

21. Click **OK**.
22. In the **Demand** menu, select **Demands**.
23. In the Demand Editor, set the Directed Demand matrix for the project so that they match those shown in Figure 2–14.

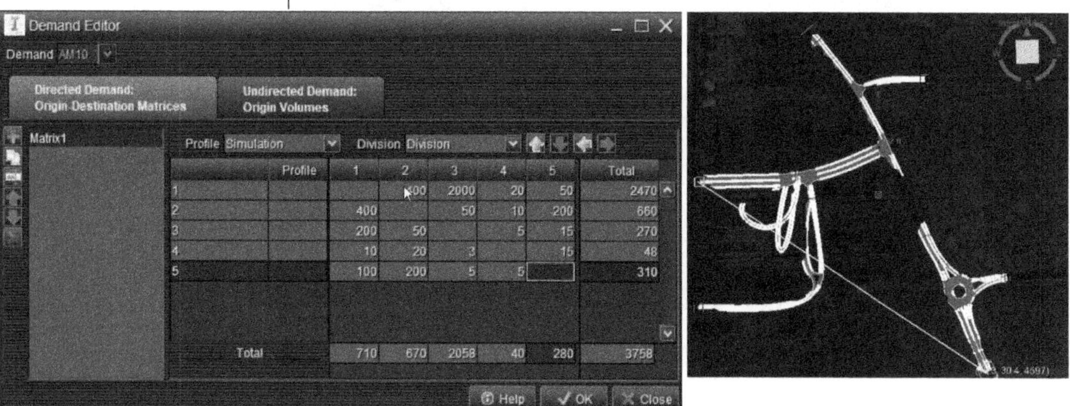

Figure 2–14

24. Click **OK**.

25. In the Traffic Analyst Panel, *Simulation* tab, click (Play). Note how the cars bunch up at the intersections and roundabout, as shown in Figure 2–15.

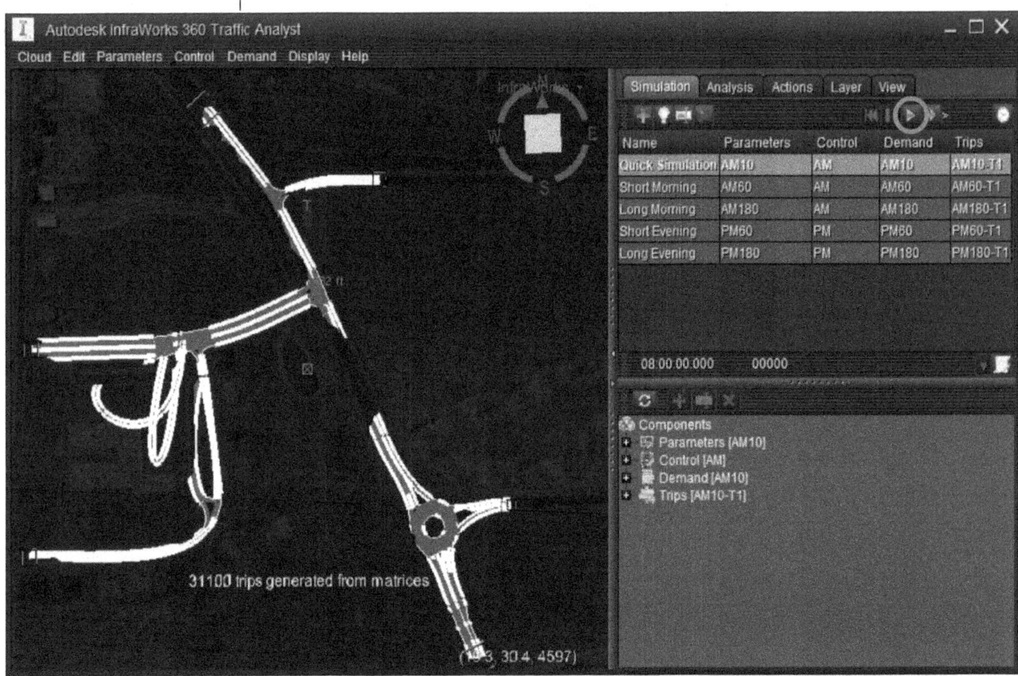

Figure 2–15

26. In the Traffic Analyst Panel, *Simulation* tab, click (Pause).

27. In the **Control** menu, select **Intersections**.

 © 2019, ASCENT - Center for Technical Knowledge®

28. In the Intersections panel:
    - In the Intersection drop-down list, select **Roundabout 6**.
    - Click (Edit Turn Lanes).
    - Three lanes have conflicts. Fix them automatically by clicking **Repair**, as shown in Figure 2–16. Click **Close**.
    - Click **OK**.

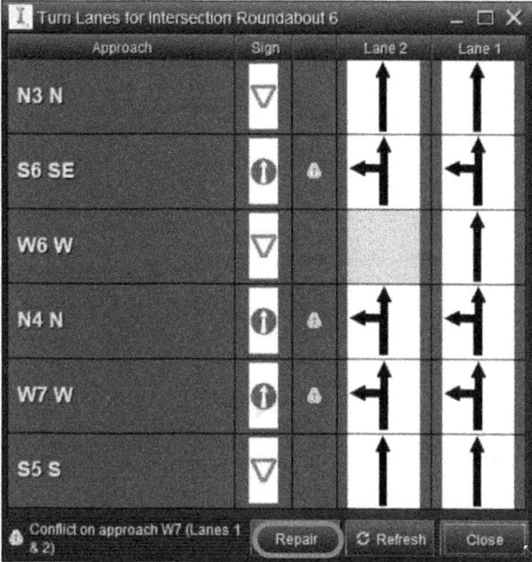

Figure 2–16

29. In the Traffic Analyst Panel, *Simulation* tab, click (Play). Note how the cars now flow better at the roundabout.

30. In the Traffic Analyst Panel, *Simulation* tab, click (Pause).

31. Close the Traffic Analyst Panel.

Running this simulation costs 1 cloud credit.

32. In the Traffic Study Area asset card, click **Run Simulation**.

33. Click **OK** in the Traffic Simulation message that displays.

You must give the simulation time to complete before you can play the animation.

34. In the Animation Player asset card, click  (Play).

    Note that if there are any Red queues, they indicate delays that exceed a threshold, as shown in Figure 2–17. This model does not have any red queues.

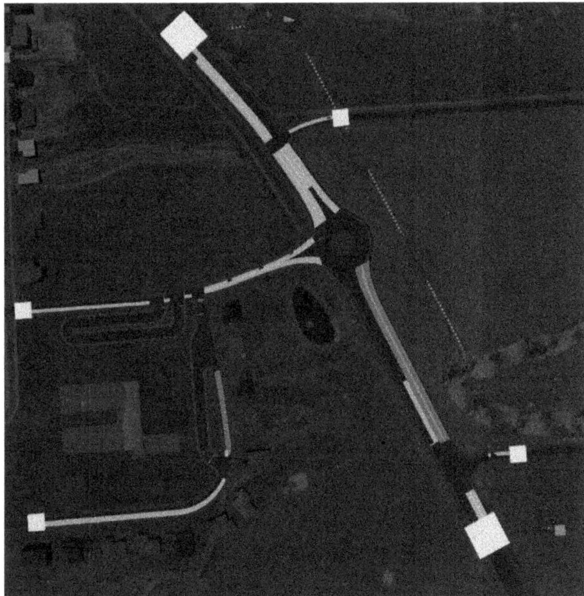

Figure 2–17

35. In the In Canvas tools, expand (Design, review and engineer roads)> (Perform analysis in preparation for road design), and click (Traffic Simulation) to toggle off the traffic simulation boundary.

© 2019, ASCENT - Center for Technical Knowledge®

2.2 Calculating Quantities

When a component road is selected, the Road asset card displays two options at the bottom of the asset card for calculating quantities, as shown in Figure 2–18.

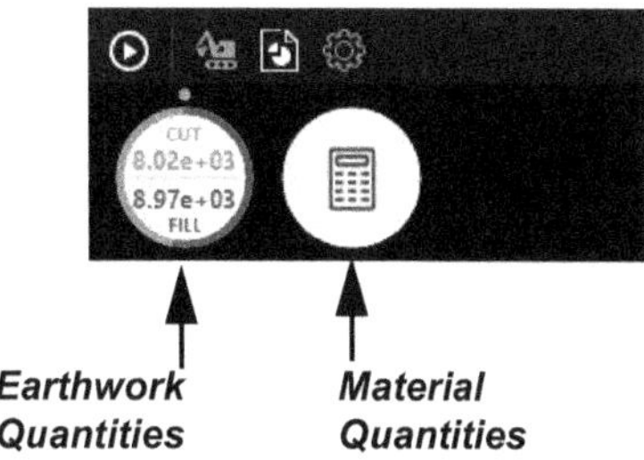

Figure 2–18

The types of materials that can be calculated include:

Road components within intersections or roundabouts are ignored.

- Earthwork Cut and Fill quantities at each sampled station along with its cumulative volume.
- The Road component's (assemblies) total length and area.
- Bridge materials.
- Drainage components, which include total length of pipe and counts of structures.
- 3D models that are used as decorations.
  - For objects spaced along an alignments, the calculations are based on the 2D length.
  - For objects at the beginning and end of the alignments, the calculations vary due to a difference in how items are placed and how the calculation handles a remainder in spacing.
  - Objects placed before the start or after the end of the alignment are not counted.

© 2019, ASCENT - Center for Technical Knowledge®

How To: Compute Earthwork Quantities

1. In the model, select the component road.
2. In the component road asset card, click (Earthwork Quantities).
3. In the component road asset card, click (Specify settings).
4. In the Earthwork Setting panel, set the *Station Increment* value and toggle on which geometry you want to sample, as shown in Figure 2–19. Close the Earthwork Setting panel.

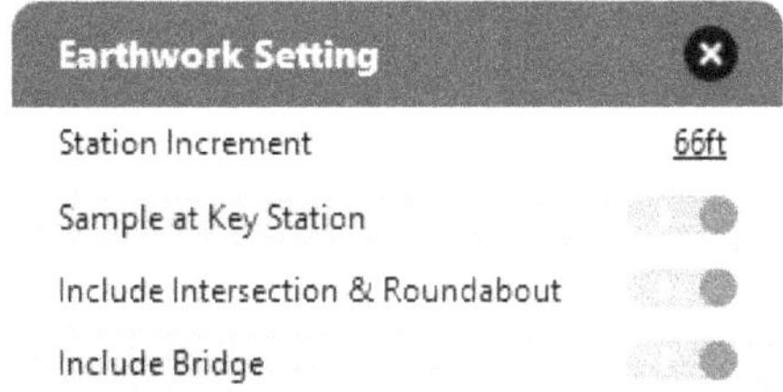

Figure 2–19

5. In the component road asset card, click (Compute earthwork quantities). Wait for it to process.
6. To see the results, in the component road asset card, click (View detail values). The Earthwork Quantities panel displays, as shown in Figure 2–20.

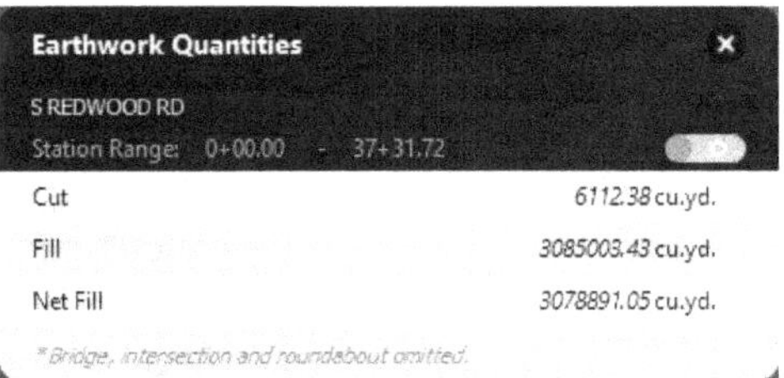

Figure 2–20

7. To create a report, in the component road asset card, click (Generate report).
8. In the Save Quantities dialog box, type a file name, browse to the folder where you want to save the file, and then click **Save**.
9. When the file is done saving, Windows Explorer automatically opens the location where you saved the file. Double-click on the file to open it in Microsoft Excel, or right-click on it and select **Open with...** to open it in a different program.

© 2019, ASCENT - Center for Technical Knowledge®

10. When opened in Microsoft Excel, the report displays similar to that shown in Figure 2–21.

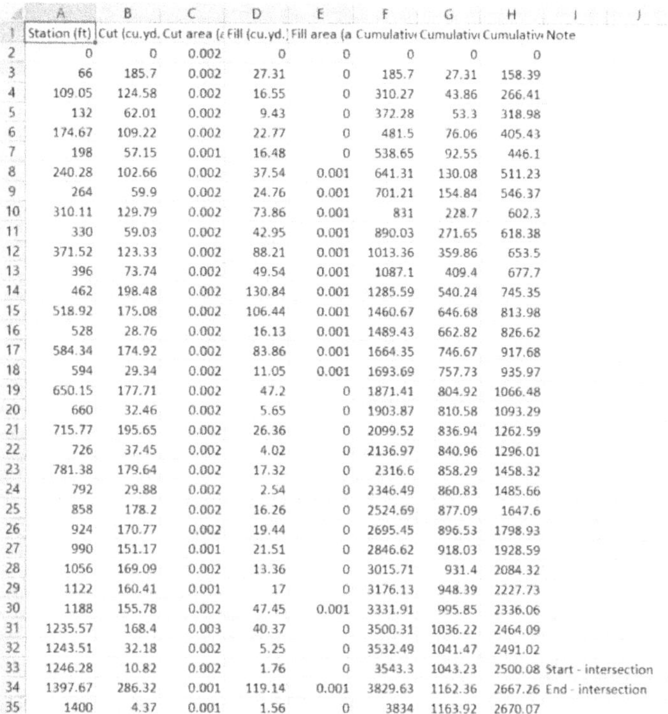

	A	B	C	D	E	F	G	H	I
1	Station (ft)	Cut (cu.yd.	Cut area (a	Fill (cu.yd.	Fill area (a	Cumulativ	Cumulativ	Cumulativ	Note
2	0	0	0.002	0	0	0	0	0	
3	66	185.7	0.002	27.31	0	185.7	27.31	158.39	
4	109.05	124.58	0.002	16.55	0	310.27	43.86	266.41	
5	132	62.01	0.002	9.43	0	372.28	53.3	318.98	
6	174.67	109.22	0.002	22.77	0	481.5	76.06	405.43	
7	198	57.15	0.001	16.48	0	538.65	92.55	446.1	
8	240.28	102.66	0.002	37.54	0.001	641.31	130.08	511.23	
9	264	59.9	0.002	24.76	0.001	701.21	154.84	546.37	
10	310.11	129.79	0.002	73.86	0.001	831	228.7	602.3	
11	330	59.03	0.002	42.95	0.001	890.03	271.65	618.38	
12	371.52	123.33	0.002	88.21	0.001	1013.36	359.86	653.5	
13	396	73.74	0.002	49.54	0.001	1087.1	409.4	677.7	
14	462	198.48	0.002	130.84	0.001	1285.59	540.24	745.35	
15	518.92	175.08	0.002	106.44	0.001	1460.67	646.68	813.98	
16	528	28.76	0.002	16.13	0.001	1489.43	662.82	826.62	
17	584.34	174.92	0.002	83.86	0.001	1664.35	746.67	917.68	
18	594	29.34	0.002	11.05	0.001	1693.69	757.73	935.97	
19	650.15	177.71	0.002	47.2	0	1871.41	804.92	1066.48	
20	660	32.46	0.002	5.65	0	1903.87	810.58	1093.29	
21	715.77	195.65	0.002	26.36	0	2099.52	836.94	1262.59	
22	726	37.45	0.002	4.02	0	2136.97	840.96	1296.01	
23	781.38	179.64	0.002	17.32	0	2316.6	858.29	1458.32	
24	792	29.88	0.002	2.54	0	2346.49	860.83	1485.66	
25	858	178.2	0.002	16.26	0	2524.69	877.09	1647.6	
26	924	170.77	0.002	19.44	0	2695.45	896.53	1798.93	
27	990	151.17	0.001	21.51	0	2846.62	918.03	1928.59	
28	1056	169.09	0.002	13.36	0	3015.71	931.4	2084.32	
29	1122	160.41	0.001	17	0	3176.13	948.39	2227.73	
30	1188	155.78	0.002	47.45	0.001	3331.91	995.85	2336.06	
31	1235.57	168.4	0.003	40.37	0	3500.31	1036.22	2464.09	
32	1243.51	32.18	0.002	5.25	0	3532.49	1041.47	2491.02	
33	1246.28	10.82	0.002	1.76	0	3543.3	1043.23	2500.08	Start - intersection
34	1397.67	286.32	0.001	119.14	0.001	3829.63	1162.36	2667.26	End - intersection
35	1400	4.37	0.001	1.56	0	3834	1163.92	2670.07	

Figure 2–21

How To: Compute Material Quantities

1. In the model, select the component road.
2. In the component road asset card, click (Material Quantities).
3. In the component road asset card, click (Show Road Quantities).

4. Review the quantities that display in the Material Quantities dialog, as shown in Figure 2–22.

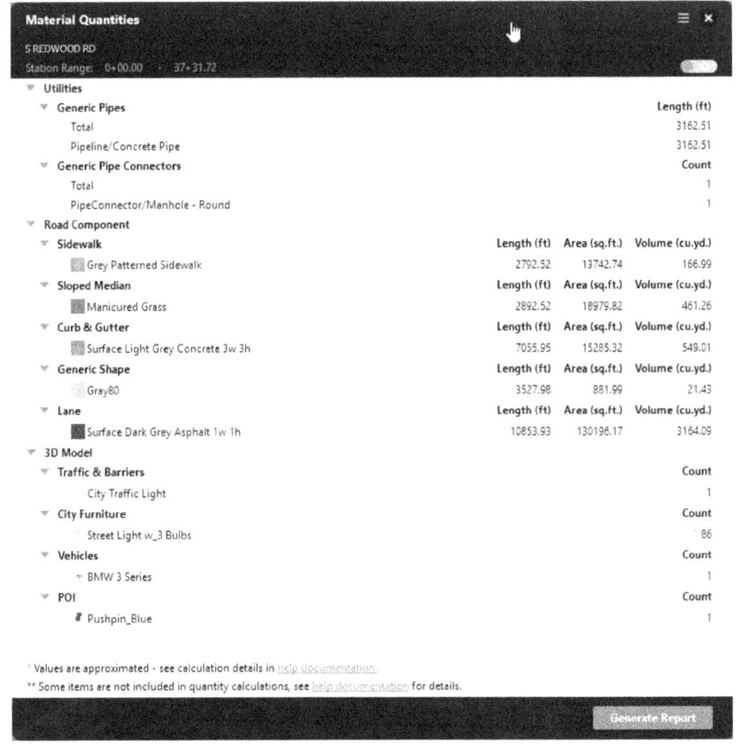

Material Quantities
5 REDWOOD RD
Station Range: 0+00.00 - 37+31.72
Utilities
Generic Pipes
Length (ft)
Total
3162.51
Pipeline/Concrete Pipe
3162.51
Generic Pipe Connectors
Count
Total
1
PipeConnector/Manhole - Round
1
Road Component
Sidewalk
Length (ft) Area (sq.ft.) Volume (cu.yd.)
Grey Patterned Sidewalk
2792.52 13742.74 166.99
Sloped Median
Length (ft) Area (sq.ft.) Volume (cu.yd.)
Manicured Grass
2892.52 18979.82 461.26
Curb & Gutter
Length (ft) Area (sq.ft.) Volume (cu.yd.)
Surface Light Grey Concrete 3w 3h
7055.95 15285.32 549.01
Generic Shape
Length (ft) Area (sq.ft.) Volume (cu.yd.)
Gray80
3527.98 881.99 21.43
Lane
Length (ft) Area (sq.ft.) Volume (cu.yd.)
Surface Dark Grey Asphalt 1w 1h
10853.93 130196.17 3164.09
3D Model
Traffic & Barriers
Count
City Traffic Light
1
City Furniture
Count
Street Light w_3 Bulbs
86
Vehicles
Count
BMW 3 Series
1
POI
Count
Pushpin_Blue
1
Values are approximated - see calculation details in help documentation.
** Some items are not included in quantity calculations, see help documentation for details.
Generate Report

Figure 2–22

5. In the Material Quantities dialog, click **Generate Report** to send the calculations to a CSV file similar to the one shown in Figure 2–23.

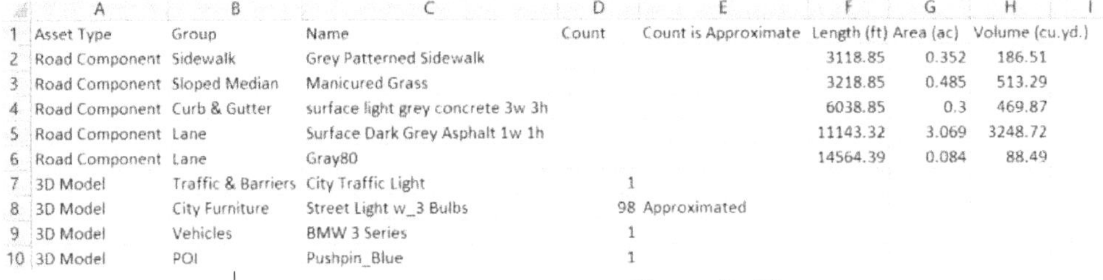

	A	B	C	D	E	F	G	H
1	Asset Type	Group	Name	Count	Count is Approximate	Length (ft)	Area (ac)	Volume (cu.yd.)
2	Road Component	Sidewalk	Grey Patterned Sidewalk			3118.85	0.352	186.51
3	Road Component	Sloped Median	Manicured Grass			3218.85	0.485	513.29
4	Road Component	Curb & Gutter	surface light grey concrete 3w 3h			6038.85	0.3	469.87
5	Road Component	Lane	Surface Dark Grey Asphalt 1w 1h			11143.32	3.069	3248.72
6	Road Component	Lane	Gray80			14564.39	0.084	88.49
7	3D Model	Traffic & Barriers	City Traffic Light	1				
8	3D Model	City Furniture	Street Light w_3 Bulbs	98	Approximated			
9	3D Model	Vehicles	BMW 3 Series	1				
10	3D Model	POI	Pushpin_Blue	1				

Figure 2–23

 © 2019, ASCENT - Center for Technical Knowledge®

Practice 2b Calculate Quantities

Practice Objective

- Calculate how much material is required to build the road.

In this practice, you will run two calculations to figure out how much material is required to build the road. First you will calculate the earthwork quantities. You will then calculate the concrete, asphalt, and other materials according to what it designed into the assemblies used in the road.

Task 1 - Calculate earthwork quantities.

To complete this practice, access to the Internet is required.

1. In the *C:\InfraWorks Design Practice Files\RoadAnalysis* folder, select **DesignRoadAnalysis.sqlite** and click **Open**.
2. In the Utility Bar, expand *Proposal* and select **B_Task1** to make it current.
3. In the Utility Bar, click (Bookmark) and select **Quantities**.
4. In the model, select **S Redwood Rd.**, running north to south to the left of the pond.
5. In the component road asset card, click (Earthwork quantities).
6. In the component road asset card, click (Specify settings).
7. In the Earthwork Setting panel, set the *Station Increment* value to **50** and toggle on all of the geometry options to sample them, as shown in Figure 2–24. Close the Earthwork Setting panel.

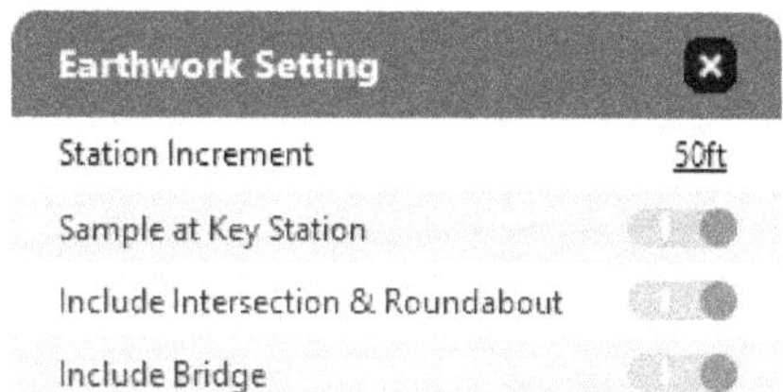

Figure 2–24

8. In the component road asset card, click (Compute earthwork quantities). Wait for it to process.

9. If the results are not showing by default, in the component road asset card, click (View detail values). The Earthwork Quantities panel displays, as shown in Figure 2–25.

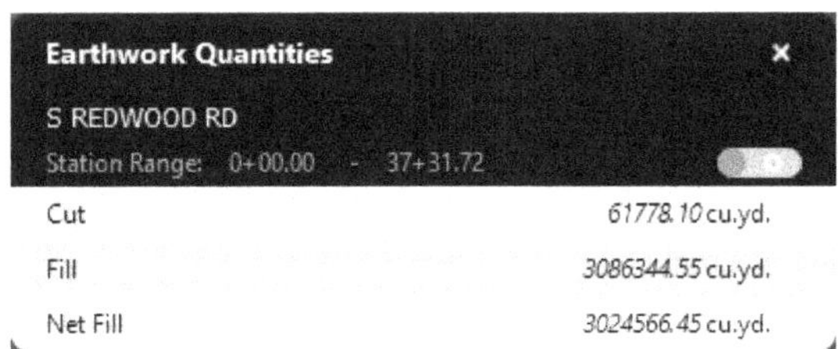

Figure 2–25

10. To create a report, in the component road asset card, click (Generate report).

11. In the Save Quantities dialog box, type a file name, browse to where the file should be saved, and click **Save**.

If Windows Explorer does not open automatically, open Microsoft Excel and open the .CSV file.

12. When the file is done saving, Windows Explorer automatically opens to the location where you saved the file. Double-click on the .CSV file to open it in Microsoft Excel. The report displays similar to that shown in Figure 2–26.

	A	B	C	D	E	F	G	H	I
1	Station (ft)	Cut (cu.yd.)	Cut area (sq.ft.)	Fill (cu.yd.)	Fill area (sq.ft.)	Cumulative Cut (cu.yd.)	Cumulative Fill (cu.yd.)	Cumulative Net (cu.yd.)	Note
2	0	0	57.79	0	17.03	0	0	0	
3	50	112.53	63.73	28.88	14.16	112.53	28.88	83.65	
4	100	117.45	63.11	27.03	15.03	229.98	55.91	174.07	
5	150	111.34	57.14	26.8	13.91	341.32	82.7	258.62	
6	200	106.4	57.78	26.63	14.85	447.73	109.33	338.4	
7	250	109.5	60.48	26.44	13.71	557.23	135.77	421.46	
8	261.93	29.6	73.5	6.9	17.53	586.83	142.67	444.16	
9	300	103.99	74.01	29.66	24.54	690.82	172.33	518.49	
10	345.71	135.64	86.22	52.62	37.62	826.46	224.95	601.5	
11	350	13.64	85.55	5.89	36.56	840.1	230.85	609.26	
12	366.67	52.26	83.71	21.81	34.06	892.36	252.65	639.71	Start - intersection
13	451.6	26.61	67.75	156.42	23.46	918.97	409.07	509.9	End - intersection
14	479.13	66.82	63.32	21.8	19.3	985.79	430.87	554.92	
15	498.24	46.05	66.79	13.07	17.61	1031.85	443.94	587.91	
16	500	4.36	67.46	1.14	17.58	1036.21	445.08	591.13	
17	541.85	132.56	103.58	32.83	24.78	1168.77	477.91	690.86	
18	550	31.11	102.58	7.34	23.85	1199.88	485.25	714.63	

Figure 2–26

 © 2019, ASCENT - Center for Technical Knowledge®

Task 2 - Calculate material quantities.

1. In the model, select **S Redwood Rd.** if not already selected.
2. In the road asset card, click (Material Quantities).
3. In the road asset card, click (Show Road Quantities).
4. Review the quantities that display in the Material Quantities dialog box, as shown in Figure 2–27.

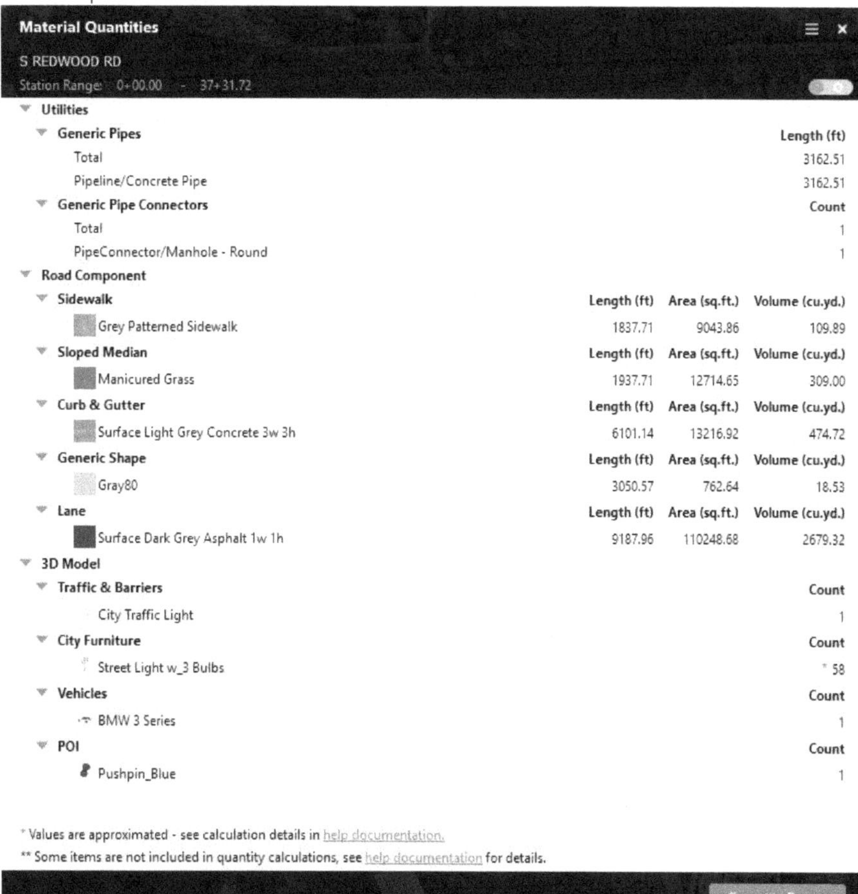

Figure 2–27

5. In the Material Quantities dialog box, click **Generate Report** to send the calculations to a CSV file.

To use this feature, access to the Internet is required.

2.3 Corridor Optimization

The Corridor Optimization module provides advanced optimization algorithms for finding an optimal horizontal roadway alignment. This cloud service uses the model terrain and other GIS information in the model to create cost effective and environmentally friendly solutions. The best available path is calculated by setting the start and end points for the road. The optimal time for performing a corridor optimization is when you are first considering the layout of the roadway.

Advanced Settings

When the Advanced Settings are expanded in the Corridor Optimization palette, additional constraints can be added to the corridor.

Cost Zones & Suitability Map

Avoidance zones can be specified to ensure that the new road corridor does not pass through environmentally sensitive or other high cost areas. These zones can be drawn in manually by selecting the **Draw avoidance zones** link. Alternatively, they can be activated by opening a suitability map by selecting **Open suitability map** then selecting the option to **Include the current suitability map**, as shown in Figure 2–28.

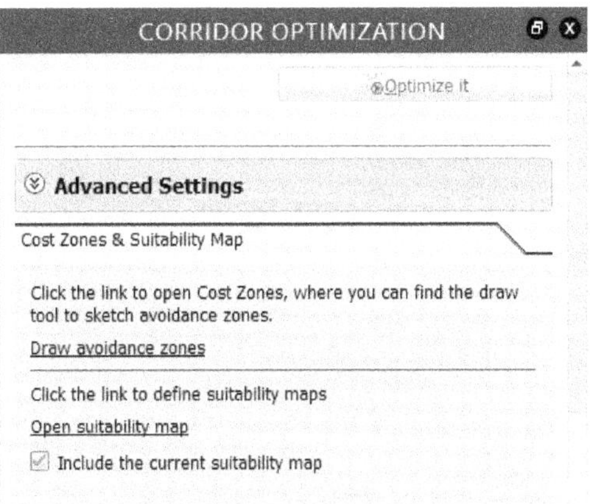

Figure 2–28

© 2019, ASCENT - Center for Technical Knowledge®

Construction Rules

Setting construction rules provides a method of ensuring bridges are placed and tunnels are cut where cut/fill heights exceed a maximum height. Additionally, roadside grading values can be set, as shown in Figure 2–29.

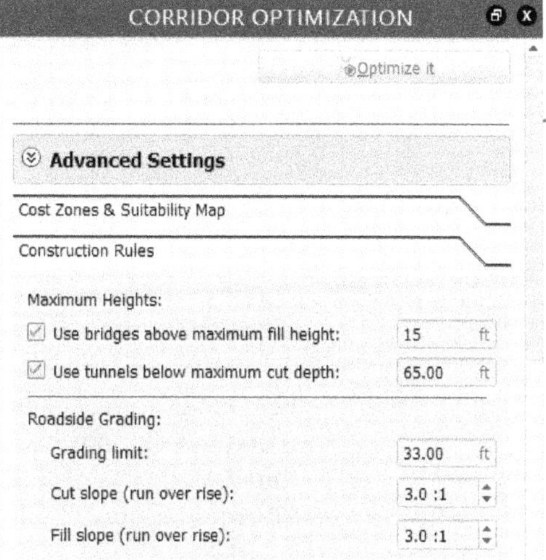

Figure 2–29

Alignment Constraints

Minimum radius can be set under the Alignment Constraints, as shown in Figure 2–30.

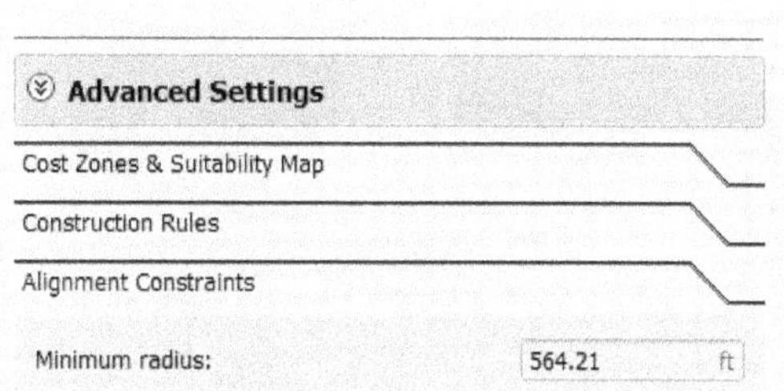

Figure 2–30

Profile Constraints

Maximum grade can be set under the Profile Constraints, as shown in Figure 2–31.

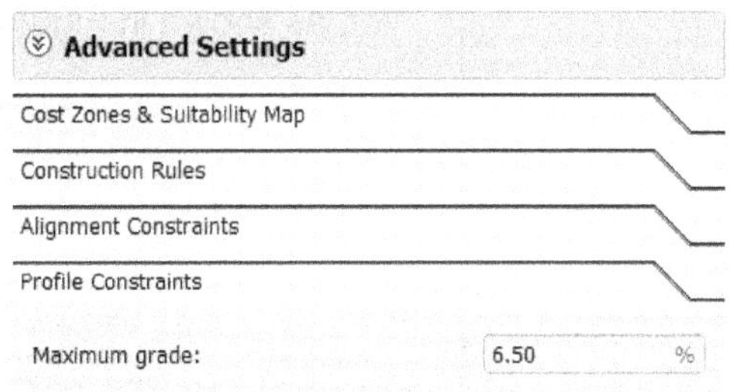

Figure 2–31

Construction & Earthwork Cost

Prices for construction and earthwork cost items can be set using the Construction & Earthwork Cost dialog box. To access this dialog box, click **Construction & Earthwork Cost**, as shown in Figure 2–32.

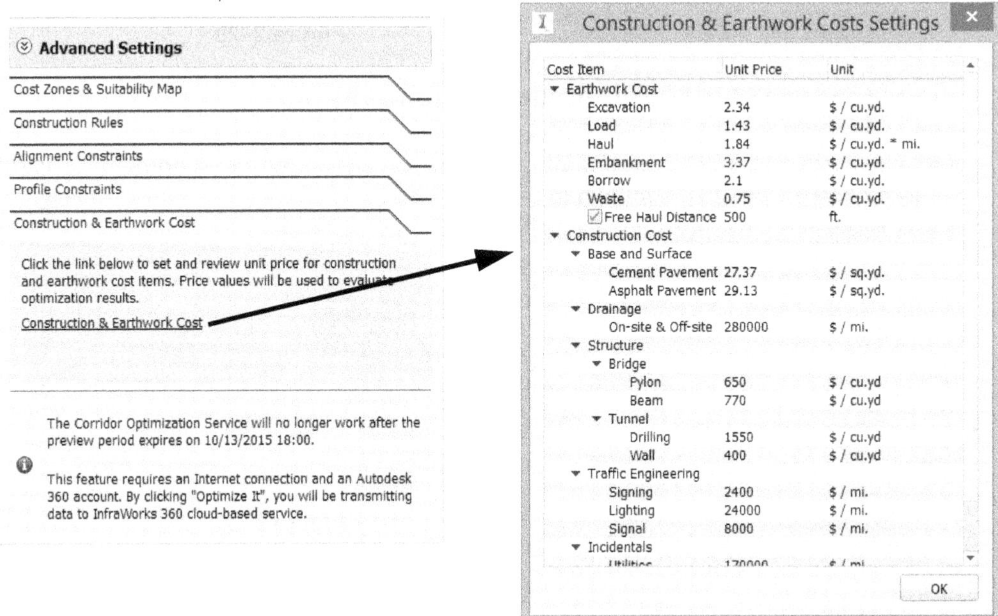

Figure 2–32

© 2019, ASCENT - Center for Technical Knowledge®

Job Monitor

The corridor optimization results are communicated through the Job Monitor panel, which displays automatically once you run an optimization. The status of all the optimizations which have been run display here, as shown in Figure 2–33.

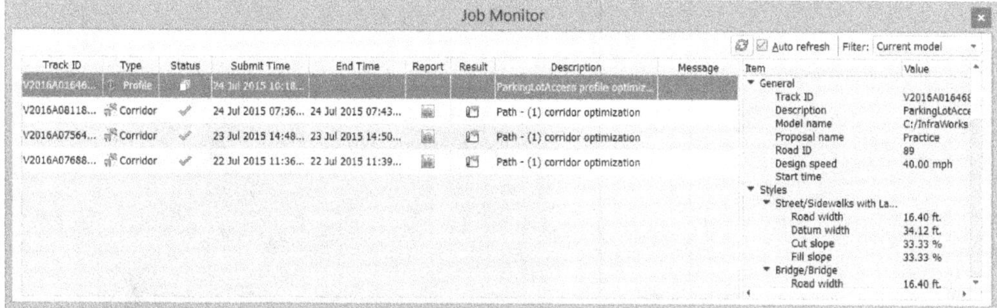

Figure 2–33

Status

The *Status* column displays the current status of your optimization. There are three status icons, which are as follows:

Icon	Status	Description
	Queued	Indicates that the profile has been sent to the cloud for computing, but has not started yet.
	In Progress	Indicates that the profile is currently being optimized in the cloud.
	Completed	Indicates that the optimization calculations are complete.

Viewing Results

The results of the optimization can be viewed by:

- Downloading a report.
- Importing the data into a new proposal in the model.

Report

In the Job Monitor panel, under the *Report* column, clicking (Click to download an optimization report) opens a file and displays the results of the calculations. This report displays items including alignment information, profile information, construction information, etc.

Figure 2–34 shows a sample report with the suggested horizontal and profile view for the component road.

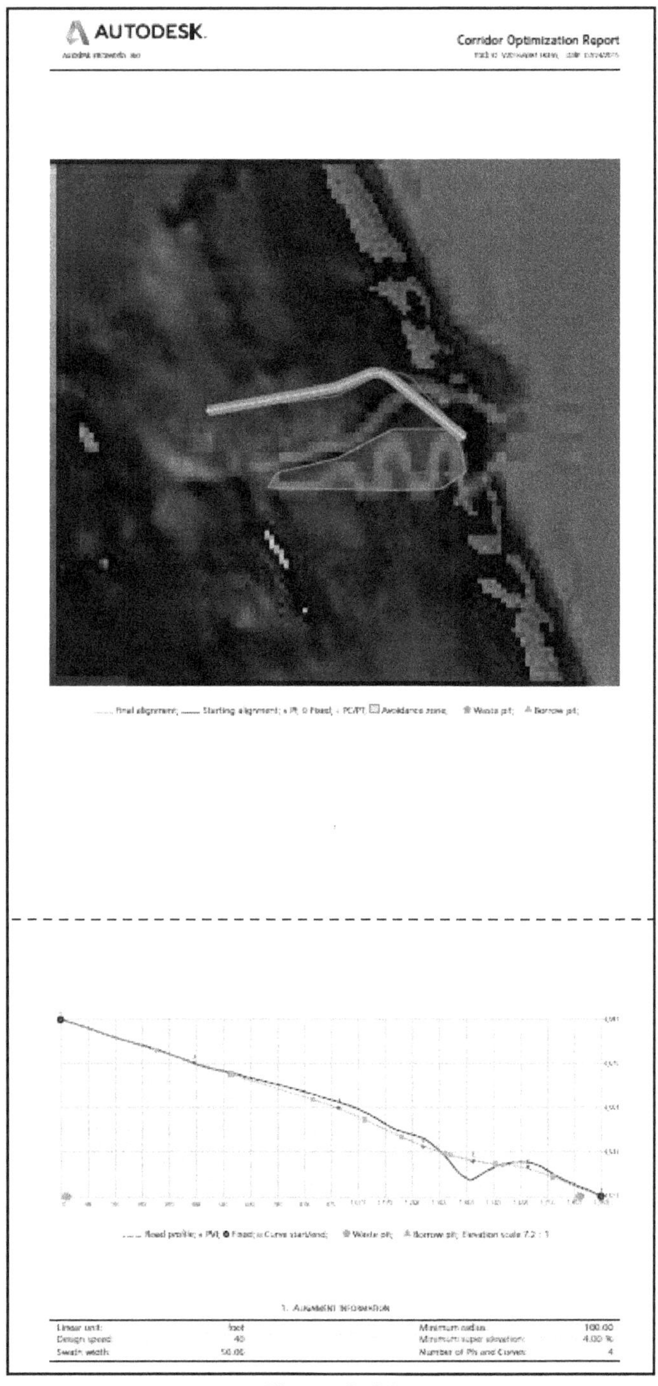

Figure 2–34

 © 2019, ASCENT - Center for Technical Knowledge®

Create a Proposal from Results

In addition to downloading the results in a file, you can also view the results by importing the roadway into a new proposal in the model. To do this, in the Job Monitor panel, in the *Results* column, click (Create a proposal to view the results in the model).

How To: Run a Corridor Optimization

1. In the In Canvas tools, expand (Design, review and engineer roads)> (Perform analysis in preparation for road design), and click (Corridor Optimization).
2. In the Corridor Optimization palette, set the following options, as shown in Figure 2–35.
    - Select an appropriate *Design speed* for the project
    - Select the *Structure styles* for the Road, Bridge, and Tunnel.
    - For the *Path*, click (Define PIs).

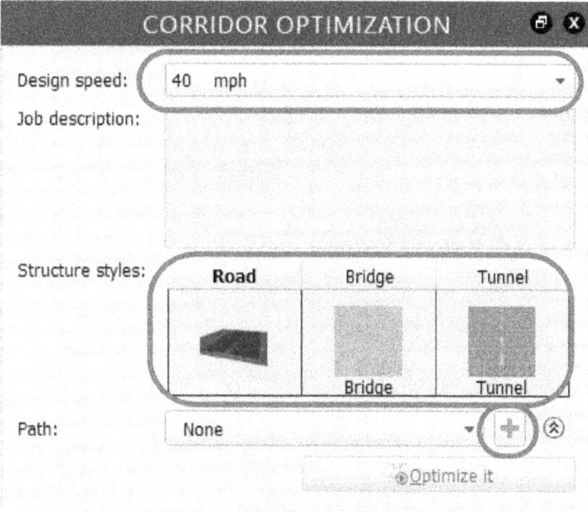

Figure 2–35

3. In the model, click to set the start PI and the end PI.
4. In the Corridor Optimization palette, expand the *Advanced Settings* area.

5. Under the Cost Zones & Suitability Map, click **Draw avoidance zones**.
6. In the Cost Zones asset card, click (Draw avoidance zones). In the model, create polylines to define areas to avoid.
7. Under the Cost Zones & Suitability Map, click **Open suitability map**.
8. In the Suitability Maps asset card, expand the Select a Map drop-down list and select the appropriate map for your needs.
9. In the Corridor Optimization palette, select the **Include the current suitability map** option.
10. In the *Construction Rules* area, set the maximum cut/fill heights and the roadside grading parameters as required.
11. In the *Alignment Constraints* area, set the minimum radius.
12. In the *Profile Constraints* area, set the maximum grade.
13. In the *Construction & Earthwork Cost* area, click **Construction & Earthwork Cost** to open the dialog box and set costing values.
14. In the Corridor Optimization palette, ensure that the correct path is selected, and then click **Optimize it**.
15. In the Job Monitor palette, under the *Report* column, click (Click to download an optimization report) to review the results in a report format.
16. In the Job Monitor palette, under the Results column, click (Create a proposal to view the result in the model).
17. Click **Yes** in the Information dialog box.
18. Type a name and click **OK** to create the proposal.

If the Job Monitor panel does not open, in the In Canvas tools, click (Design, review, and engineer roads)> (Review and modify roadway designs)> (Job Monitor).

© 2019, ASCENT - Center for Technical Knowledge®

Practice 2c Identify the Best Location for a New Roadway

Practice Objective

- Locate the best location for a roadway based on a suitability map.

After seeing the plan, the approving agency requires another option for the roadway that accesses the white water park parking lot. In this practice, you will use a suitability map in the corridor optimization to find the best location for a new roadway.

To complete this practice, access to the Internet is required.

Task 1 - Run a corridor optimization.

1. Continue working in the same model as the previous practice. If you did not complete the previous practice, in the Utility Bar, expand *Proposal* and select **C_Task1** to make it current.
2. In the Utility Bar, click (Bookmark) and select **River**.
3. In the In Canvas tools, expand (Design, review and engineer roads)> (Perform analysis in preparation for road design), and click (Corridor Optimization).
4. In the Corridor Optimization palette, set the following options, as shown in Figure 2–36:
    - *Design speed*: **40 mph**
    - *Road Structure style:* **Two Lanes**
    - For the *Path*, click (Define PIs).

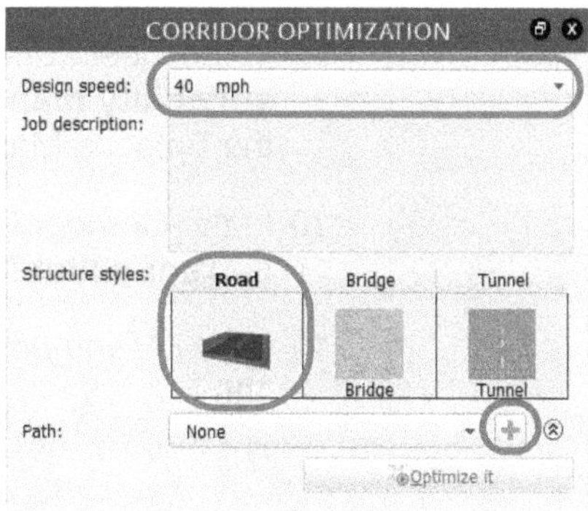

Figure 2–36

5. In the model, click to set the start PI at the roundabout and the end PI on the north-west corner of the proposed parking lot, as shown in Figure 2–37.

Figure 2–37

6. In the Corridor Optimization palette, expand the *Advanced Settings* area.
7. In the *Cost Zones & Suitability Map* area, click **Draw avoidance zones**.
8. In the Cost Zones asset card, click (Draw avoidance zones). In the model, create the area shown in Figure 2–38. Ensure that you double-click to finish the boundary.

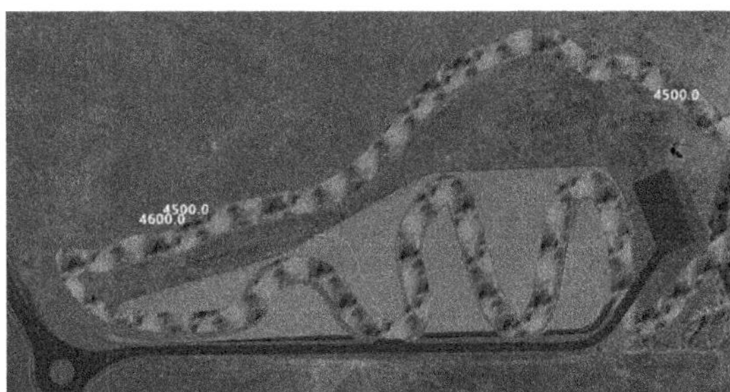

Figure 2–38

9. In the *Cost Zones & Suitability Map* area, click **Open suitability map**. In the Suitability Maps asset card, expand the Select a Map drop-down list and select **Water Features**.
10. In the Corridor Optimization palette, select the **Include the current suitability map** option.
11. In the *Alignment Constraints* area, set the minimum radius to **100**.

 © 2019, ASCENT - Center for Technical Knowledge®

This could take as much as 25 minutes, depending on the current load in the cloud.

12. In the Corridor Optimization palette, ensure that **Path - (1)** is selected. Leave all other constraints as they are and click **Optimize it**.
13. If the Job Monitor panel does not open, in the In Canvas tools, click (Design, review, and engineer roads)> (Review and modify roadway designs)> (Job Monitor).
14. In the Job Monitor palette, under the Report column, click (Click to download an optimization report) to review the results in a report.
15. In the Job Monitor palette, under the Results column, click (Create a proposal to view the result in the model). Click **Yes** in the Information dialog box.
16. Type **NewCorridor** for the name and click **OK** to create the proposal.

Since the optimal results (shown in Figure 2–39) indicate that the best route crosses the pier road, you decide to just create a road from the beginning of the pier to the parking lot rather than on the south side of the river. For time's sake, this is done for you in preparation for the next exercise.

Figure 2–39

© 2019, ASCENT - Center for Technical Knowledge®

2.4 Balance Cut and Fill Along the Roadway

Profile Optimization

To use this feature, access to the Internet is required.

Multiple vertical design options can be calculated quickly using profile optimization tools. Running a profile optimization enables you to enter specific cost information for the project area. This information is used to reduce haul charges, thus decreasing the cost of the project. During the analysis process, certain parameters can be set to ensure that project constraints are met.

Profile Constraints

A number of profile constraints can be set under the *Advanced Settings* of the Profile Optimization panel, including:

- Maximum grade
- Minimum PVI spacing
- Required drainage grade
- PVI frequency
- Anchored PVIs

Anchored PVIs are required when the component road must match existing or proposed conditions, such as when the road crosses another road, or requires a specific clearance. The *Profile Constraints* area of the Profile Optimization panel is shown in Figure 2–40.

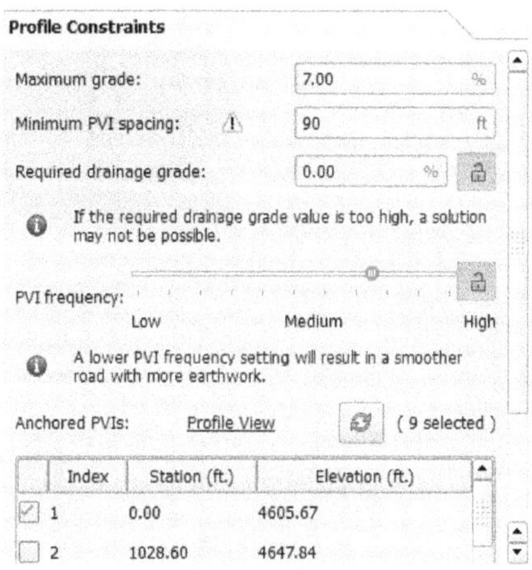

Figure 2–40

© 2019, ASCENT - Center for Technical Knowledge®

Quantities Options

Borrow and waste pits can be added to the model at specific stations to reduce mass haul charges. The capacity of each pit and the access distance from the road can both be set in the *Quantities Options* area, as shown in Figure 2–41.

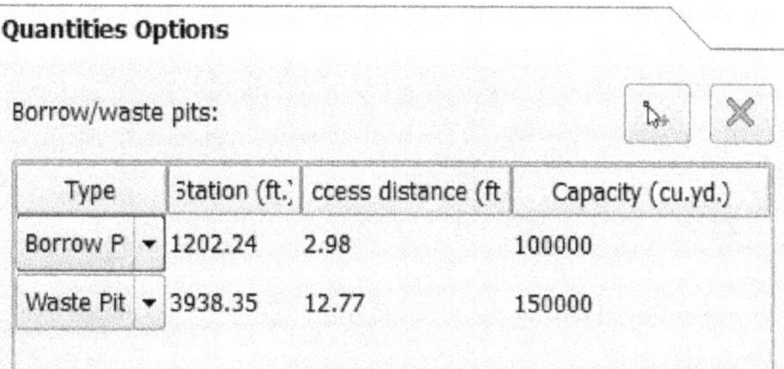

Quantities Options
Borrow/waste pits:
Type
Station (ft.
ccess distance (ft
Capacity (cu.yd.)
Borrow P
1202.24
2.98
100000
Waste Pit
3938.35
12.77
150000

Figure 2–41

Construction Rules

Construction rules can be set to determine what to do when a cut or fill becomes excessive. If a fill height is above the specified value, a bridge is used rather than fill material. Alternatively, if a cut depth is beyond the specified value, a tunnel is used to reduce the environmental impact. This is set in the *Construction Rules* area of the Profile Optimization panel, as shown in Figure 2–42.

Figure 2–42

Construction and Earthwork Cost

The cost of the project can be estimated by entering construction and earthwork costs for the area where the project is located. These are defined in the Construction & Earthwork Costs Settings dialog box, as shown in Figure 2–43.

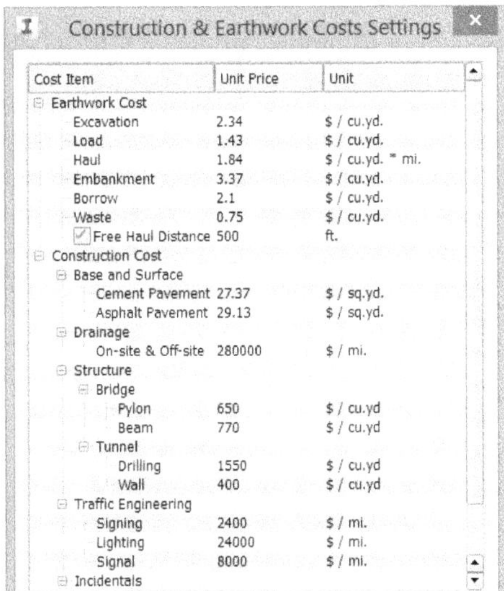

Construction & Earthwork Costs Settings
Cost Item
Unit Price
Unit
Earthwork Cost
Excavation 2.34 $ / cu.yd.
Load 1.43 $ / cu.yd.
Haul 1.84 $ / cu.yd. * mi.
Embankment 3.37 $ / cu.yd.
Borrow 2.1 $ / cu.yd.
Waste 0.75 $ / cu.yd.
Free Haul Distance 500 ft.
Construction Cost
Base and Surface
Cement Pavement 27.37 $ / sq.yd.
Asphalt Pavement 29.13 $ / sq.yd.
Drainage
On-site & Off-site 280000 $ / mi.
Structure
Bridge
Pylon 650 $ / cu.yd
Beam 770 $ / cu.yd
Tunnel
Drilling 1550 $ / cu.yd
Wall 400 $ / cu.yd
Traffic Engineering
Signing 2400 $ / mi.
Lighting 24000 $ / mi.
Signal 8000 $ / mi.
Incidentals

Figure 2–43

Cloud Credits

When you click **Optimize It** within the Profile Optimization panel, your design is transmitted to the Autodesk® InfraWorks® cloud-based service. The cloud-based service runs the calculations enabling you to continue working on the design. Since this command uses the cloud, cloud credits are required to optimize the profile. The number of credits that are required varies according to the length of the road, and the amount of vertical change that is happening in the project. The exact amount of credits can be calculated by clicking **Click here to check** in the Profile Optimization panel, below the *Construction and Earthwork Cost* area, as shown in Figure 2–44.

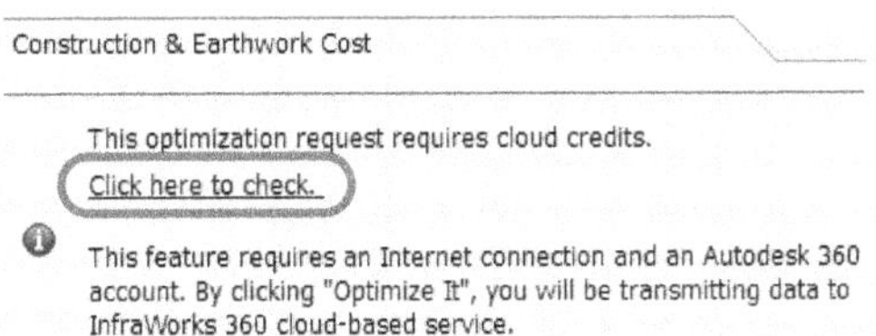

Figure 2–44

 © 2019, ASCENT - Center for Technical Knowledge®

Optimize It

Once you have entered all of the information, you can send the roadway to the cloud for calculating. Do this by clicking **Optimize It** in the Profile Optimization panel, as shown in Figure 2–45.

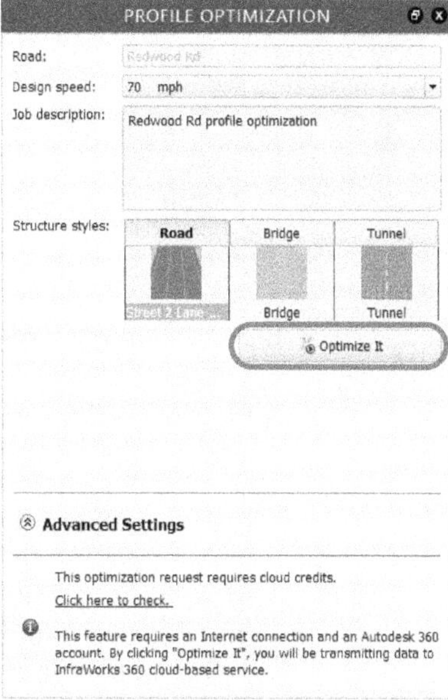

Figure 2–45

Job Monitor

Viewing Results

Similar to a Corridor Optimization, the results of the profile optimization can be viewed in two different ways:

- Downloading a report.
- Importing the data into a new proposal in the model.

Report

In the Job Monitor panel, in the *Report* column, clicking (Click to download an optimization report) opens Adobe Reader or PDF Reader and displays the results of the calculations. This report displays:

- Total project cost
- Total construction cost
- A haul diagram
- Cut and fill quantities along the roadway
- Additional information

Figure 2–46 shows a sample report with the suggested profile view for the component road.

Create a Proposal from Results

In addition to downloading the results in a file, you can also view the results by importing the corrected profile into a new proposal in the model. To do this, in the Job Monitor panel, in the *Results* column, click (Create a proposal to view the results in the model).

© 2019, ASCENT - Center for Technical Knowledge®

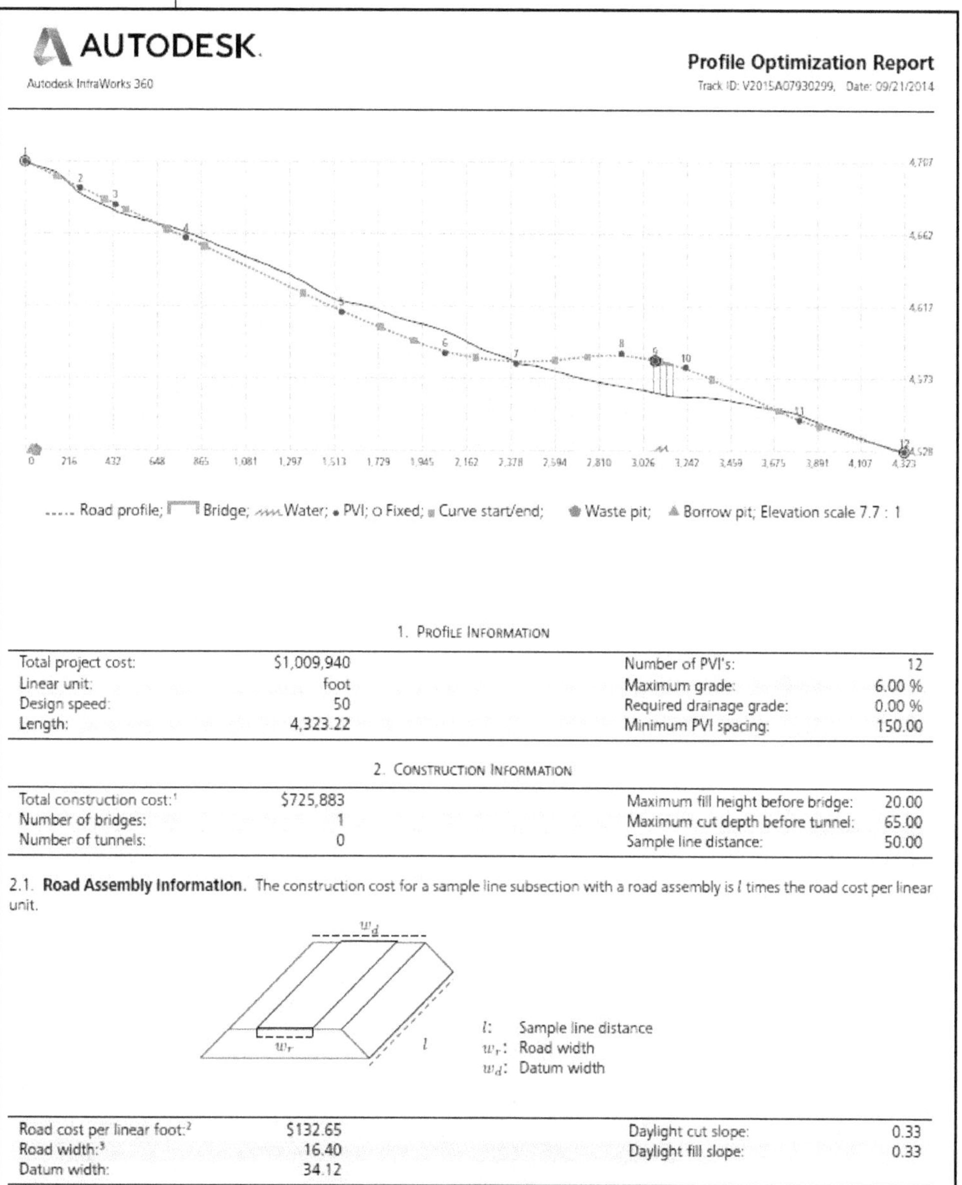

AUTODESK.

Autodesk InfraWorks 360

Profile Optimization Report

Track ID: V2015A07930299, Date: 09/21/2014

..... Road profile; Bridge; Water; • PVI; o Fixed; ▪ Curve start/end; Waste pit; Borrow pit; Elevation scale 7.7 : 1

1. Profile Information

Total project cost:	$1,009,940	Number of PVI's:	12
Linear unit:	foot	Maximum grade:	6.00 %
Design speed:	50	Required drainage grade:	0.00 %
Length:	4,323.22	Minimum PVI spacing:	150.00

2. Construction Information

Total construction cost:[1]	$725,883	Maximum fill height before bridge:	20.00
Number of bridges:	1	Maximum cut depth before tunnel:	65.00
Number of tunnels:	0	Sample line distance:	50.00

2.1. **Road Assembly Information.** The construction cost for a sample line subsection with a road assembly is l times the road cost per linear unit.

l: Sample line distance
w_r: Road width
w_d: Datum width

Road cost per linear foot:[2]	$132.65	Daylight cut slope:	0.33
Road width:[3]	16.40	Daylight fill slope:	0.33
Datum width:	34.12		

Figure 2–46

Practice 2d Perform a Vertical Optimization

Practice Objective

- Balance the cut and fill quantities for a design roadway.

In this practice, you will run a vertical optimization for the parking lot access road. You will then import the new proposal to view the results, shown in Figure 2–47.

To complete this practice, access to the Internet is required.

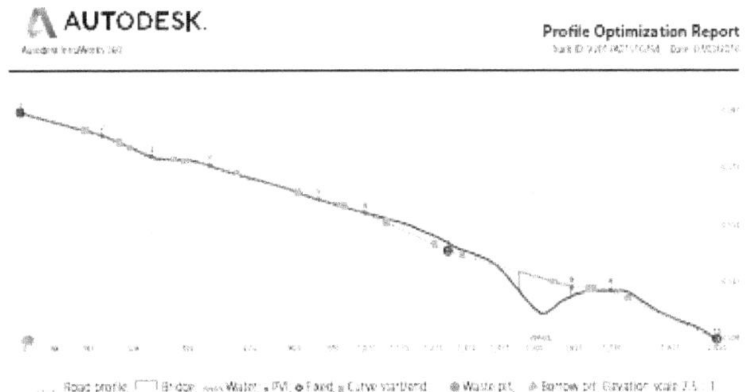

Figure 2–47

Task 1 - Run a vertical optimization.

In order to save time, a new road was added as indicated at the end of the last exercise.

1. Continue working in the same model as the last practice. In the Utility Bar, expand *Proposal* and select **D_Task1** to make it current.
2. In the Utility Bar, click (Bookmark) and select **River**.
3. In the model, select the parking lot access road shown in Figure 2–48.

Figure 2–48

© 2019, ASCENT - Center for Technical Knowledge®

4. In the In Canvas tools, click (Design, review, and engineer roads)> (Review and modify roadway designs)> (Profile Optimization).

5. In the Profile Optimization panel, set the *Design speed to* **40 mph** and the *Structure styles* to **Road**, as shown in Figure 2–49. Then expand the *Advanced Settings* area.

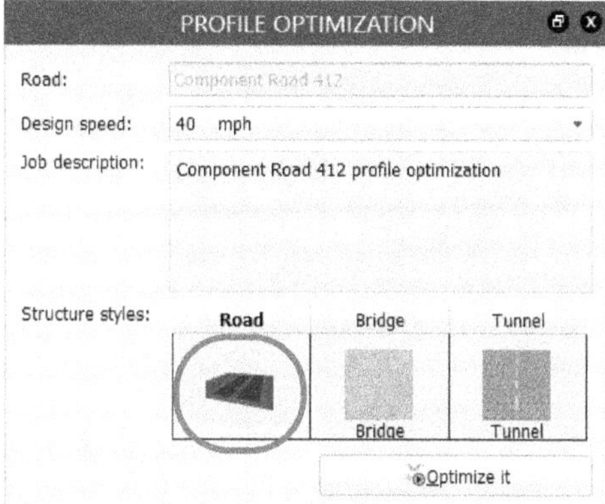

Figure 2–49

6. In the Profile Optimization panel, under *Advanced Settings*, expand Profile Constraints and set the *Maximum grade* to **6**. In the *Anchored PVIs* area, uncheck PVIs **2** and **3**, as shown in Figure 2–50. Leave all other settings as the default.

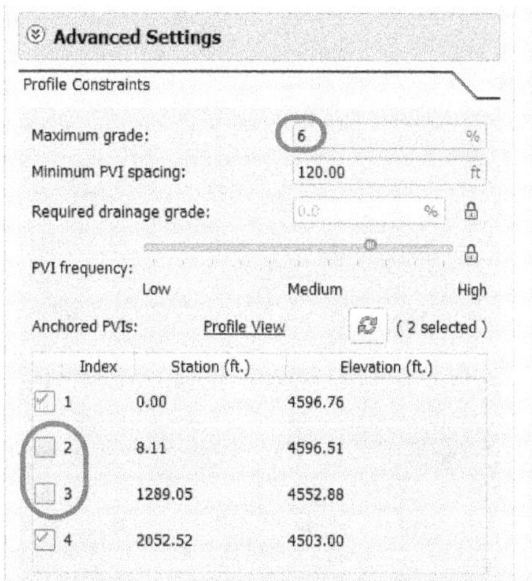

Figure 2–50

This costs 100 cloud credits. If you want to save your credits, a copy of the report is available in the class files and a proposal with the results is available called ***Profile OptimizationResults.***

7. In the Profile Optimization panel, leave all other settings as is, scroll to the top, and click **Optimize It**.
8. If the Job Monitor panel does not open, in the In Canvas tools, click (Design, review, and engineer roads)> (Review and modify roadway designs)> (Job Monitor).
9. In the Job Monitor palette, under the Report column, click (Click to download an optimization report) to review the results in a report format.
10. In the Job Monitor palette, under the Results column, click (Create a proposal to view the result in the model). Click **Yes** in the Information dialog box.
11. Type **NewProfile** for the name and click **OK** to create the proposal.
    - Note: You might have to return to Steps 8 to 11 once the cloud finishes processing of the profile.

© 2019, ASCENT - Center for Technical Knowledge®

2.5 Sight Distance Analysis

Roadway Sight Distance Analysis

A sight distance analysis is run on component roads to identify blind spots and sight failure zones, where a driver's line of sight is compromised by obstructions. There are six visual options for roadway analysis:

- **Sight Zones:** Displays colors on the analyzed lane to indicate safe and compromised sight zones.
- **Accident Zones:** Darkens portions of the analyzed lane to indicate where sight problems make accidents likely.
- **Sight Envelopes:** Displays colors on a range of required sight distances beyond the road boundary, and shows the effect of obstructions.
- **Sight Regions:** Displays sight regions relative to manually placed sight pins. Darkened areas indicate where the sight line is compromised by obstructions.
- **Sight Lines:** Displays the sight line from the eye point to the target point at the required sight distance. If any obstructions within sight regions negatively affect visibility at the eye point where the sight pin is placed, the first and last blocked sight lines are also shown.
- **Distance Line:** Displays a line from the eye height of manually placed sight pins, to the required sight distance.

© 2019, ASCENT - Center for Technical Knowledge®

Intersection Sight Distance Analysis

Running a sight distance analysis on intersections provides visual cues for sight triangles, as shown in Figure 2–51. Both visible areas and obstructions display in the model using a set color coding system.

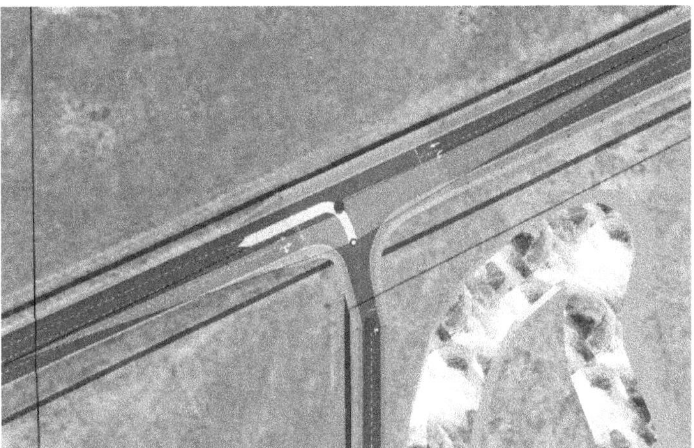

Figure 2–51

The table below lists the color codes used for sight distance analysis for both roadways and intersections.

Color	Description
Light blue	Indicates zones with clear visibility.
Yellow	Indicates sight failure zones.
Red	Indicates obstructions.

How To: Conduct a Sight Distance Analysis on a Roadway

1. In the model, select the component road.
2. In the In Canvas tools, click (Design, review, and engineer roads)> (Review and modify roadway designs)> (Sight Distance).

© 2019, ASCENT - Center for Technical Knowledge®

3. Set the following settings in the Sight Distance panel (shown in Figure 2–52):
   - *Method:* Select either **Stopping Sight Distance**, or **Passing Sight Distance**.
   - *Direction:* The direction of travel (**Forward** or **Backward**).
   - *Lane:* Select which lane to analyze. Note: **Lane (1)** is the lane that is closest to the centerline.
   - *Obstruction Types:* Select or clear the **Road Decorations** option.
   - Select the obstruction types you want to include in the analysis. The options available in the Obstruction Types area vary depending on the road type used, and includes trees, barriers, lamps, and other common road elements.

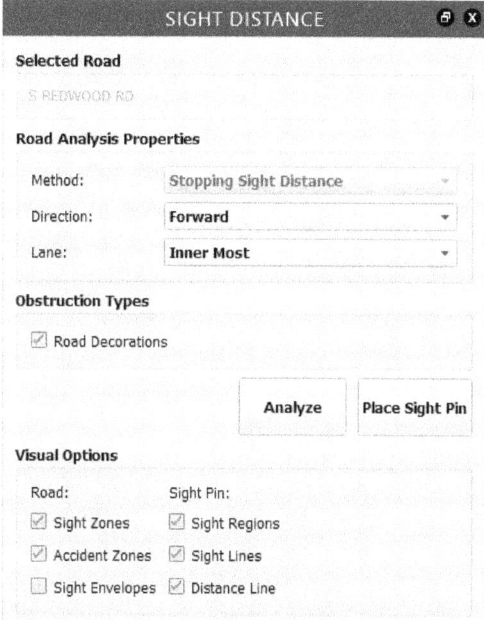

Figure 2–52

4. Click **Analyze**.
5. Select or clear the items in the *Visual Options* area that you want to include in the analysis. The items are toggled on/off in the model. You do not need to rerun the analysis if you change the items that display in the model.
6. Click **Place Sight Pin** to place any required sight pins in the model.
7. Close the Sight Distance panel to clear the sight analysis.

How To: Conduct a Sight Distance Analysis on an Intersection Object

1. In the model, select the intersection object.
2. In the In Canvas tools, click (Design, review, and engineer roads)> (Review and modify roadway designs)> (Sight Distance).
3. Set the following settings in the Sight Distance panel (shown in Figure 2–53):
   - *Approach:* Select the approach road
   - *Traffic control:* **Stop**, **Yield**, or **No control**
   - *Maneuver:* Select a maneuver pattern from those available.
   - *Obstruction Types:* Select or clear the **Road Decorations** option.
   - Select which obstruction types to include in the analysis.
   - Click **Analyze**.
   - Select or clear the *Visual Options* you want to include in the analysis.

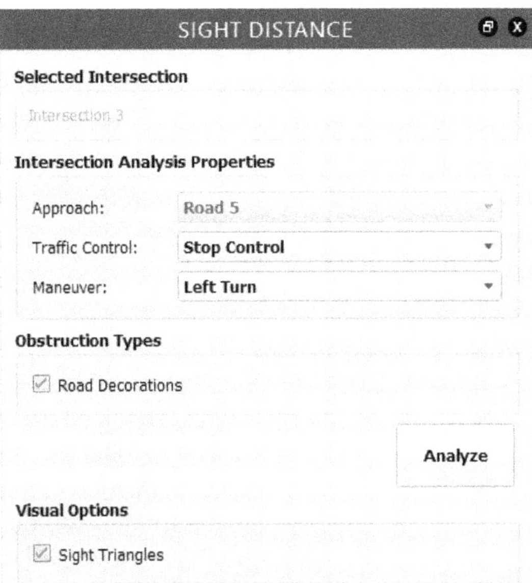

Figure 2–53

4. Close the Sight Distance panel to clear the sight analysis.

© 2019, ASCENT - Center for Technical Knowledge®

Practice 2e Analyze Sight Distance

Practice Objective

- Analyze the roadway and the intersection for sight distance obstructions.

In this practice, you will complete a sight distance analysis for the design roadway and the intersection of the new road with S Redwood Rd., shown in Figure 2–54.

Figure 2–54

Task 1 - Analyze the roadway.

1. Continue working in the same model as the previous practice. In the Utility Bar, expand *Proposal* and select **E_Task1** to make it current.
2. In the Utility Bar, click (Bookmark) and select **ProjectArea**.
3. In the model, select the component road shown in Figure 2–55.

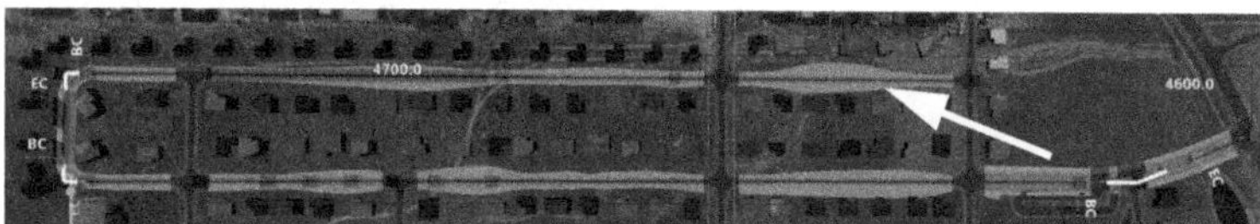

Figure 2–55

4. In the In Canvas tools, click (Design, review, and engineer roads)> (Review and modify roadway designs)> (Sight Distance).

5. In the Sight Distance panel, set the following options:
   - Method: **Stopping Sight Distance**
   - Direction: **Forward**
   - Lane: **Inner Most**
   - Obstruction Types: Select **Road Decorations**
6. Click **Analyze**.
7. Select the Visual Options shown in Figure 2–56.

If the driving side of the road is set in the Road Design Standards in the Model Properties dialog box, you might not see the option to set the driving side in the Sight Distance dialog box.

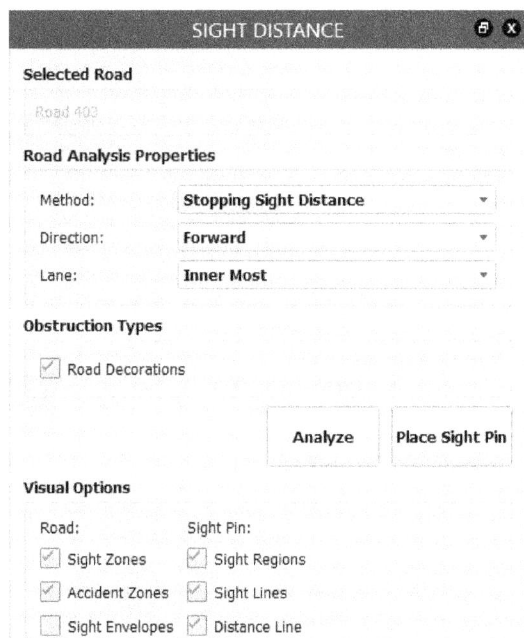

Figure 2–56

8. Close the Sight Distance panel to clear the sight analysis.
9. In the Sight Distance asset card, click **Place Sight Pin**.
10. Click various points in the model to place sight pins and display the results.

© 2019, ASCENT - Center for Technical Knowledge®

Chapter Review Questions

1. When running a traffic simulation, where do you control the traffic per intersection?
   a. Traffic Simulation asset card
   b. Traffic Analyst panel
2. Where can you find the tools to calculate earthwork and material quantities?
   a. (Design, review, and engineer roads)> 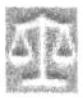 (Review and modify roadway designs).
   b. Component Road asset card.
   c. (Design, review and engineer roads)> (Perform analysis in preparation for road design).
3. When is the optimal time to perform a corridor optimization?
   a. When you are first considering where to layout the roadway.
   b. After you have laid out a few alternatives, and are ready to compare them.
   c. Right before creating the profile view.
   d. After you have cut plan and profile sheets.
4. Cut and Fill quantities can be balanced automatically using which of the following tool(s)?
   a. 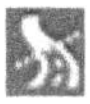
   b.
   c. 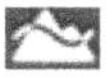
5. Which of the following visual options can be selected when running a sight distance analysis on an intersection?
   a. Sight Zones
   b. Accident Zones
   c. Sight Regions
   d. Sight Triangles

Command Summary

Button	Command	Location
	Corridor Optimization	• **In Canvas Tools:** Design, review, and engineer roads>Perform Analysis in preparation for road designs
	Earthwork Quantities	• **Design Road Asset Card:** Geometry stack • **Component Road Asset Card**
	Job Monitor	• **In Canvas Tools:** Design, review, and engineer roads>Review and modify roadway designs
	Material Quantities	• **Design Road Asset Card:** Geometry stack • **Component Road Asset Card**
	Profile Optimization	• **In Canvas Tools:** Design, review, and engineer roads>Review and modify roadway designs
	Sight Distance	• **In Canvas Tools:** Design, review, and engineer roads>Review and modify roadway designs
	Traffic Simulation	• **In Canvas Tools:** Design, review, and engineer roads>Perform Analysis in preparation for road designs

© 2019, ASCENT - Center for Technical Knowledge®

Introduction to Bridge Design

The Bridge Design tools enable you to add bridges to component roads and the rule-based tool sets enable you to lay out bridges. During the creation process, you can instantly visualize the designed bridge in context with its surroundings.

Learning Objectives in this Chapter

- Describe many of the bridge components that are inserted when a bridge is added to a component road.
- Add bridges to a component road over waterways, railways, or other roadways.
- Edit bridges using gizmos and bridge asset cards.
- Analyze the bridge line girders for structural strength.
- Send design bridges to other software for the detailed design phase.

© 2019, ASCENT - Center for Technical Knowledge®

3.1 Bridge Components

The Bridge Design tools in Autodesk® InfraWorks® enable you to add bridge structures to any component road. Bridges can be used for overpasses, for roads crossing a river or ravine, or for roads intersecting a railway without interfering with traffic. Bridges are very complex structures that contain multiple sub-components. Figure 3–1 illustrates many of these components.

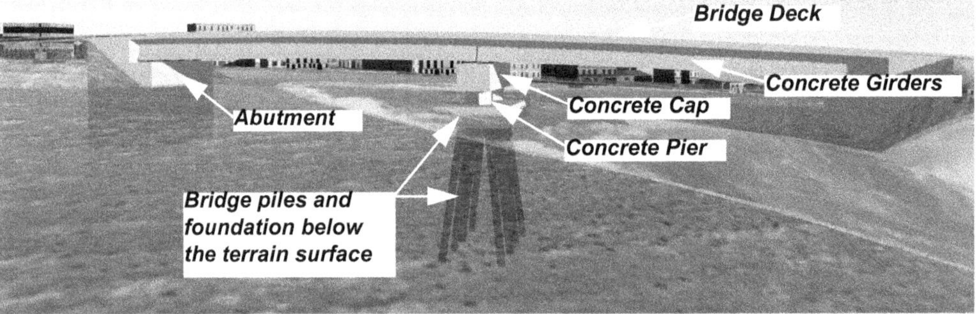

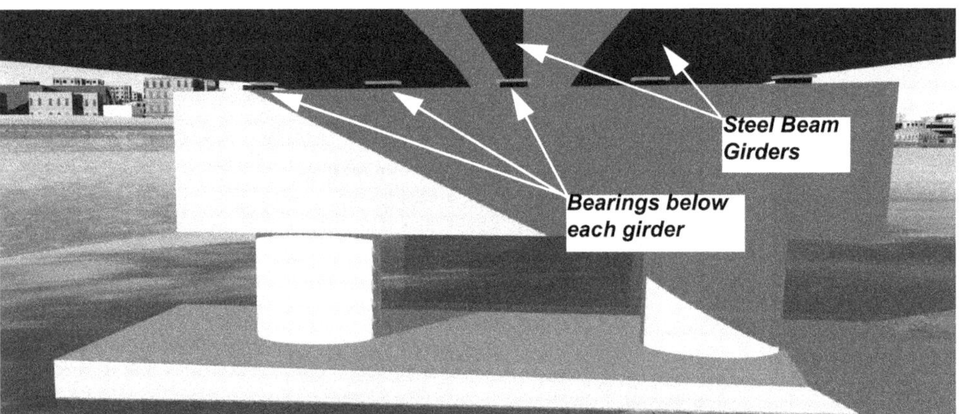

Figure 3–1

© 2019, ASCENT - Center for Technical Knowledge®

Before you can add a bridge to the model, you must have a component road.

How To: Add a Bridge to a Component Road

1. In the model, draw a component road.
2. In the In Canvas tools, click (Design, review and engineer bridges)> (Design bridges).
3. In the expanded tool group, click the (Precast | Girder Bridge) or (Steel Plate Girder Bridge) for the type of bridge you want to create, as shown in Figure 3–2.

Figure 3–2

4. In the model, click on the component road at the station where you want to start the bridge. Alternatively, you can type the starting station and press <Enter>.

5. In the model, click on the component road at the station where you want the bridge to end. Alternatively, you can press <Tab> and type the bridge length, or you can press <Tab> twice to type the ending station, then press <Enter>, as shown in Figure 3–3.

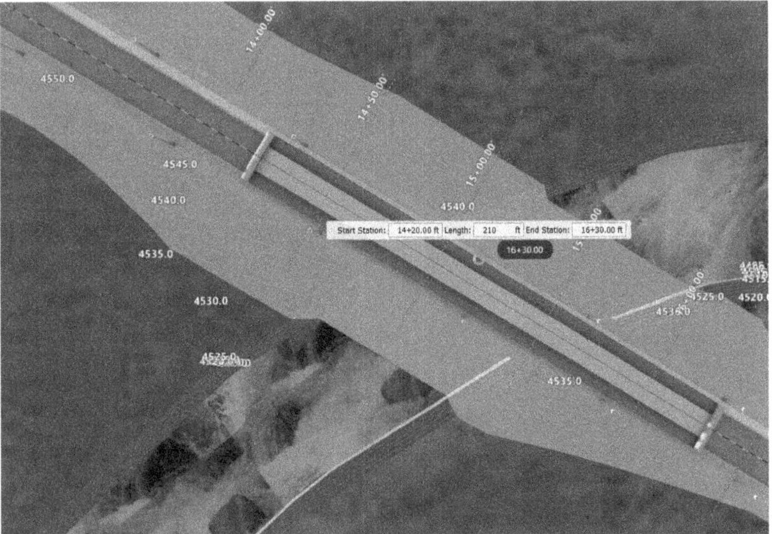

Figure 3–3

© 2019, ASCENT - Center for Technical Knowledge®

3.2 Modify Bridges

Once a bridge has been created, it can be modified using the Bridge asset card, (selected component) stacks, or gizmos.

Bridge Asset Card

When any part of the bridge is selected by clicking once, it is referred to as a Bridge asset card. When anything else on the bridge is selected by clicking twice, it is referred to as the "(Selected Component) stack".

The Bridge asset card enables you to change the type of bridge being modeled, the number of piers used to support the bridge, the clearance below the bridge, or the deck and bearing attributes, as shown in Figure 3–4.

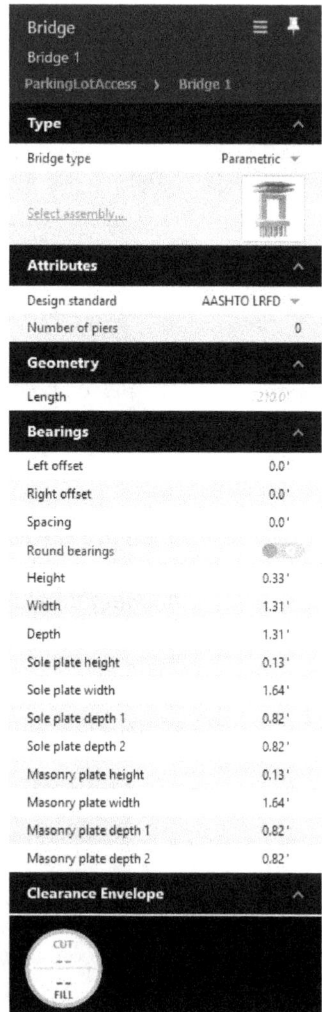

Figure 3–4

Bridge Clearance

To ensure that the bridge has the correct clearance for traffic below it, the clearance envelope can be displayed in the model. The clearance envelope is a purple box that indicates the clearance height required for the bridge. The **Show clearance envelope** option is found in the Bridge asset card, as shown in Figure 3–5.

Figure 3–5

Once the **Show clearance envelope** option is toggled on, all of the values within the *Clearance* area can be modified. Changing the *Height* value changes the height of the clearance envelope only. To change the height of the bridge, you must right-click on the bridge deck in the model and select **Update Vertical Profile**, as shown in Figure 3–6. This causes the profile of the road to adjust to accommodate the clearance envelope.

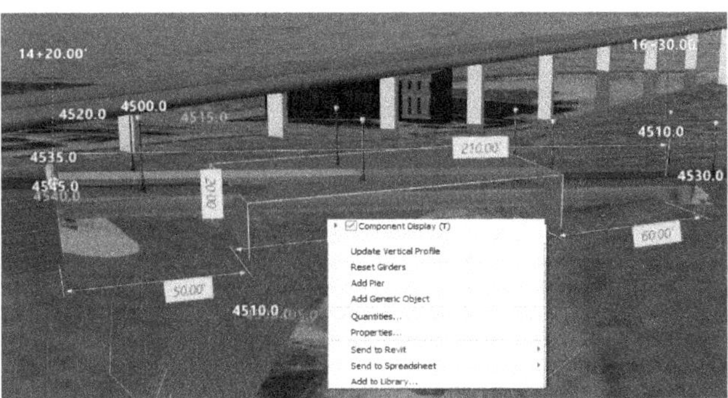

Figure 3–6

© 2019, ASCENT - Center for Technical Knowledge®

How To: Modify the Number of Bridge Piers Using the Bridge Asset Card

1. In the model, select the design bridge. The Bridge asset card displays.
2. In the Bridge asset card, change *Number of piers*, as shown in Figure 3–7.

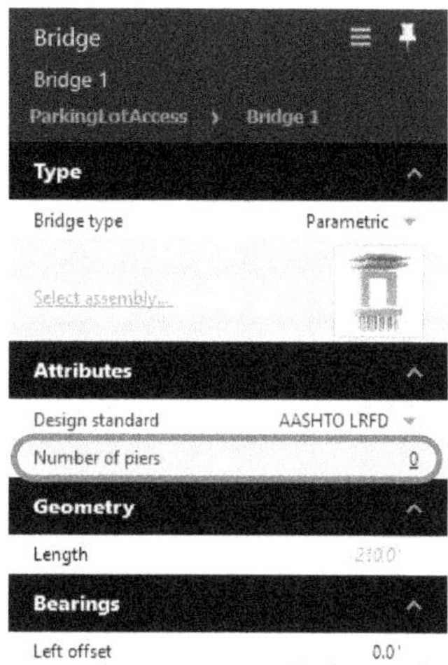

Figure 3–7

3. Press <Esc> to clear the bridge selection.

Bridge Gizmos

When the bridge is selected, gizmos display at the beginning and ending stations of the bridge. Selecting either gizmo enables you to change the station for that specific gizmo, as shown in Figure 3–8.

Figure 3–8

If both the beginning and ending stations require changing, the space between the two gizmos can be selected. This enables you to change both stations at the same time, as shown in Figure 3–9.

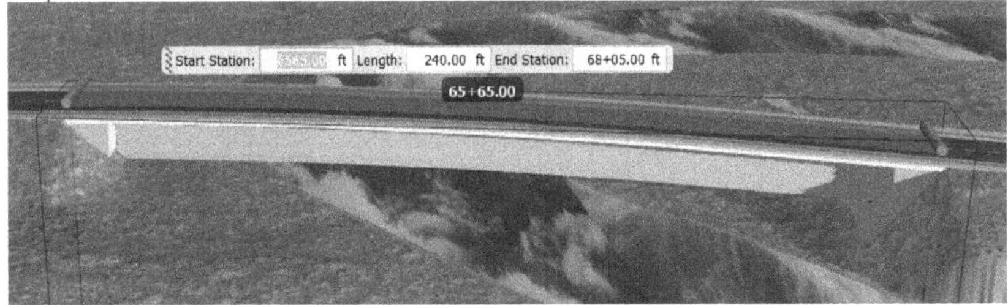

Figure 3–9

Selecting a pier causes a control gizmo to display. Clicking (Control Gizmo) for the pier enables you to change the location of the pier. Additionally, you can rotate each pier with the (Rotate Gizmo), as shown in Figure 3–10.

Figure 3–10

How To: Modify the Bridge Using Gizmos

1. In the model, select the design bridge, and then click on the bridge beginning or ending station gizmo.
2. Drag the bridge gizmo to a new location to change the length of the bridge. Alternatively, you can type a new station value for the beginning or ending station and press <Enter>, as shown in Figure 3–11.

© 2019, ASCENT - Center for Technical Knowledge®

Figure 3–11

3. Press <Esc> to clear the bridge selection.

Bridge Properties

Properties for each component of a bridge can be modified using the component stack (asset card). Select the bridge component that needs to be modified to display its stack. Different properties are available depending upon which component of the bridge is selected in the model, as shown in Figure 3–12.

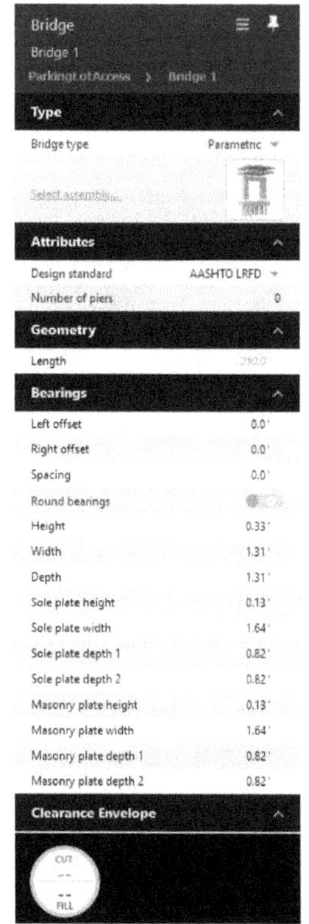

Bridge stack

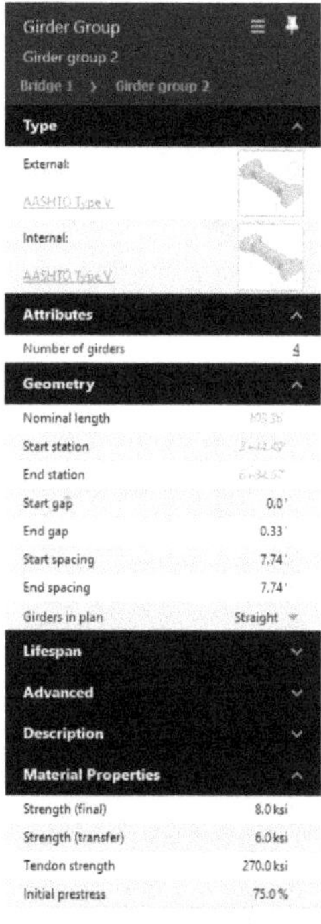

Girder Group stack

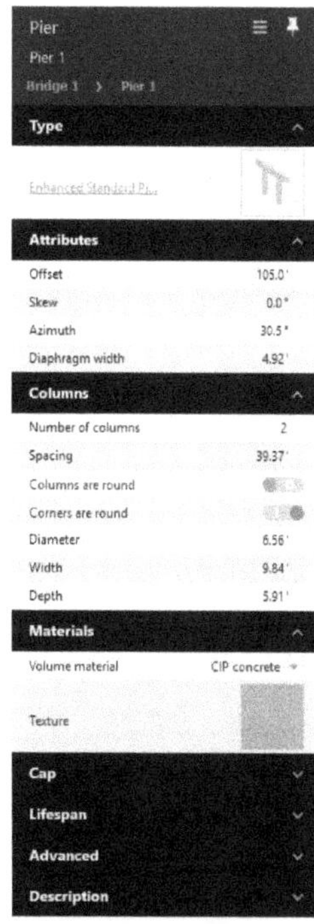

Pier stack

Figure 3–12

Bridge Styles and Templates

In the Style Palette, the *Bridge* and *Bridge Template* tabs enable you to modify bridge components. The *Bridge Template* tab houses different parts for bridges that follow specific standards. Figure 3–13 shows some of the settings that can be modified for a bridge in the Bridge Style dialog box.

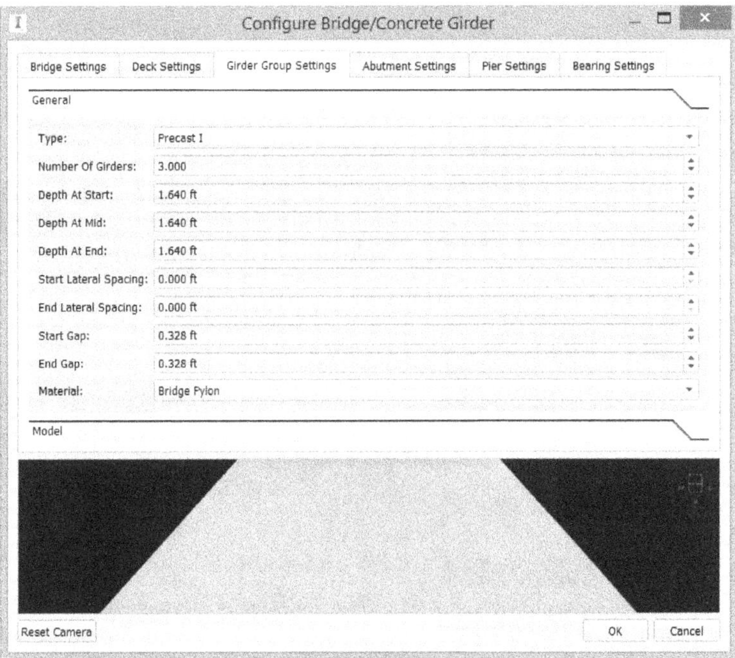

Figure 3–13

© 2019, ASCENT - Center for Technical Knowledge®

Parametric Models

Parametric bridge model components can be created for use in Autodesk InfraWorks. The advantage of using parametric models is that you can use the same component part for multiple sizes of the same component, as shown in Figure 3–14. This is similar to a dynamic block in AutoCAD.

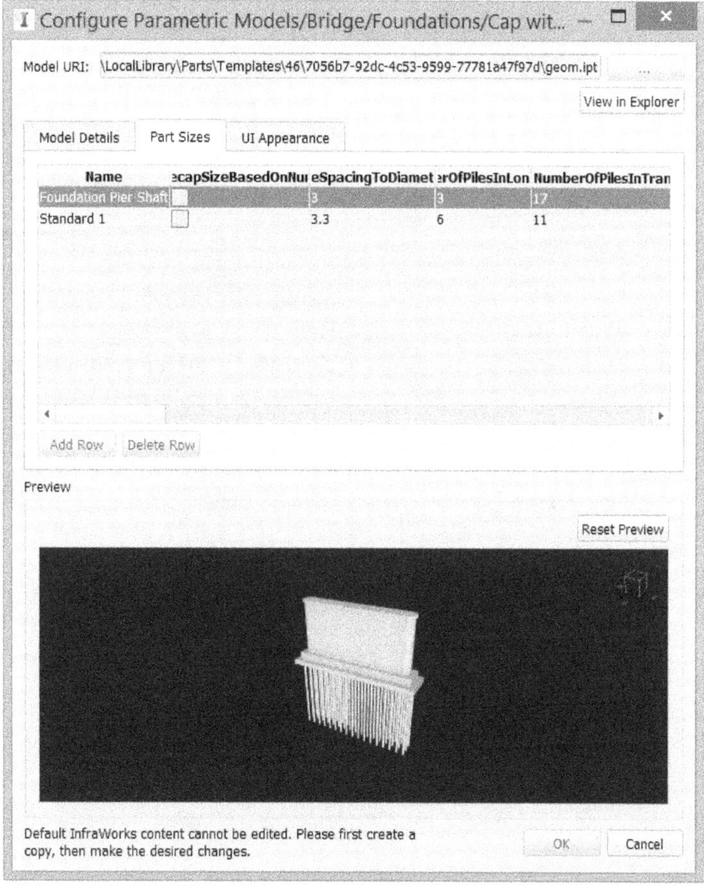

Figure 3–14

See the Autodesk InfraWorks Online Help for information on installing the Infrastructure Part Shape Utilities plug-in.

Autodesk® Inventor® is used to create and configure parametric models in the form of .IPT files. You must use the Infrastructure Part Shape Utilities plug-in for Autodesk Inventor to make these files usable in InfraWorks.

How To: Add Parametric Bridge Components to the Style Palette

1. Open Autodesk Inventor.
2. Create a parametric model that fits your needs using Autodesk Inventor.
3. Use the Infrastructure Part Shape Utilities plug-in for Autodesk Inventor to specify key dimensions that can be viewed and edited in the Autodesk InfraWorks software.
4. Use the Infrastructure Part Shape Utilities plug-in for Autodesk Inventor to export the parametric bridge component model to an .IPT file format.
5. Open the Autodesk InfraWorks software.
6. In the In Canvas tools, click (Build, manage, and analyze your infrastructure model)> (Create and manage your model)> (Style Palette).
7. Select the *Parametric Models* tab and double-click on **Bridge**. From here, you can modify several parametric bridge components, as shown in Figure 3–15.

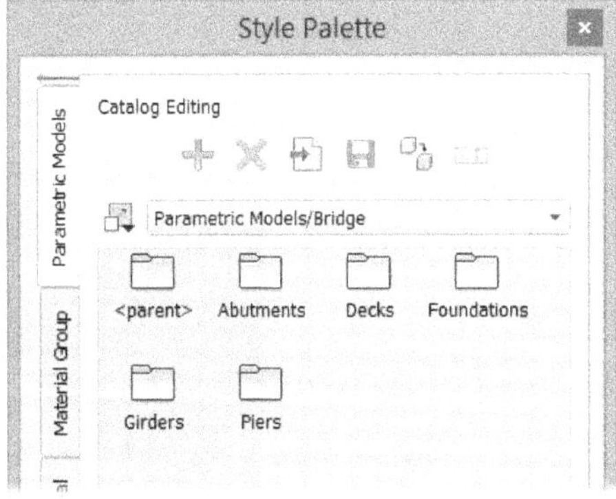

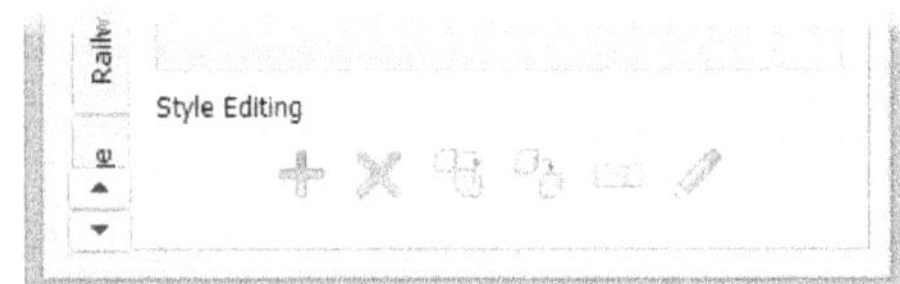

Figure 3–15

8. In the Styles Palette, *Parametric Models* tab>Bridges, double-click on the type of bridge component (Abutments, Decks, Foundations, Girders, or Piers) for which you plan to create a parametric style.
9. At the bottom of the Styles Palette, click (Add new style) in the *Style Editing* area.

© 2019, ASCENT - Center for Technical Knowledge®

Note that the Units field is not editable.

10. In the Configure Parametric Models dialog box, click ... (Browse) to select an .IPT file that has been exported from Inventor using the Infrastructure Part Shape Utilities.
11. In the *Model Details* tab, fill in the *Name*, *Description*, *Domain*, and *Component type*, as shown in Figure 3–16.

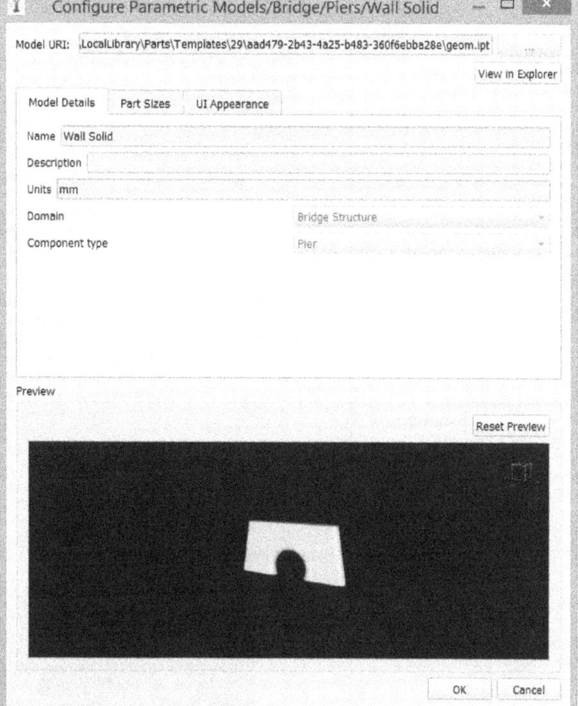

Figure 3–16

12. In the Configure Parametric Models dialog box, click the *Part Sizes* tab.

13. In the *Part Sizes* tab, do the following, as shown in Figure 3–17:
    - Click **Add Row** to add a new part size.
    - Each column represents a key dimension. Fill in each of the measurements across the row.
    - Continue adding rows for each part size.

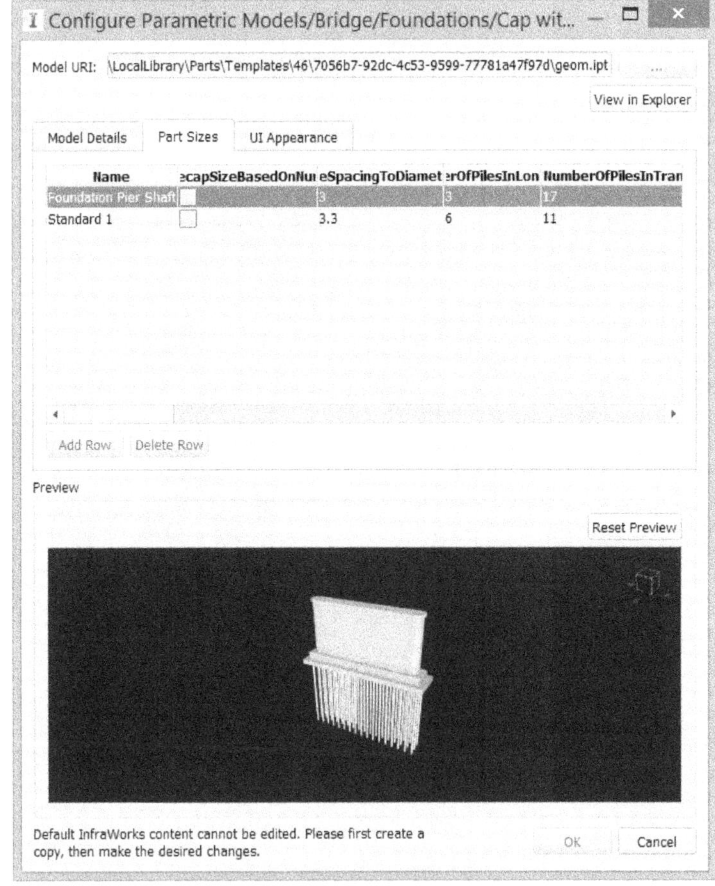

Figure 3–17

14. In the Configure Parametric Models dialog box, click the *UI Appearance* tab.

© 2019, ASCENT - Center for Technical Knowledge®

15. In the *UI Appearance* tab, customize how attributes display in the component stack, as shown in Figure 3–18.

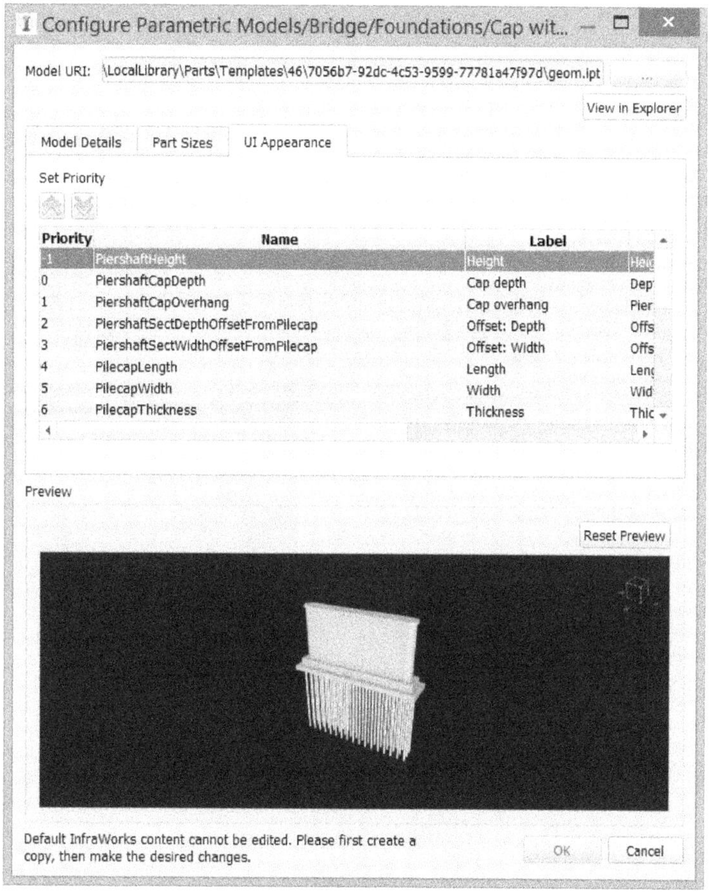

Figure 3–18

16. Click **OK**.

Practice 3a Work with Bridges

Practice Objectives

- Add a bridge to the Component road to provide passage over the river.
- Modify the design bridge to change the starting and ending stations and number of piers.

In this practice, you will add a bridge to the Component road where the road crosses the white water river, as shown in Figure 3–19. This river is part of the development, and the road provides access for rafters and kayakers to the future parking area near the take out point.

Figure 3–19

Task 1 - Create a design bridge.

1. In the Home Screen, click (Open).
2. In the *C:\InfraWorks Design Practice Files\Bridges* folder, select **DesignBridges.sqlite** and click **Open**.
3. In the Utility Bar, click (Bookmark) and select **DesignBridge**. Also ensure that **A_Task1** is the current proposal.
4. In the In Canvas tools, click (Design, review and engineer bridges)> (Design bridges)> (Precast | Girder Bridge).
5. In the model, click on the Component road that crosses the white water river and connects to the pedestrian fishing pier (ParkingLotAccess).

 © 2019, ASCENT - Center for Technical Knowledge®

6. In the *Start Station* field, type **1420**. Press <Tab> twice, and in the *Length* field, type **210**, as shown in Figure 3–20. Press <Enter>.

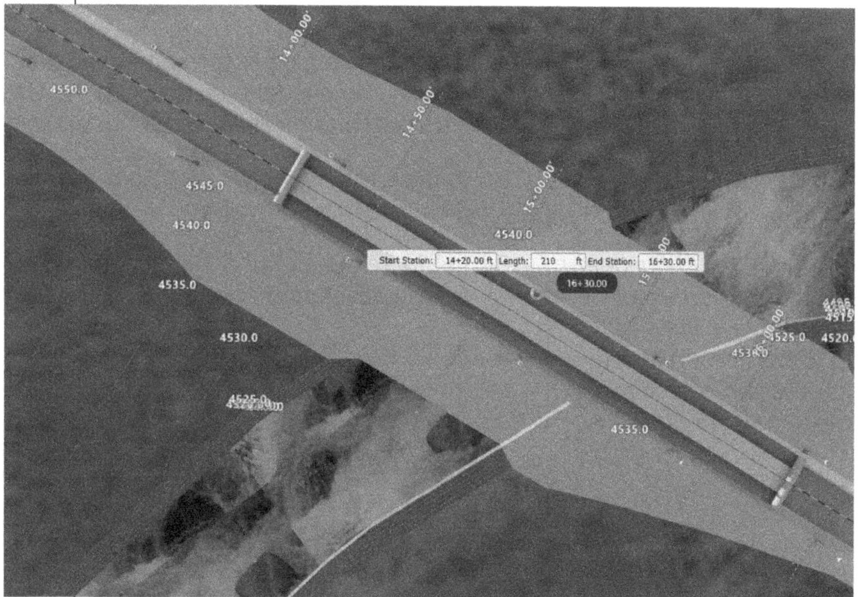

Figure 3–20

7. In the Select Bridge asset card, under Bridge type, click **Select assembly**.

8. In the Select Template palette, click **BridgeTemplate>AASHTO I Beams with Pier Shafts**, as shown in Figure 3–21. Click **OK**.

Figure 3–21

9. Press <Esc> to clear the selection of the bridge.

Note that the bridge deck remains the same as the rest of the road. All that changed is the supporting structure below the road.

© 2019, ASCENT - Center for Technical Knowledge®

Task 2 - Modify the bridge to remove the pier.

In this task, you will modify the bridge using the Bridge asset card to remove the pier.

1. Continue working in the same model as the last task. If you did not complete the last task, in the Utility Bar, expand *Proposal* and select **A_Task2** to make it current.
2. In the Utility Bar, click (Bookmark) and select **DesignBridgeElevation**.

If you click on the bridge deck, the Road asset card displays instead. To avoid this, ensure you click on part of the supporting structure.

3. In the model, click on the design bridge pier to display the Bridge asset card.
4. In the Bridge asset card, change the *Number of piers* to **0**, as shown in Figure 3–22. Press <Enter> to accept the change.

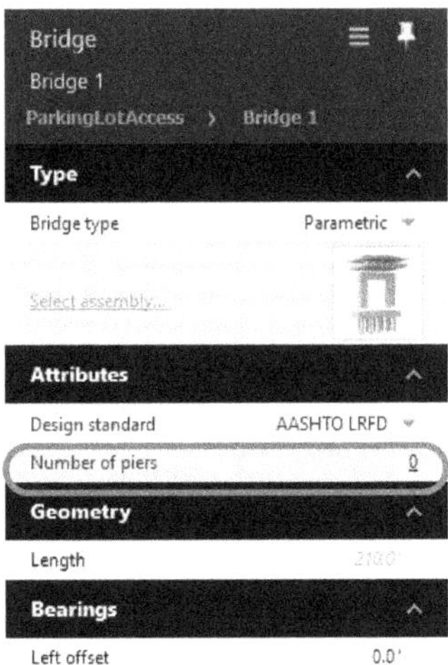

Figure 3–22

5. Press <Esc> to release the bridge selection.

© 2019, ASCENT - Center for Technical Knowledge®

3.3 Bridge Line Girder Analysis

Girders

Girders can be edited individually or in groups (interior and exterior). Autodesk InfraWorks contains multiple precast girder styles.You can assign different girder styles to each girder in a bridge, or assign styles to a group of girders.

- Clicking on a bridge girder once selects the bridge and displays the Bridge asset card.
- Clicking on a bridge girder a second time selects a bridge girder group and displays the Girder Group stack.
- Clicking on a specific girder displays the Girder stack.

The Girder Group stack and the Girder stack are shown in Figure 3–23.

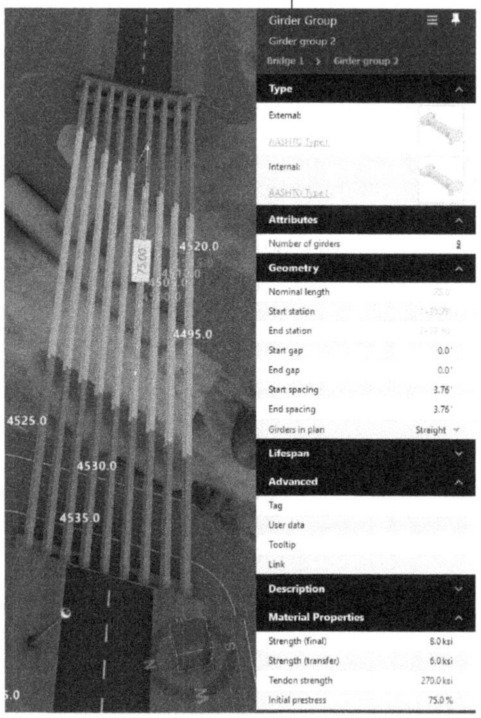

Girder Group stack

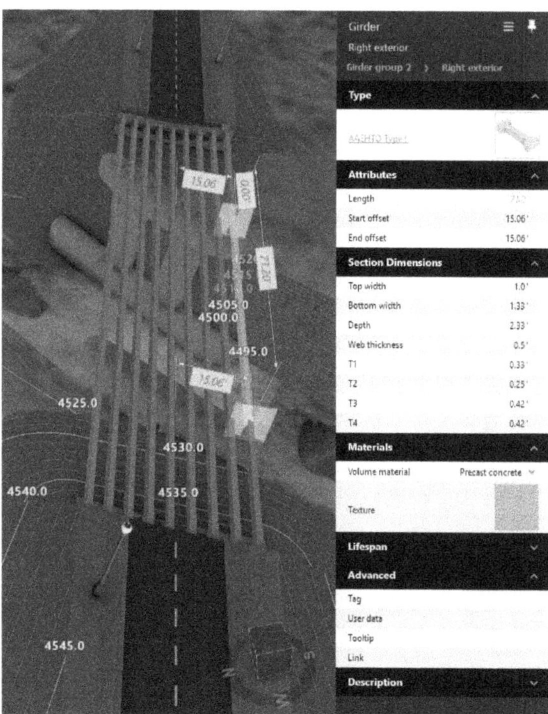

Individual Girder stack

Figure 3–23

In the Girder stack, in the *Type* area, when you click inside the girder image, a girder schematic palette displays, as shown in Figure 3–24.

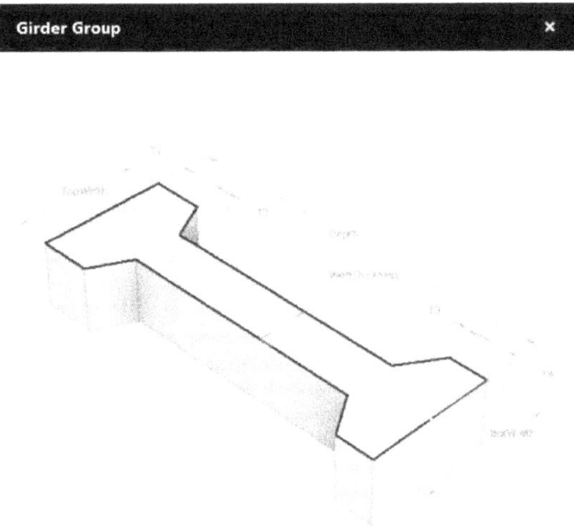

Figure 3–24

Girder Analysis

To use this feature, access to the Internet is required.

The structural strength of pre-stressed concrete bridge girders can be verified using the Autodesk InfraWorks cloud service. Initial results can be viewed in the model. A full girder design document can be purchased using cloud credits. The design optimization is computed using the Autodesk Structural Bridge Design.

© 2019, ASCENT - Center for Technical Knowledge®

Project Information

Information provided during the analysis displays in the final *.PDF report. By completing as much information as possible, others reading the report can identify the project it belongs to and the company that created the report. The following information can be added to the report, as shown in Figure 3–25:

- Job name
- Job number
- Project name
- Company name
- Address
- Logo file
- User name
- User initials

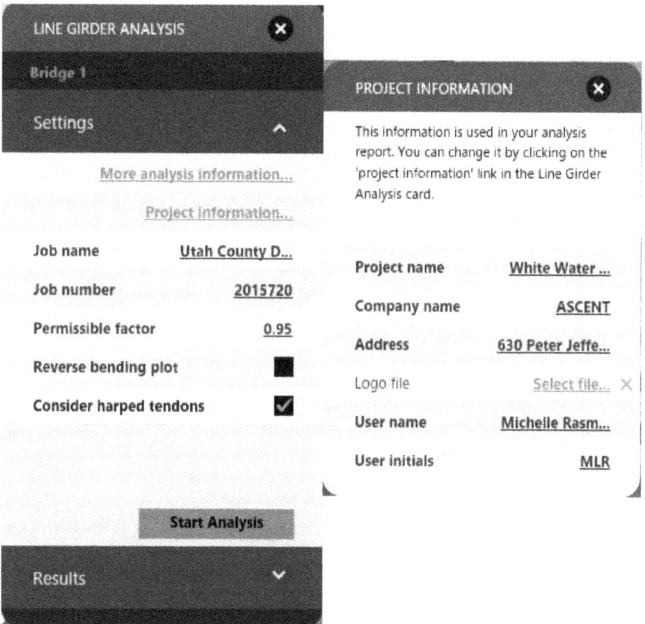

Figure 3–25

Once an analysis is complete, selecting any girder displays the results of the analysis in the Line Girder Analysis stack, as shown in Figure 3–26.

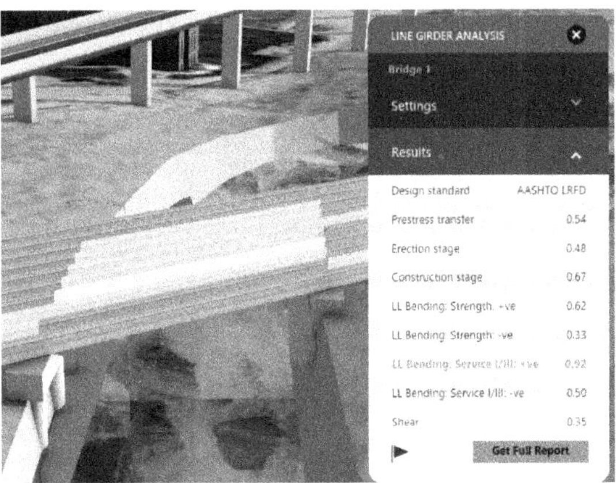

Figure 3–26

Additional analysis information can be viewed by clicking **Get Full Report**. A sample report is shown in Figure 3–27.

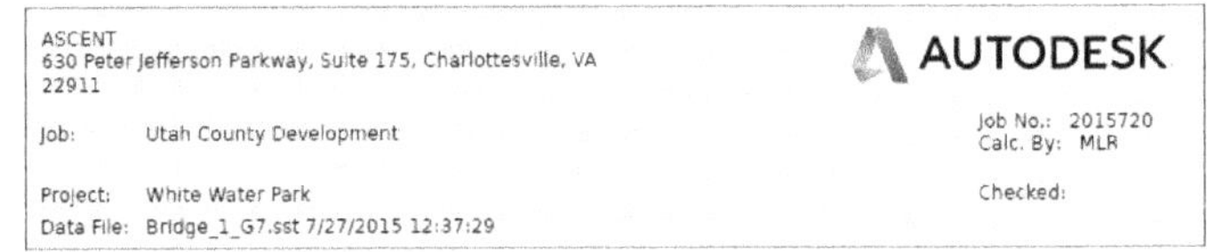

ASCENT
630 Peter Jefferson Parkway, Suite 175, Charlottesville, VA 22911

AUTODESK

Job: Utah County Development — Job No.: 2015720 — Calc. By: MLR

Project: White Water Park — Checked:

Data File: Bridge_1_G7.sst 7/27/2015 12:37:29

Girder Design Summary

Descending Performance Ratios

Span	Girder	Performance	Analysis Type	Limit State	Loadcase
S2	L2	0.92	Live Load Bending	Service I/III	Max +ve
		0.67	Construction Stage	Service I/III	-
		0.62	Live Load Bending	Strength	Max +ve
		0.54	Prestress Transfer	Service I/III	-
		0.50	Live Load Bending	Service I/III	Max -ve
		0.48	Erection Stage	Service I/III	-
		0.35	Shear	Strength	-
		0.33	Live Load Bending	Strength	Max -ve

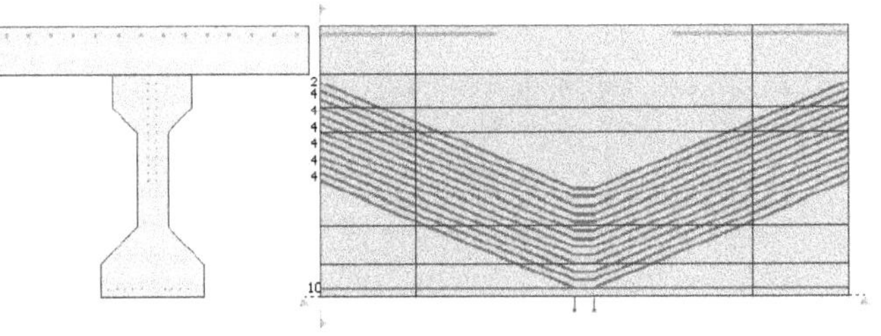

Figure 3–27

 © 2019, ASCENT - Center for Technical Knowledge®

To use this feature, access to the Internet is required.

How To: Run a Bridge Line Girder Analysis

1. In the model, select the bridge you want to analyze.
2. In the In Canvas Tools, click (Design, review and engineer bridges)> (Perform analysis on your bridge design)> (Line Girder Analysis).
3. In the Line Girder Analysis stack, enter the *Job name* and *Job number*.
4. In the Line Girder Analysis stack, click **Project Information**.
5. In the Project Information asset card, enter all of the available project information. Close the card.
6. In the Line Girder Analysis stack, enter a *Permissible Factor*. This factor is applied to the permissible values during the tendon design.
7. Check or clear **Reverse bending plot**.
    - This affects the graphic representations that are received in the detailed girder documentation (full report). It changes the direction of bending moments but not the direction of torsion moments.
8. Check or clear **Consider harped tendons**. This sets whether harping is considered in the tendon design.
9. Click **Start Analysis.**
10. Once complete, select a girder to view the results in the Line Girder Analysis stack.
11. Click **Get Full Report** to view the full PDF report.

Cloud credits might be charged when you get the full report.

Practice 3b Run a Girder Analysis

Practice Objective

- Analyze the bridge girders for structural strength.

In this practice, you will analyze the bridge girders for structural strength.

Task 1 - Analyze a design bridge.

To complete this practice, access to the Internet is required.

1. Continue working in the same model as the previous practice. If you did not complete the previous practice, in the Utility Bar, expand *Proposal* and select **B_Task1** to make it current.

2. In the Utility Bar, click (Bookmark) and select **DesignBridgeElevation**.

3. In the model, select the design bridge. Right-click and expand *Component Display (T)*. Clear the selection of **Road** and **Deck** (as shown in Figure 3–28) to make it easier to see the girders.

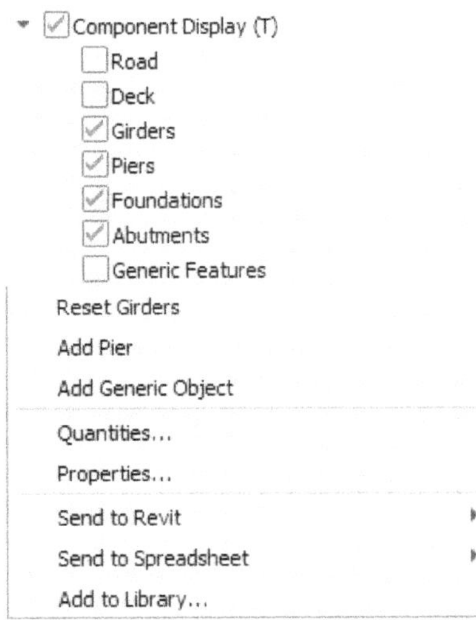

Figure 3–28

© 2019, ASCENT - Center for Technical Knowledge®

4. In the In Canvas tools, click (Design, review and engineer bridges)> (Perform analysis on your bridge design)> (Line Girder Analysis).
5. In the Line Girder Analysis stack, set the following:
   - *Job name*: **Utah County Development**
   - *Job number:* **2015720**
6. In the Line Girder Analysis stack, click **Project Information**.

If this information is already present, it is because the last person to use your computer already filled it in. The information remains on the system for convenience.

7. Enter the following information in the Project Information asset card:
   - *Project name*: **White Water Park**
   - *Company name*: **ASCENT**
   - *Address*: **630 Peter Jefferson Parkway, Suite 175, Charlottesville, VA 22911**
   - *User name*: Enter your name
   - *User initials*: Enter your initials
   - Close the Project Information asset card

Once you start the analysis, it will take some time to process.

8. In the Line Girder Analysis stack, leave all other settings as they are and click **Start Analysis**.

When the analysis is complete, it should return **2 Girders analyzed, 0 Girders satisfy design requirements**.

9. Press <Esc> to clear the selection of the bridge.

Hint: Analysis Time Requirements

If the analysis is taking too long, you can open the next proposal to see the results.

1. In the Utility Bar, expand *Proposal* and select **B_Task2** to make it current.
2. In the model, click on the bridge twice to select it. The results display in the Line Girder Analysis stack.

© 2019, ASCENT - Center for Technical Knowledge®

Task 2 - Add a pier and rerun the girder analysis.

1. Continue working in the same model as the previous task. If you did not complete the previous practice, in the Utility Bar, expand *Proposal* and select **B_Task2** to make it current.
2. In the Utility Bar, click (Bookmark) and select **DesignBridgeElevation**.
3. In the model, select the bridge.
4. In the model, click the start and end gizmos and change the starting station to **1450** and the ending station to **1600**.
5. In the Bridge asset card, set the number of piers to **2**.
6. In the model, select each pier and rotate it so that it is parallel to the river banks, as shown in Figure 3–29.

Figure 3–29

© 2019, ASCENT - Center for Technical Knowledge®

7. Select the left pier and in the Pier stack, set its offset to **40'**. Then select the right pier and set its offset to **115'**, as shown in Figure 3–30.

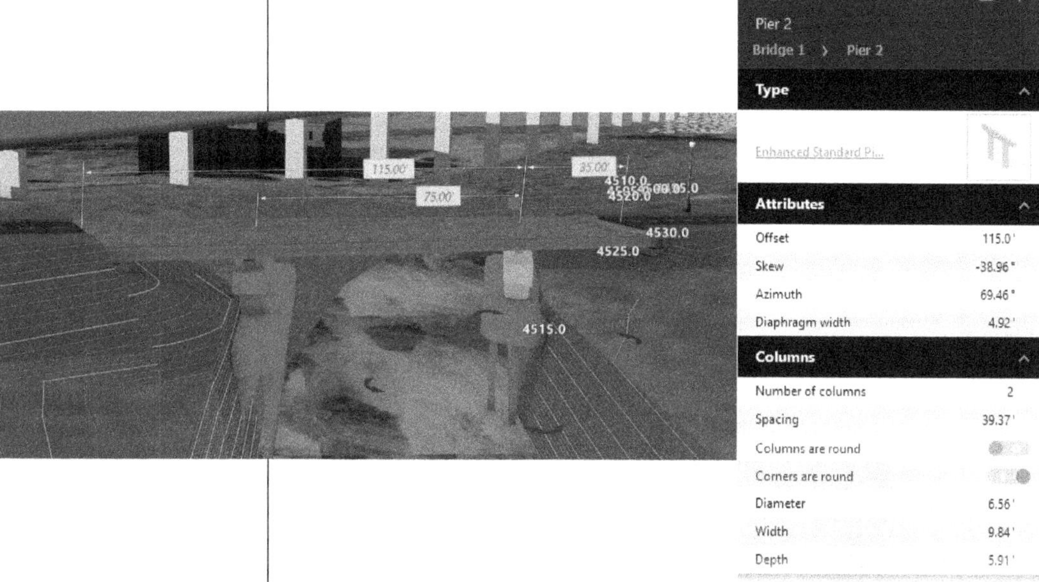

Figure 3–30

8. Select the left foundation and in the Foundation stack, set its *Height above ground* to **-24**, as shown in Figure 3–31.

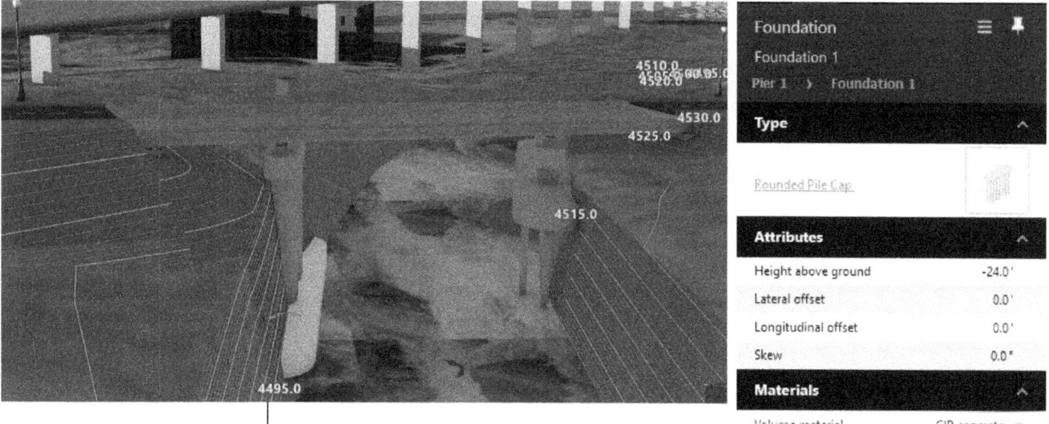

Figure 3–31

9. Similarly, select the Foundation on the right and set the *Height above ground* to **-20**.

10. Press <Esc> to release the foundation and select bridge.

11. With the bridge still selected, in the In Canvas Tools, click (Design, review and engineer bridges)> (Perform analysis on your bridge design)> (Line Girder Analysis).

12. In the Line Girder Analysis stack, leave all the settings as they are and click **Start Analysis**.

    When the analysis is complete, it should return **27 Girders analyzed, 10 Girders satisfy design requirements**.

*If you click **Get Full Report,** you might be charged cloud credits. As of the release of this guide, these cloud credits have been listed as **Free**.*

13. In the model, select one of the center girders to display the results in the Line Girder Analysis stack, as shown in Figure 3–32.

- Processing the full report can take as long as 10-15 minutes for this specific project. Other projects might take more or less time depending on complexity and cloud service processing load.

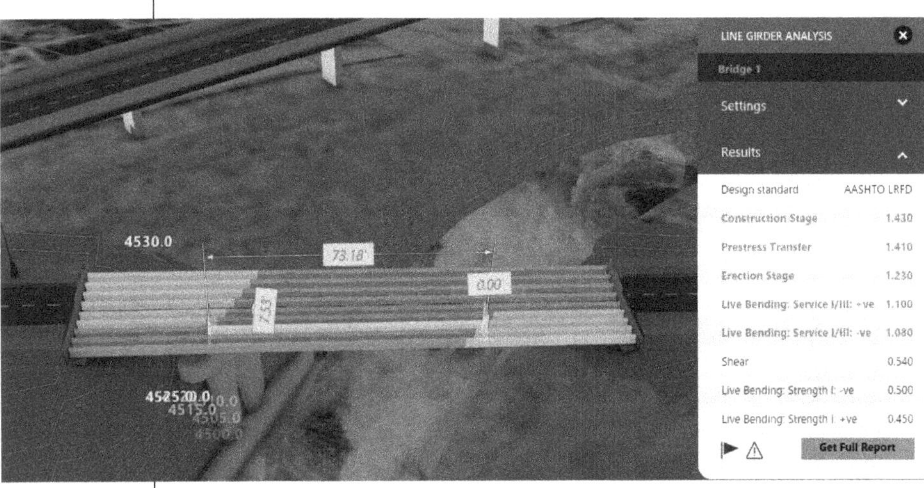

Figure 3–32

Hint: Analysis Time Requirements

If the analysis is taking too long, you can open the next proposal to see the results.

1. In the Utility Bar, expand *Proposal* and select **C_Task1** to make it current.
2. In the model, click on the bridge twice to select it. The results display in the Line Girder Analysis stack.

 © 2019, ASCENT - Center for Technical Knowledge®

3.4 Detail Design for Bridges

A key benefit to designing the bridge in the InfraWorks software is the ability to view the bridge in the context of its surroundings without losing any time on the design. When you are ready to proceed into the detailed design phase for the bridge, you can move the design easily into the Autodesk Revit or Autodesk Navisworks software.

Send a Bridge to Autodesk Revit

The Autodesk Revit software provides many more tools for designing bridges than the Autodesk InfraWorks software. Fortunately, you can send the bridge from InfraWorks to Revit with a simple right-click command. When doing so, you have two options on how they are included in the Autodesk Revit software:

- As Revit Families
- As Direct Shape

How To: Send a Bridge to Autodesk Revit

1. In the model, click once to select a Component road.
2. Click to select the bridge deck.
3. Right-click on the bridge and select **Send to Revit**, as shown in Figure 3–33.

You must have the Autodesk Revit software installed on the machine to complete this.

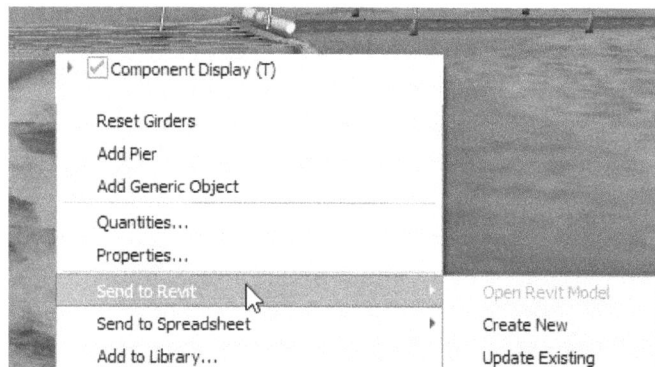

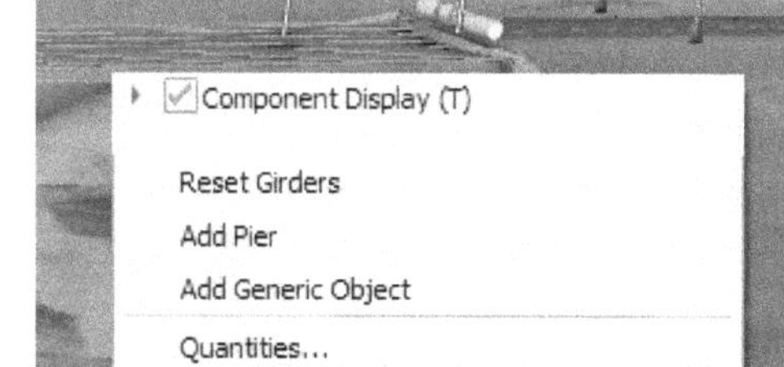

Figure 3–33

The Create Revit Model dialog box opens, as shown in Figure 3–34. When the command is complete, the Autodesk Revit software should open the new *.RVT file.

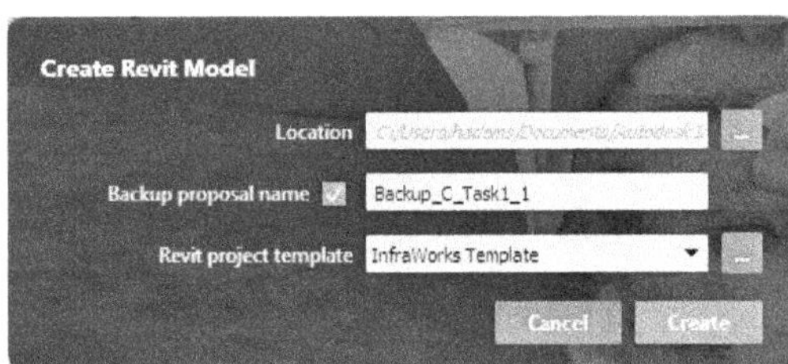

Figure 3–34

Open a Bridge in Autodesk Navisworks

The design can be opened directly in the Navisworks software to uncover design problems and constructibility issues more effectively and plan the construction sequencing. There are two options when porting an Autodesk InfraWorks model to Autodesk Navisworks.

- **Option 1:** First, open the bridge in Autodesk Civil 3D. Then, open the DWG file in Navisworks.
- **Option 2:** From Autodesk InfraWorks, export a 3D Model which you can append to the Autodesk Navisworks file.

If a 3D model is used to import a design into Autodesk Navisworks, you can export the model as a single file or multiple files. The benefit of using multiple files is that you can select which features in the model to export.

© 2019, ASCENT - Center for Technical Knowledge®

How To: Export an Autodesk InfraWorks Model to Autodesk Navisworks

1. In the In Canvas Tools, click (Settings and Utilities)> (Export 3D Model).
2. In the Export to 3D Model File dialog box, do the following, as shown in Figure 3–35:
   - Define the area to export.
   - Set the Target Coordinate System.
   - Determine if you want a single file or multiple files.
   - Click Export.

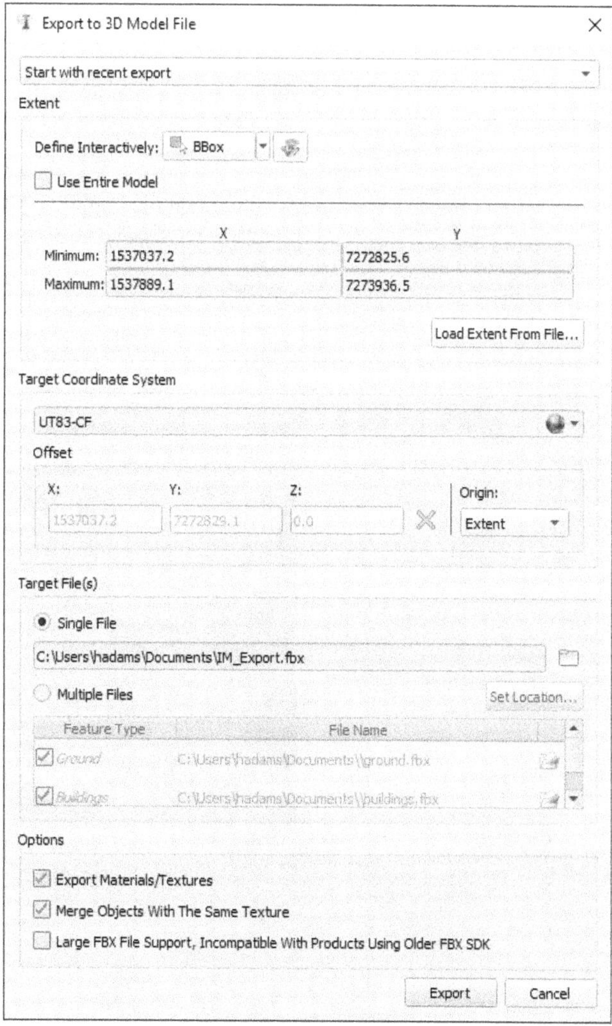

Figure 3–35

Practice 3c Send the Bridge to the Detailed Design Phase

Practice Objectives

- Send a bridge to the Autodesk Revit software for the detailed design.
- Create a 3D model of the bridge for the Autodesk Navisworks software.

In this practice, you will analyze the bridge girders for structural strength.

To complete this practice, access to the Internet and Autodesk® Revit® software is required.

Task 1 - Send a bridge to Autodesk Revit.

1. Continue working in the same model as the previous practice. If you did not complete the previous practice, in the Utility Bar, expand *Proposal* and select **C_Task1** to make it current.
2. In the Utility Bar, click (Bookmark) and select **DesignBridgeElevation**.
3. In the model, select the design bridge.
4. Right-click on the bridge and select **Send to Revit>Create New**, as shown in Figure 3–36.

You must have the Autodesk Revit software installed on your machine to complete this step.

Note: Although the deck was toggled off, the deck is included in the export.

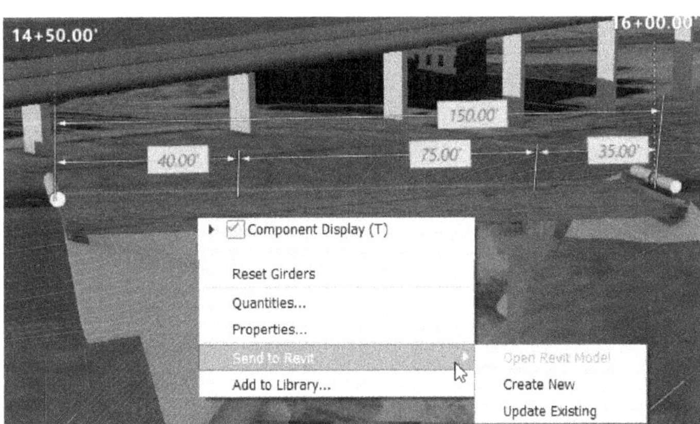

Figure 3–36

© 2019, ASCENT - Center for Technical Knowledge®

5. In the Create Revit Model dialog box, accept the defaults for the Location, Backup Proposal name, and Revit project template to use, as shown in Figure 3–37. Click **Create**.

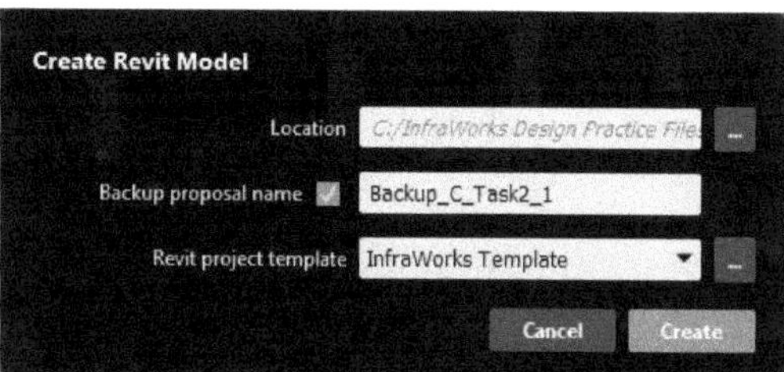

Figure 3–37

Task 2 - Send a bridge to Autodesk Navisworks.

1. In the In Canvas Tools, click (Settings and Utilities)> (Export 3D Model).
2. In the Utility Bar, click (Bookmark) and select **River**.
3. Next to *Define Interactively*, select **BBox**. Define the bounding box, as shown in Figure 3–38.

Figure 3–38

4. Ensure that the Target Coordinate System is set to **UT83-CF**, as shown in Figure 3–39:

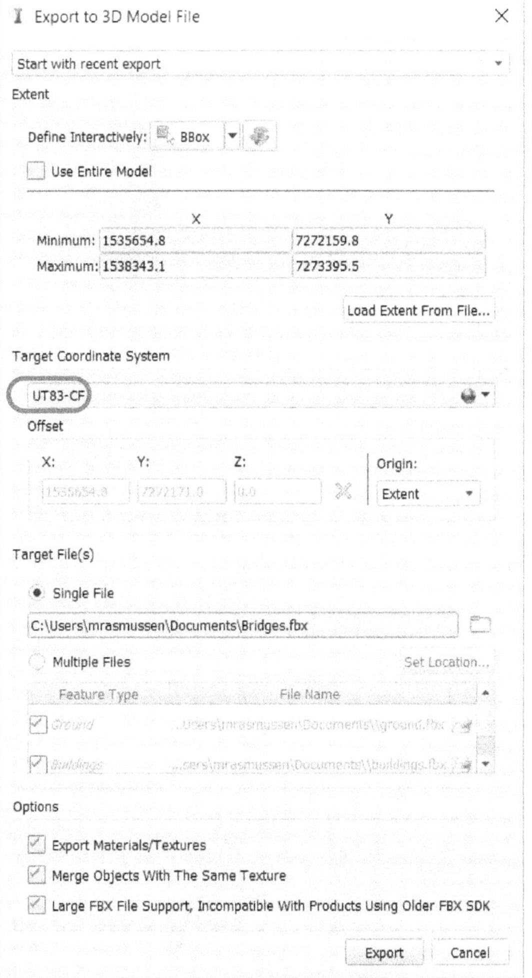

Figure 3–39

5. Ensure that *Target Files* is set to **Single File**. Set the file path to *C:\InfraWorks Design Practice Files\Bridges*.

6. Now the file can be imported into the Autodesk Navisworks or the Autodesk 3ds Max software. Click **Export**.

© 2019, ASCENT - Center for Technical Knowledge®

Chapter Review Questions

1. What key component do you need in the model before you can create a bridge?
   a. Component Road
   b. River
   c. Railway
   d. None of the above
2. What bridge component do you select in the model in order to change to the bridge beginning station?
   a. Girder
   b. Pier
   c. Bridge Deck
   d. Abutment at the beginning of the bridge
3. How would you change the number of piers that support the bridge?
   a. Select the pier and make copies to add more piers or press delete to remove piers
   b. Select the bridge deck and in the Bridge asset card, change the value in the Number of piers field.
   c. Modify the Bridge style in the Styles palette.
   d. You cannot change the number of piers.
4. How would you change the type of bridge in the model once it has been added to a Component road? (Select all that apply.)
   a. Right-click on the bridge deck and select Properties. In the Properties palette, change the manual style.
   b. You cannot change the bridge type once it has been created.
   c. Drag and drop a different style from the *Bridge* tab of the Style palette.
   d. Select the bridge deck. In the Bridge asset card, change the value in the *Bridge Type* field.
5. What type of bridge girders can you run a Line Girder Analysis on?
   a. Concrete
   b. Steel

© 2019, ASCENT - Center for Technical Knowledge®

6. When you run a Line Girder Analysis, it costs cloud credits every time you make an adjustment and preview the results in the model.
   a. True
   b. False

© 2019, ASCENT - Center for Technical Knowledge®

Command Summary

Button	Command	Location
	**Export 3D Model**	• **In Canvas Tools: Settings and Utilities**
	Line Girder Analysis	• **In Canvas Tools: Design, review and engineer bridges>Perform analysis on your bridge design**
	**Precast | Girder Bridge**	• **In Canvas Tools:** Design, review, and engineer bridges>Design bridges
	**Steel Plate Girder Bridge**	• **In Canvas Tools:** Design, review, and engineer bridges>Design bridges

© 2019, ASCENT - Center for Technical Knowledge®

© 2019, ASCENT - Center for Technical Knowledge®

Introduction to Drainage Design

The Drainage Design tools enable you to add drainage features to component roads. You can use the rule-based tool sets to lay out a drainage network and then follow a four-step process to identify and analyze watersheds and their stream flows, create and modify culverts, create pavement drainage networks, and review the quantities of materials for culverts or pavement drainage networks by road, type, and number.

Learning Objectives in this Chapter

- Determine the extents of a watershed area.
- Create and modify culverts.
- Design pavement drainage along a component road.
- Calculate quantities for a drainage network.

4.1 Watershed Analysis

Determining the discharge of a stream is important for designing culverts and other structures used to protect transportation systems from ponding, freezing, and water runoff damage. With the Drainage Design for InfraWorks module, you can add drainage networks to the model. Before creating the drainage network, it is important to run a watershed analysis to determine the extents of a watershed area. By running a watershed analysis, the watershed extents and stream locations display in the model. Additionally, pins are placed where the streams cross a component road to indicate that either a culvert or bridge is required.

Running a watershed analysis requires cloud credits because the calculations are done in the cloud.

The analysis identifies the existing drainage patterns prior to road placement and design. Therefore, it uses the original terrain surface that was in the model before any component roads were created. A single analysis can identify multiple watersheds, each of which is a selectable feature. During the analysis process, square grids of terrain are sampled. The grid spacing and stream threshold can each be adjusted in the Create Watershed asset card, as shown in Figure 4–1. Lowering the values finds smaller streams, but also requires more analysis. Raising the value finds larger streams and reduces the analysis.

- **Grid Spacing:** Controls the size of the square grids sampled for the terrain.
- **Stream Threshold:** Sets the number of grid cells used to define streams. For example, a stream threshold of 50 indicates that a stream is created once there are a minimum of 50 upstream grid squares flowing into a stream's starting point.

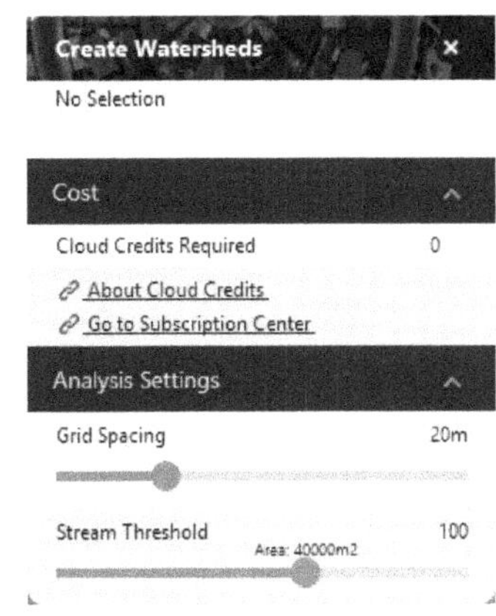

Figure 4–1

© 2019, ASCENT - Center for Technical Knowledge®

Modify Peak Flows

Once a watershed is created, it contains a Watershed asset card. Within the Watershed asset card, the peak flows can only be modified if *Hydrology Method* is set to **User Defined**. However, two other methods are available which cause the *Peak Flows fields to calculate automatically*, as shown in Figure 4–2:

- **Regression** analysis is available for select areas. It enables you to set the state and region.
- **Rational** analysis enables you to enter a *Runoff Coefficient* and a *Rainfall Intensity* for 100 year storms.

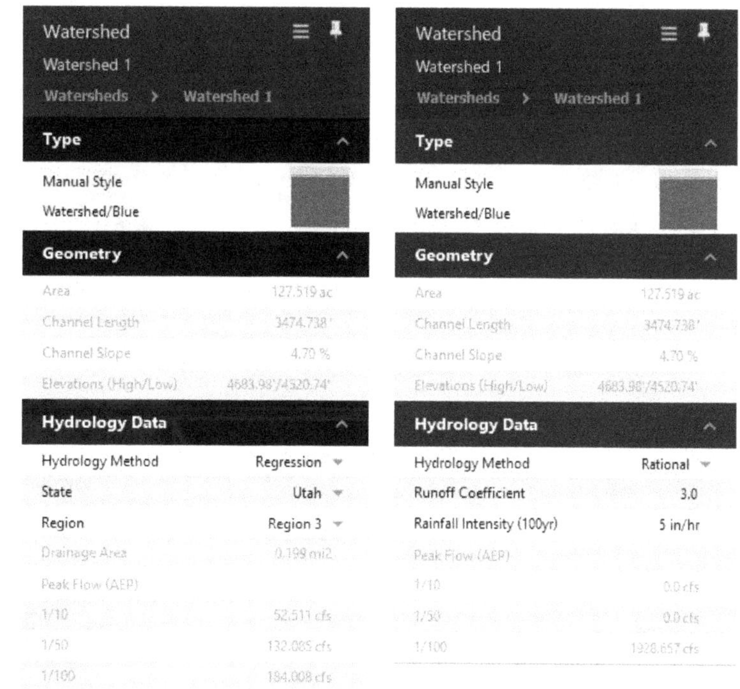

Figure 4–2

How To: Run a Watershed Analysis to a Component Road

1. In the In Canvas tools, click (Design, review and engineer drainage)> (Design drainage).
2. In the expanded tool group, click (Create Watersheds). In the model, all of the component roads are highlighted, as shown in Figure 4–3.

Figure 4–3

3. Select how you want to calculate the watershed:

To calculate a watershed...	Start the analysis by...
Upstream from a point	Double-clicking on a point in a valley or low-lying area.
Along a component road	Select a component road and press <Enter>. The watershed is calculated upstream from the selected road.
Along a region of a component road	Selecting a component road, clicking to select the start and end points of the region, and then pressing <Enter>. The watershed is calculated upstream from the selected road.

4. In the Create Watershed asset card, set the *Grid Spacing* and the *Stream Threshold* sliders according to the terrain being analyzed, as shown in Figure 4–4.

© 2019, ASCENT - Center for Technical Knowledge®

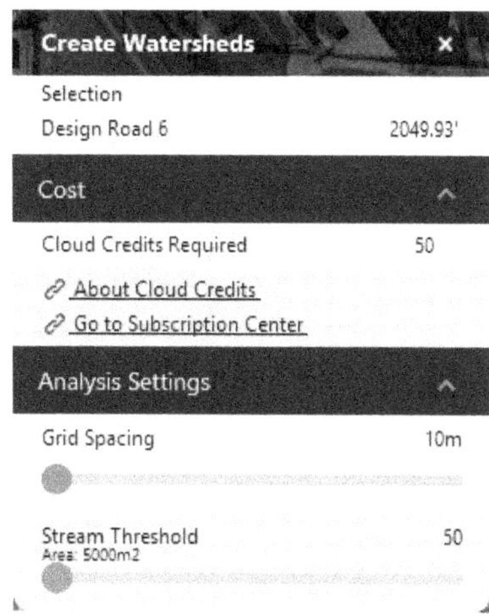

Figure 4–4

5. Once the analysis is complete, the watershed boundary and stream network display in the model, as shown in Figure 4–5. Additionally, a pin should display in the model at the point that a stream crosses the road.

Figure 4–5

6. In the model, select the watershed area.

7. In the Watershed asset card, do the following:
    - Set the *Hydrology Method*.
    - Set additional field values according to the Hydrology Method selected.

8. Press <Esc> to clear the selection of the watershed area.

9. To control the watershed area display, do the following, as shown in Figure 4–6:

   - In the Utility Bar, click (Control, display, and selectability of features).
   - In the Model Explorer, right-click on *Surface Layers* and select **Surface Layers**.
   - In the Surface Layers palette, click / .(Show/Hide data source contents).

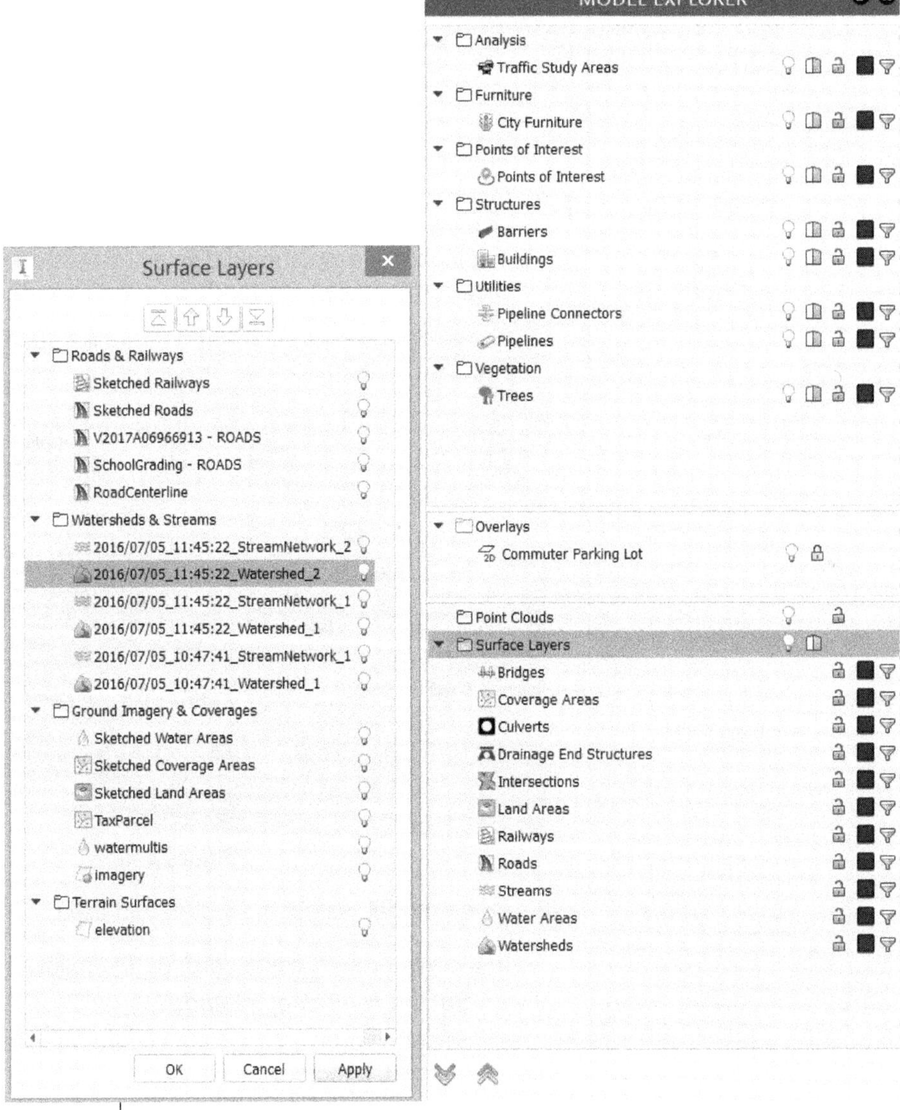

Figure 4–6

© 2019, ASCENT - Center for Technical Knowledge®

Practice 4a Create a Watershed

Practice Objective

- Create a watershed upstream from a component road.

In this practice, you will create a watershed, as shown in Figure 4–7.

To use this feature, access to the Internet is required.

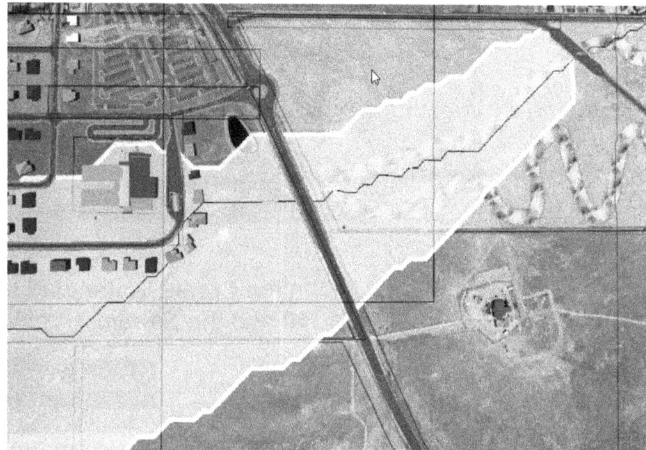

Figure 4–7

Task 1 - Create a watershed for a component road.

1. In the Home Screen, click **Open**.
2. In the *C:\InfraWorks Design Practice Files\DrainageDesign* folder, select **DrainageDesign.sqlite** and click **Open**.
3. In the Utility Bar, click (Bookmark) and select **River**. Ensure that **A_Task1** is the current proposal.
4. In the In Canvas tools, click (Design, review and engineer drainage)> (Design drainage)> (Create Watersheds).
5. In the message that displays, click **OK**.

© 2019, ASCENT - Center for Technical Knowledge®

6. The component roads are highlighted in the model.Select the component road with a bridge (Road 6). Then select the section shown in Figure 4–8.

Figure 4–8

7. In the Create Watershed asset card, set the *Grid Spacing* to **10** and the *Stream Threshold* to **50**, as shown in Figure 4–9.

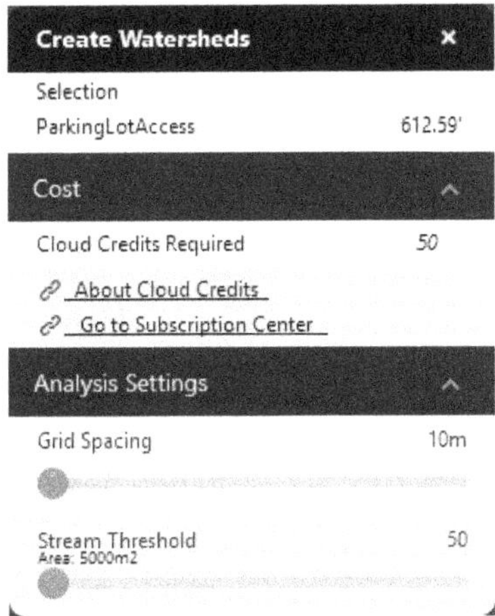

Figure 4–9

The analysis costs 50 cloud credits.

8. Press <Enter> to analyze the bridge section of road.
9. In the message that displays, click **OK**.
10. In the model, select the watershed area.

© 2019, ASCENT - Center for Technical Knowledge®

11. In the Watershed asset card, set the following options, as shown in Figure 4–10:
    - *Hydrology Method*: **Regression**
    - *State*: **Utah**
    - *Region:* **Region 3**

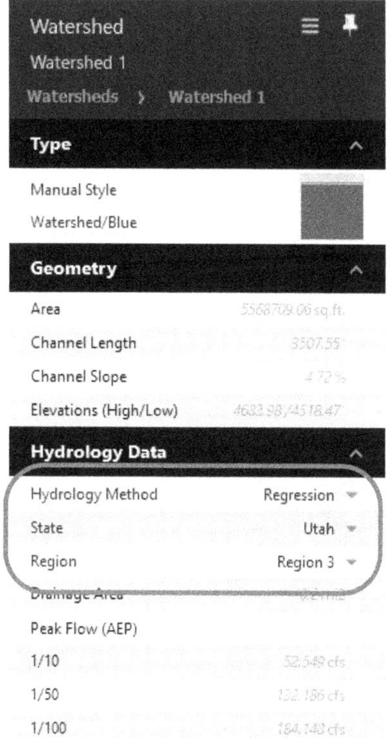

Figure 4–10

12. Press <Esc> to clear the selection of the watershed area.

4.2 Create and Modify Culverts

Add Culverts Automatically

Once a watershed analysis has been run, one or more culverts can be added to the model anywhere that streams cross the component road. Once added, the culvert information displays in the model in the form of tooltips, as well as in the Culvert asset card, as shown in Figure 4–11.

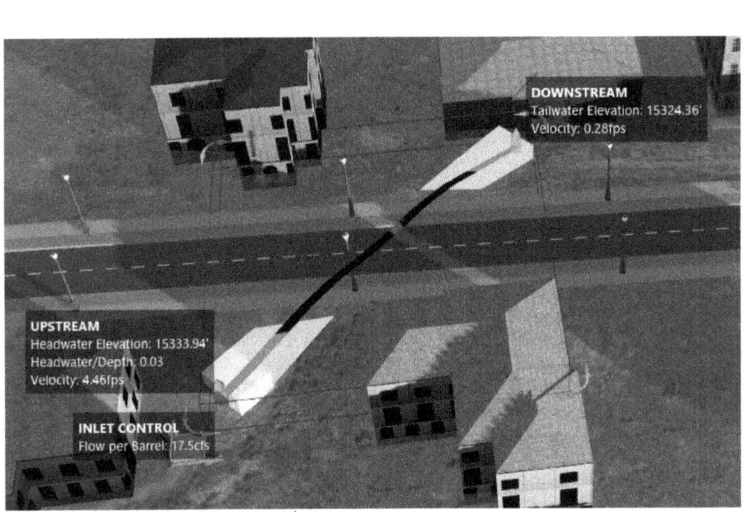

Figure 4–11

© 2019, ASCENT - Center for Technical Knowledge®

How To: Add Culverts at Stream Crossings Automatically

1. In the model, run a watershed analysis using the (Create Watersheds) tool.
2. In the model, select the component road.
3. Right-click on the component road and select **Drainage>Add Culverts**, as shown in Figure 4–12.

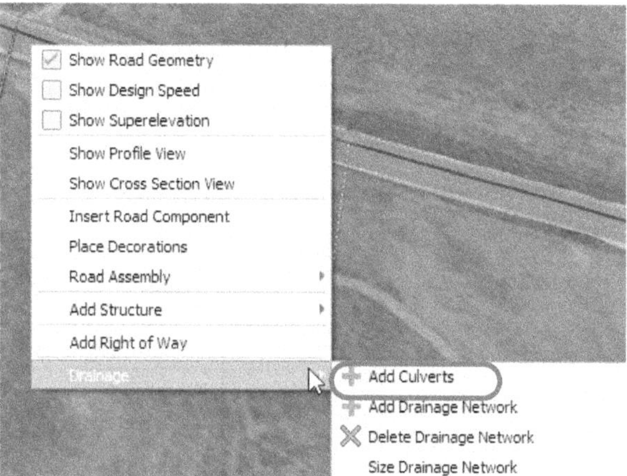

Figure 4–12

4. Culverts display in the model at each of the stream crossing pins that were placed during the watershed analysis. To clear the culvert selection, press <Esc>.

Create Culverts Manually

Culverts can be added automatically or manually. The benefit of adding a culvert manually is that it can be added to objects other than component roads.

How To: Create a Culvert Manually

1. In the In Canvas tools, click (Design, review and engineer drainage)> (Design drainage)> (Culverts).
2. Click two points in the model to place the beginning and ending points for the culvert.
3. Press <Esc> to clear the culvert selection.

Modify a Culvert

Culverts can be modified by gizmos or the Culvert asset card. If the culverts were created automatically using the **Add Culverts** command, then they can be updated automatically as well. If the road style or number of lanes are changed for a component road, the culvert length, slope, and invert elevations change to match the new design.

The gizmos available for editing culverts manually are described in the table below.

Gizmos	Transformation	Description
	Elevation/ Control Point	Stretches culverts horizontally and vertically, changing the elevation or beginning/ending point location.
	Headwall Height	Stretches the headwall height without changing its length or width.
	Move	Moves a culvert without changing its size or shape.
	Rotate	Rotates a culvert around its Z-axis.
	Size	Changes the size of the barrel.

The following features and options of a culvert can be modified using the Culvert asset card, shown in Figure 4–13:

- **Number of Barrels:** 1 or 2
- **Shape:** Box or Circular
- **Material:** Concrete or Corrugate Metal
- **Manning's n**
- **End Treatment:** Headwall Height and Flare Angle
- **Show Analysis results**
- **Tailwater Condition:** (dc+D)/2, Crown, Critical, Normal, or User Defined

 © 2019, ASCENT - Center for Technical Knowledge®

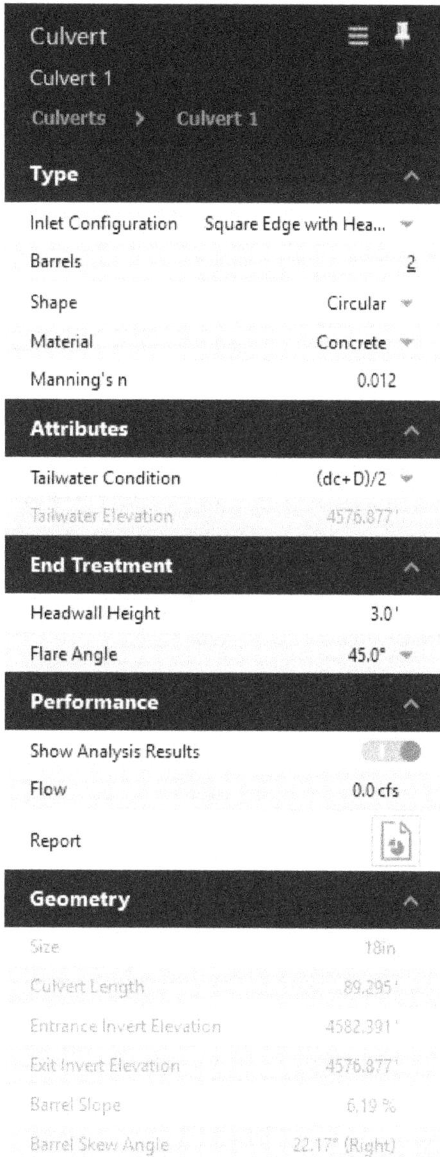
Culvert
Culvert 1
Culverts > Culvert 1
Type
Inlet Configuration Square Edge with Hea...
Barrels 2
Shape Circular
Material Concrete
Manning's n 0.012
Attributes
Tailwater Condition (dc+D)/2
Tailwater Elevation 4576.877'
End Treatment
Headwall Height 3.0'
Flare Angle 45.0°
Performance
Show Analysis Results
Flow 0.0 cfs
Report
Geometry
Size 18in
Culvert Length 89.295'
Entrance Invert Elevation 4582.391'
Exit Invert Elevation 4576.877'
Barrel Slope 6.19 %
Barrel Skew Angle 22.17° (Right)

Figure 4–13

Practice 4b Create a Culvert

Practice Objective

- Create a culvert to a component road.

In this practice, you will create a culvert, as shown in Figure 4–14.

Figure 4–14

Task 1 - Add a culvert to a component road.

1. In the Home Screen, click **Open**.
2. In the *C:\InfraWorks Design Practice Files\DrainageDesign* folder, select **DrainageDesign.sqlite** and click **Open**.
3. In the Utility Bar, click (Bookmark) and select **Bridge**. Ensure that **B_Task1** is the current proposal.
4. In the model, select **S Redwood Rd.** Right-click and select **Drainage>Add Culverts**, as shown in Figure 4–15.

© 2019, ASCENT - Center for Technical Knowledge®

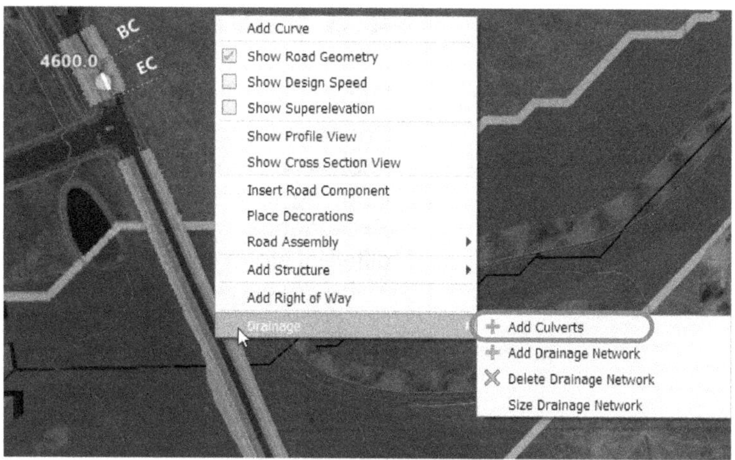

Figure 4–15

5. In the model, select the culvert (you can find it by zooming in on where the black watershed stream crosses S Redwood Rd).

6. In the Culvert asset card, set *Barrels* to **2**.

7. In the model, click (Control gizmo) to extend the end of the culvert past the daylight line on each side of the road, as shown in Figure 4–16.

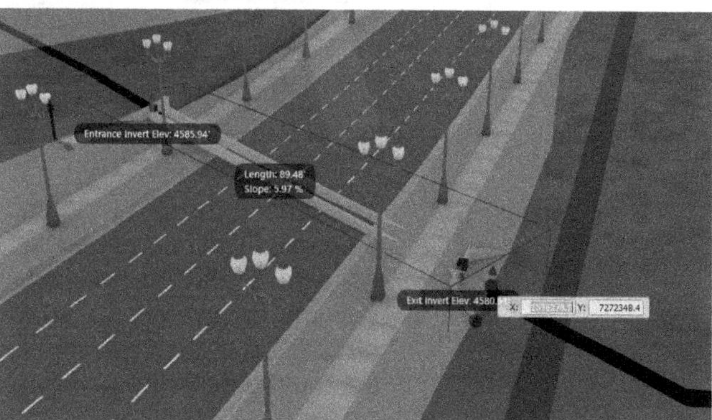

Figure 4–16

8. In the model, click (Move in the Z axis gizmo) to move the culvert in the Z direction down 4 feet.

9. To clear the culvert selection, press <Esc>.

4.3 Pavement Drainage

In this course, structure refers to either an inlet or a manhole which is at the end of a pipe in the drainage network.

Industry standard rules and calculations inside the Autodesk Drainage Design module for InfraWorks® software provides analysis-driven design for pavement drainage networks. By inputting various coefficients and varying the AEP (Annual Exceedance Probability) setting, you can examine pipe runs in different storm level conditions. The data displays in the model or in the drainage structure's asset card, as shown in Figure 4–17.

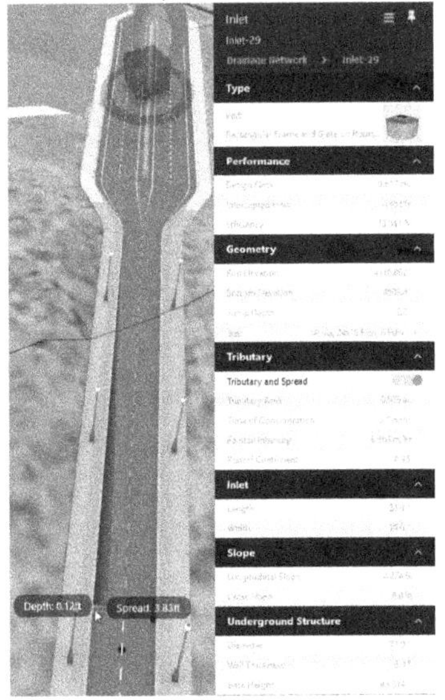

Visual Inspection of Inlet Performance

Hydraulic Performance of a Pipe

Figure 4–17

General Workflow

The order in which commands are used for setting up the pavement drainage network is important. Certain commands do not work if specific steps are not completed first. For example, you cannot analyze the surface drainage unless you have already sized the pavement drainage. The following steps should be completed in the following order.

1. Create the conceptual design by adding pavement drainage to a component road.
2. Modify the design by moving, adding, and removing pipes and structures, as required.
3. Fine-tune the changes that have been made by sizing pavement drainage.
4. Analyze the surface drainage between inlets to verify performance of pipe runs.

© 2019, ASCENT - Center for Technical Knowledge®

Input Rainfall Quantities

A rainfall editor enables you to customize the rainfall content for a model.

How To: Customize Rainfall Content

1. In the In Canvas tools, click (Design, review and engineer drainage)> (Analyze your model)> (Rainfall Content).
2. In the Rainfall Content palette, double-click on any of the existing tables to open it for editing.
    - Alternatively, click (Add a new empty rainfall content of the current rainfall type) to create a new table.
3. In the Rainfall Editor panel, click in any of the fields that require editing and type in the new values, as shown in Figure 4–18.

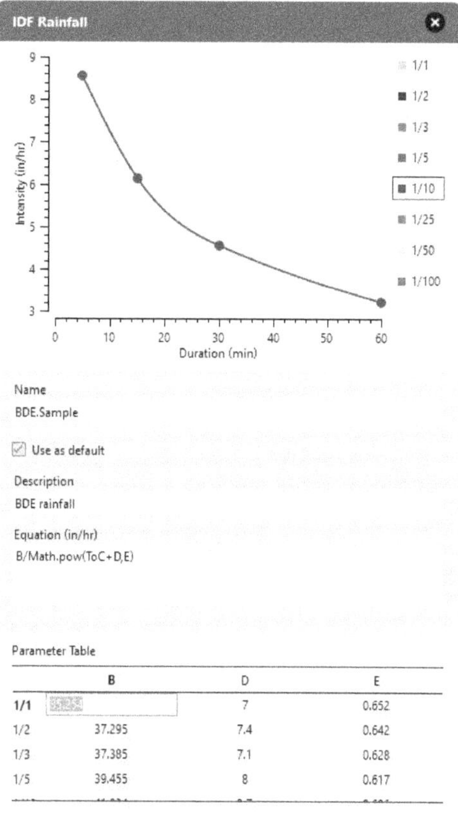

Figure 4–18

Create a Network

A component road must exist before a pavement drainage network can be added to the model. To add a network, simply edit the component road.

How To: Create a Pavement Drainage Network

1. In the model, select a component road.
2. Right-click on the component road and select **Drainage>Add Drainage Network**, as shown in Figure 4–19.

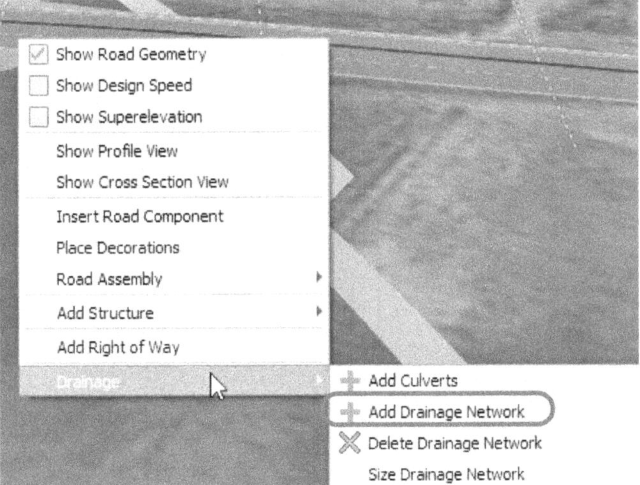

Figure 4–19

3. Press <Enter> to accept the selection and create the drainage.

© 2019, ASCENT - Center for Technical Knowledge®

Modify Drainage Networks

Similar to the other features in the Autodesk InfraWorks software, drainage networks can be modified using gizmos.

Gizmo	Transformation	Description
	Elevation/ Control Point	Displays at each point of intersection along a pipe or at the center of each structure. In a 3D View, it can stretch features horizontally or vertically by changing the elevation of the vertex. In plan view, it becomes a Control Point.
	Rotate	Rotates a feature around the Z-axis.
	Control Point	Displays at each point of intersection of pipes, or center of structure. Stretches pipes by moving the selected vertex of the pipe. Moves the location of structures. Note: Additional control points can be added by holding <Alt> and selecting the new control point location.
	Move	Moves the selected feature or vertex.

When a pipe is selected in the model, the Pipe asset card displays. This asset card enables you to change the material of the pipe, size, and invert elevations, as shown in Figure 4–20. The length and slope are calculated values.

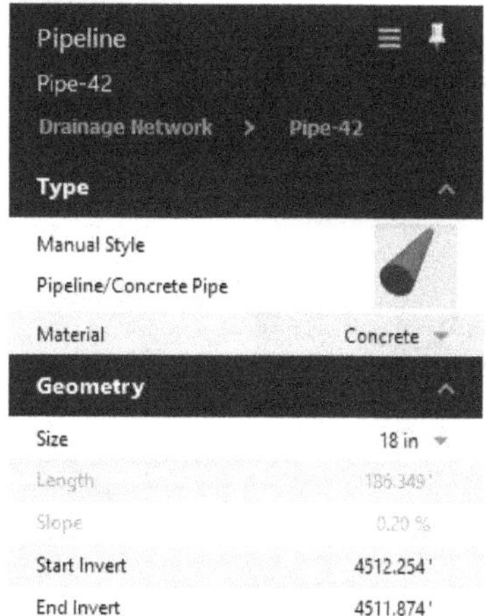

Figure 4–20

When a structure is selected in the model, the appropriate asset card displays, enabling you to change the type and the size of structure, as shown in Figure 4–21. If the *Type* field is selected, the Select Component asset card displays, which enables you to select from a number of predefined structure types.

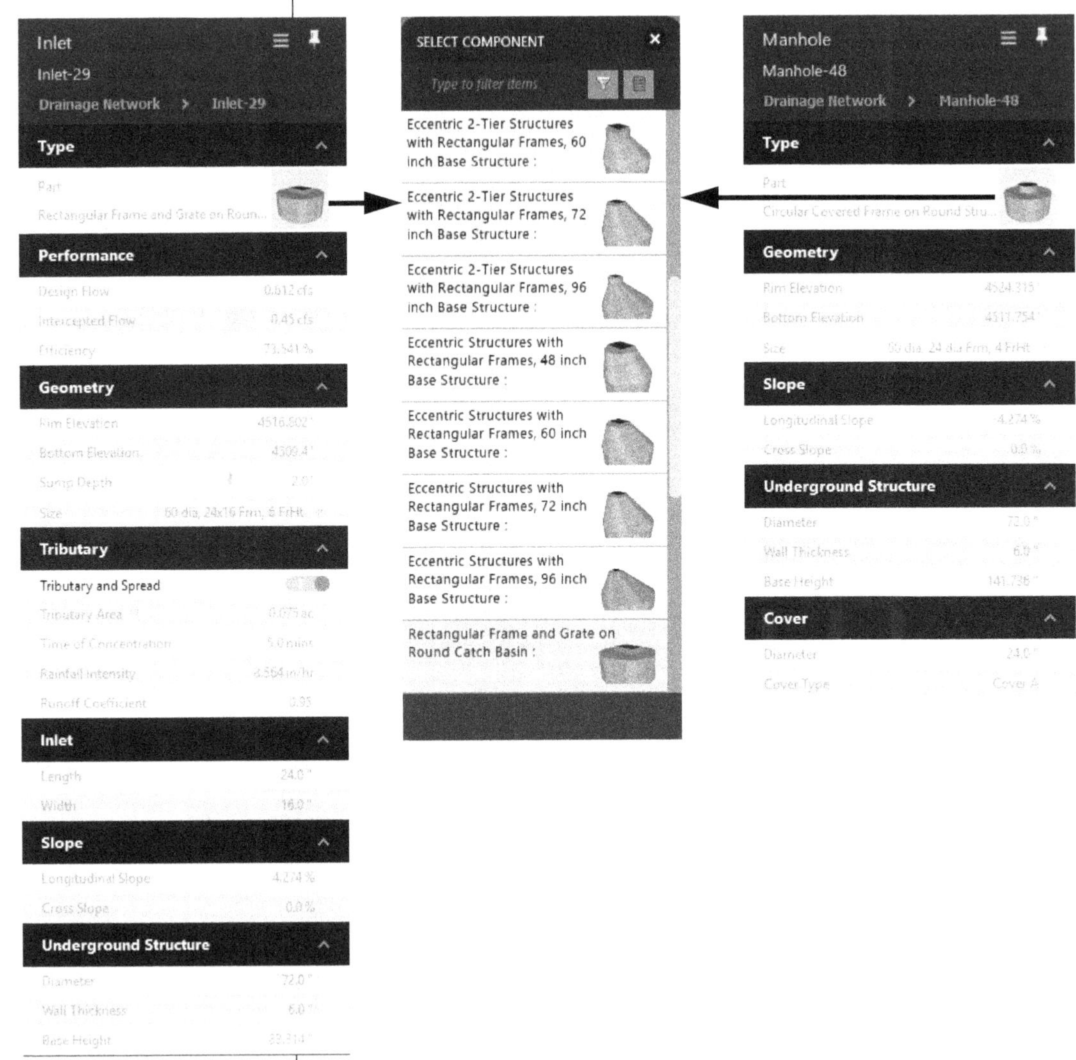

Figure 4–21

Hint: Component Road Changes

If you want to change a component road that already has pavement drainage added to it, do not modify the drainage network. It is best to delete the drainage network and add a new drainage network to any revised component roads.

 © 2019, ASCENT - Center for Technical Knowledge®

How To: Add Drainage Features to an Existing Network

1. In the In Canvas tools, click (Design, review and engineer drainage)> (Design drainage)> (Drainage Networks).
2. In the Sketch Drainage Network asset card, set the appropriate inlet, manhole, and pipe types, sizes, and other parameters, as shown in Figure 4–22.

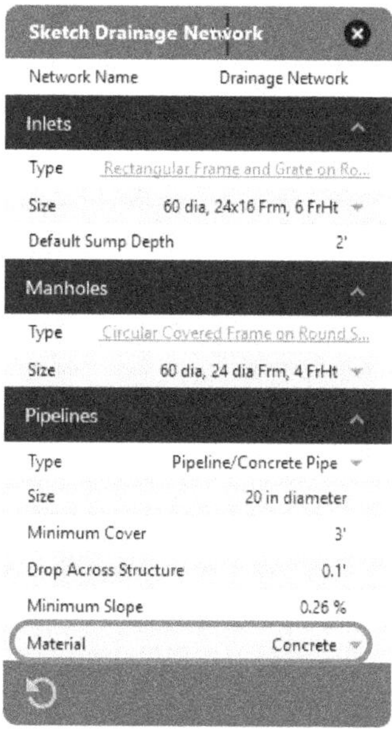

Figure 4–22

3. In the model, click to place the features. Right-click to change the feature(s) being placed or to enable the **Show high and low points** option, as shown in Figure 4–23.

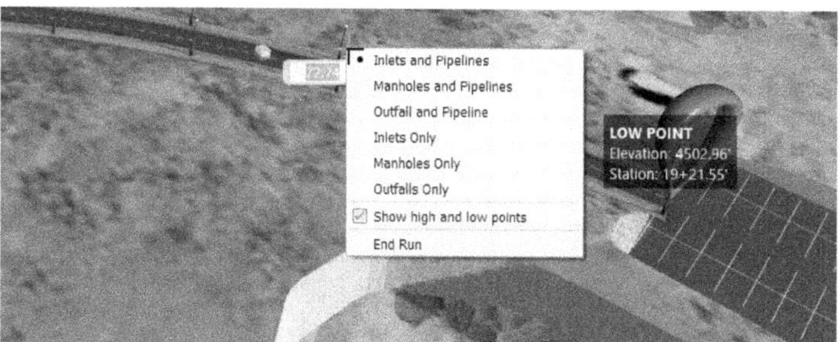

Figure 4–23

4. Double-click to place the last feature or right-click and select **End Run**.

Size Pavement Drainage

After moving structures or adding additional structures to a design, it is necessary to fine-tune the placement and sizing of the structures. You can do this by running the **Size Pavement Drainage** command. This recalculates the pipe diameters, adjusts pipe slopes, and resizes connectors as required to accommodate any changes.

How To: Size Pavement Drainage

1. In the model, select the component road.
2. Right-click and select **Drainage>Size Drainage Network**, as shown in Figure 4–24.

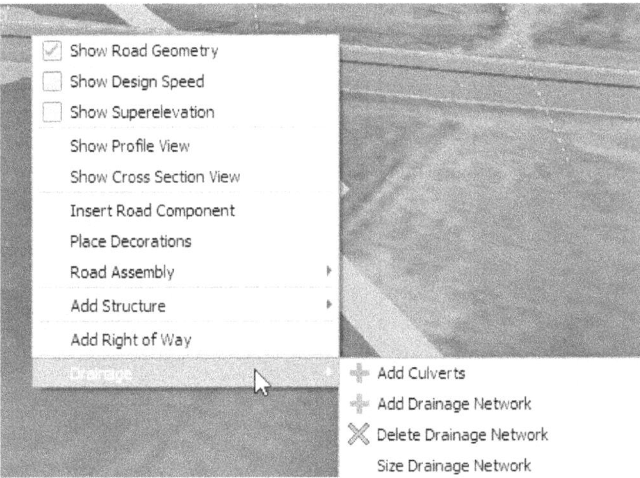

Figure 4–24

© 2019, ASCENT - Center for Technical Knowledge®

Analyze Pavement Drainage

Visual Inspection of Inlet Performance

Inlets are analyzed in real-time by the Autodesk InfraWorks software. By selecting an inlet, you can visually inspect it to ensure that its performance meets the design parameters. When selected, the Inlet asset card displays along with the water capture, spread, and bypass, as shown in Figure 4–25.

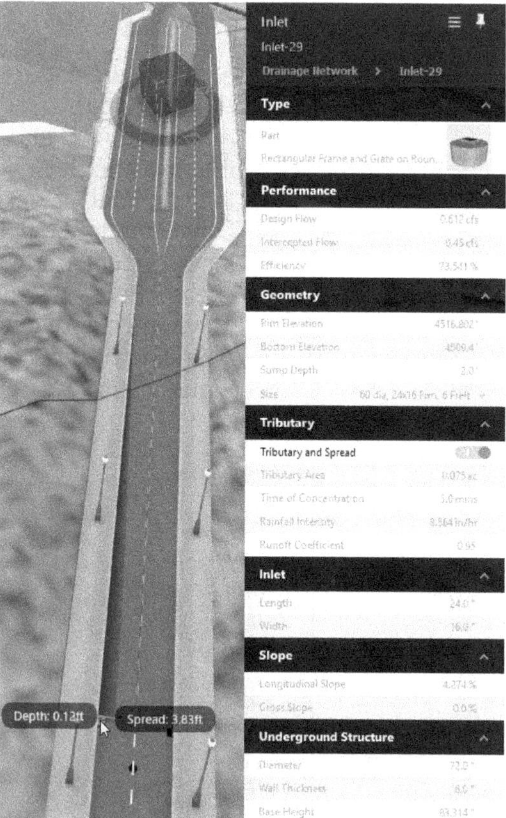

Figure 4–25

Hydraulic Performance of a Pipe

Flooded manholes and surcharged pipes can be identified visually in the model. After running an analysis, the EGL, HGL, and the Obvert of pipe elevations can be viewed by moving the cursor over the hatched area over the analyzed pipes.

How To: Analyze Pavement Drainage

1. Navigate the view below the terrain surface so that underground pipes and structures are displayed and selectable.
   - Alternatively, you can decrease the opacity of the surface to see below the ground.
2. In the In Canvas tools, click (Design, review, and engineer drainage)> (Analyze your model)> (Inspect Performance).
3. Adjust the AEP and Tailwater Condition values as required in the Analysis Settings asset card.
4. In the model, select one of the pipe connectors that are connected to the pipe you want to analyze. Then select the pipe connector on the opposite side of the pipe.
5. Press <Enter> to analyze the pipe.
6. Move the cursor over the vertical bar along the hatched bounding box to view analysis result, as shown in Figure 4–26.

Figure 4–26

- The blue bar indicates the hydraulic gradeline (water depth in the pipe).
- The green line represents the obvert (inside) of the pipe.
- The yellow line represents the energy gradeline.

© 2019, ASCENT - Center for Technical Knowledge®

Practice 4c Create a Pavement Drainage Network

Practice Objectives

- Add a pavement drainage network to a component road.
- Add inlets, pipes, and manholes to a drainage network.
- Size a pavement drainage network.
- Analyze a pavement drainage network.
- Calculate quantities for a drainage network.

In this practice, you will create a pavement drainage network. You will then analyze it for performance, as shown in Figure 4–27.

Figure 4–27

Task 1 - Add a pavement drainage network to a component road.

1. In the Home Screen, click **Open**.
2. In the *C:\InfraWorks Design Practice Files\DrainageDesign* folder, select **DrainageDesign.sqlite** and click **Open**.
3. In the Utility Bar, click (Bookmark) and select **Bridge**. Ensure that **C_Task1** is the current proposal.

4. In the model, select **S Redwood Rd.**, right-click and select **Drainage>Add Drainage Network**, as shown in Figure 4–28.

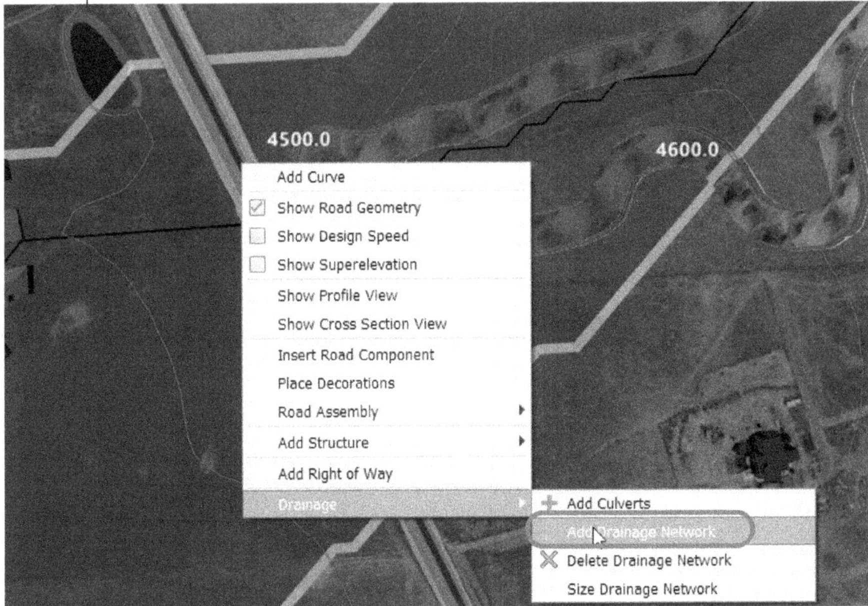

Figure 4–28

5. Accept all the defaults in the Add Drainage Network asset card and press <Enter> to add pavement drainage.

6. In the Add Drainage Network message box, click **OK**.

Task 2 - Modify pavement drainage.

1. Continue working in the same model as the previous task. If you did not complete the previous task, set **C_Task2** as the current proposal.

2. In the Utility Bar, expand the View Style drop-down and click (Configure current view). In the View Settings asset card, click (Change navigation and application feedback settings) to open the *Interaction* stack.

© 2019, ASCENT - Center for Technical Knowledge®

3. Under *Navigation*, toggle off the **Lock Mouse Above Ground** slider if it is on, as shown in Figure 4–29.

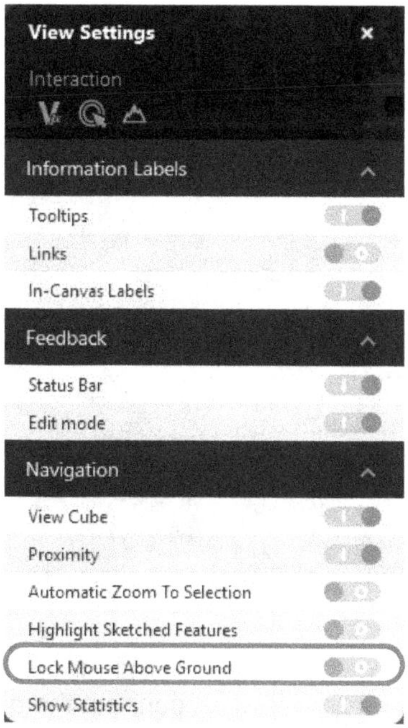

Figure 4–29

4. Close the View Settings asset card.

5. In the Utility Bar, click (Bookmark) and select **MissingDrainage**.

Even though there are outlets on each network, the approving agency wants the two networks to be connected and one more manhole and two more inlets to be added.

6. In the Utility Bar, click (Bookmark) and select **AddDrainage**.

7. In the In Canvas tools, click  (Design, review and engineer drainage)>  (Design drainage)> (Drainage Network).

8. In the Create Drainage Network asset card, accept the default inlet, manhole, pipe types, sizes, and other parameters.

© 2019, ASCENT - Center for Technical Knowledge®

9. In the model, click to place the first inlet on the north-east side of the road just north of the intersection, as shown in Figure 4–30. Right-click and select **Manholes and Pipelines**.

Figure 4–30

10. In the model, click the inlet you placed in the previous step to connect the pipe to it. Move the cursor south and click to place the manhole in the center of the intersection. Double-click on the manhole created in the last task, as shown in Figure 4–31.

When placing inlets, ensure that you select a point on the pavement and not the curb.

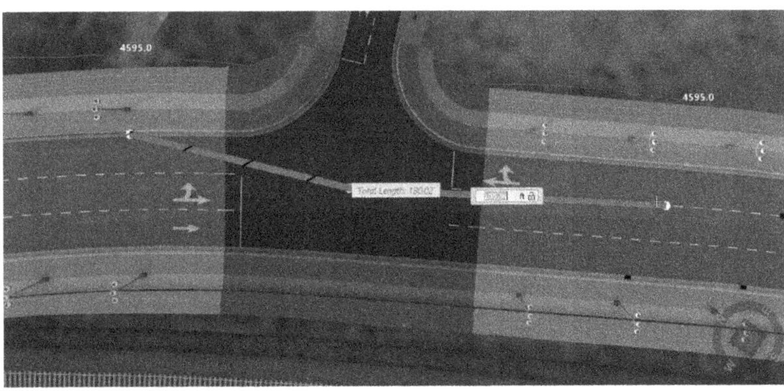

Figure 4–31

© 2019, ASCENT - Center for Technical Knowledge®

11. Right-click and select **Inlets and Pipelines**. Click to place an inlet across from the other one you created. Double-click on the manhole you created to end the pipe, as shown in Figure 4–32.

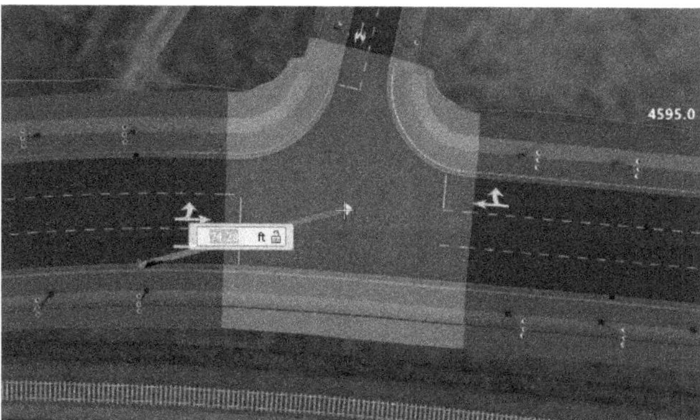

Figure 4–32

12. Repeat the previous steps to add two more inlets and a manhole to the drainage network, as shown in Figure 4–33. Then connect the new manhole to the two other manholes indicated. Figure 4–33 shows the results you should see below ground once everything is connected.

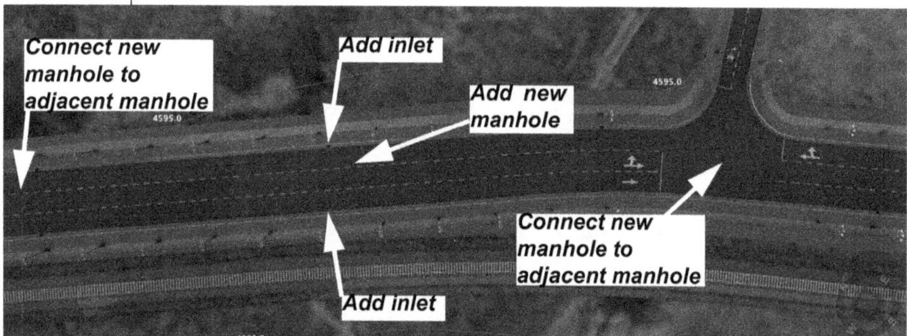

Above Ground-Plan View

Below Ground-Profile View

Figure 4–33

13. Press <Esc> twice to exit the command.

Task 3 - Size pavement drainage.

1. Continue working in the same model as the previous task. If you did not complete the previous task, set **C_Task3** as the current proposal.
2. In the model, select **S Redwood Rd.**
3. Right-click and select **Drainage>Size Drainage Network**, as shown in Figure 4–34.

*If you get the message "Missing Outfall in sub-network, skipping relevant calculations. Do you want to continue?", click **Yes**.*

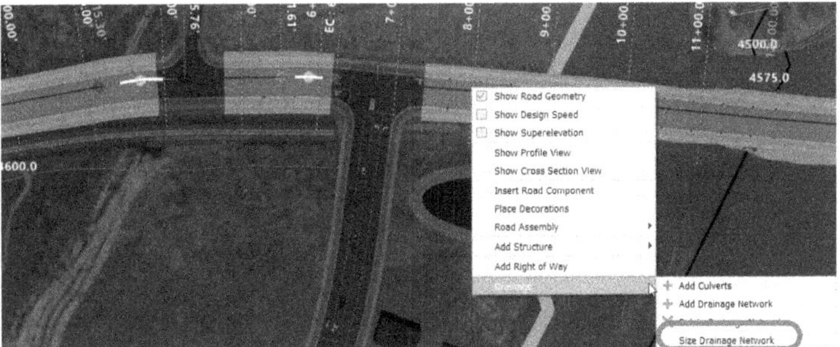

Figure 4–34

4. Press <Enter> to accept the default values in the Size Drainage Network asset card.

Task 4 - Analyze pavement drainage.

1. Continue working in the same model as the previous task. If you did not complete the previous task, set **C_Task4** as the current proposal.
2. Select one of the inlet structures to view its asset card and the water capture, spread, and bypass measurements.
3. In the Utility Bar, click (Bookmark) and select **AnalyzeDrainage**.
4. In the In Canvas tools, click (Design, review, and engineer drainage)> (Analyze your model)> (Inspect Performance).
5. In the Analysis Settings asset card, change *AEP* to **1/5**.

© 2019, ASCENT - Center for Technical Knowledge®

6. In the model, select the second manhole you created earlier. Then select the manhole on the opposite side of the pipe, as shown in Figure 4–35.

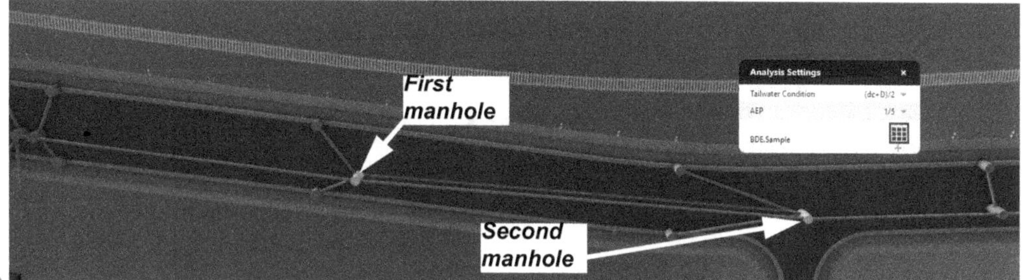

Figure 4–35

7. Press <Enter> to analyze the pipe.

8. Pivot the view to see above ground. Move the cursor over the vertical bar along the hatched bounding box to view analysis result, as shown in Figure 4–36.

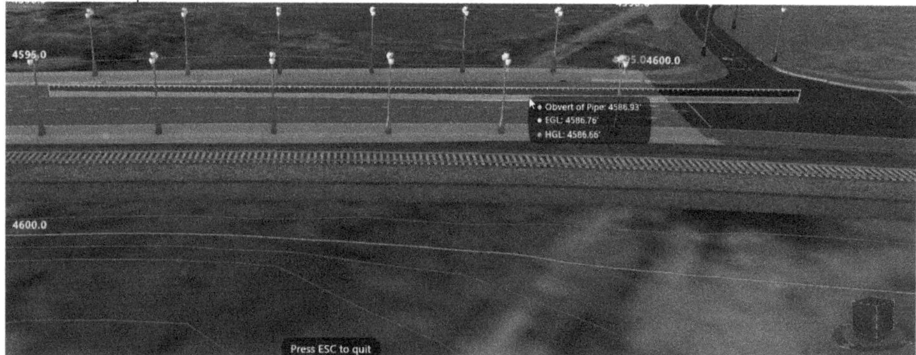

Figure 4–36

9. Press <Esc> when done.

Chapter Review Questions

1. Watershed areas can be calculated for the following. (Select all that apply)
   a. A single-low lying point
   b. A single-high point
   c. An entire component road
   d. A select station range of a component road
2. Culverts can be added to component roads automatically.
   a. True
   b. False
3. Which of the following must you do before you can analyze the surface drainage between inlets to verify the performance of pipe runs?
   a. Create the conceptual design by adding pavement drainage to a component road.
   b. Modify the design by moving, adding, and removing, pipes and structures, as required.
   c. Run the (Create Watersheds) command.
   d. Fine-tune the changes that have been made by sizing pavement drainage.
4. How do you find the overt value of a pipe?
   a. Run the (Create Watersheds) command.
   b. Run the (Drainage Network) command.
   c. Run the (Inspect Performance) command.
   d. Select the pipe to open the Pipe asset card.

© 2019, ASCENT - Center for Technical Knowledge®

5. How do you size pavement drainage?
   a. Select the component road and right-click.
   b. Select a network feature and right-click.
   c. Run the (Drainage Network) command.
   d. Run the (Inspect Performance) command.

© 2019, ASCENT - Center for Technical Knowledge®

Command Summary

Button	Command	Location
	Create Watersheds	• **In Canvas Tools:** Design, review, and engineer drainage>Design drainage • **In Canvas Tools:** Design, review, and engineer drainage>Analyze your model
	Culverts	• **In Canvas Tools:** Design, review, and engineer drainage>Design drainage
	Drainage Network	• **In Canvas Tools:** Design, review, and engineer drainage>Design drainage
	Inspect Performance	• **In Canvas Tools:** Design, review, and engineer drainage>Analyze your model
	Rainfall Content	• **In Canvas Tools:** Design, review, and engineer drainage>Analyze your model

© 2019, ASCENT - Center for Technical Knowledge®

Chapter 5

Point Cloud Modeling

Reality Capture software is steadily becoming more a part of the engineering workflow as the technology continues to improve. The Autodesk® InfraWorks® software has the ability to import point cloud data and model objects from it.

Learning Objectives in this Chapter

- Import point cloud data into Autodesk InfraWorks.
- Extract features from point cloud data.

© 2019, ASCENT - Center for Technical Knowledge®

5.1 Point Cloud Preparation

Point Clouds are the byproduct of laser scanners, photogrammetry, LiDAR and other sources. They are used to document realistic conditions of a given environment (existing conditions). Whether you are scanning a building or modeling critical infrastructure, Autodesk InfraWorks has the ability to utilize point clouds in their models, as shown in Figure 5–1. Before importing a point cloud, it must be processed in the Autodesk ReCap program and saved as either an .RCS (ReCap Scan) or an .RCP (ReCap Project) file.

Figure 5–1

Import

Point clouds are one of the few data types that can be imported into an empty Autodesk InfraWorks model. They can be used to create a terrain surface as a base for the new InfraWorks model.

© 2019, ASCENT - Center for Technical Knowledge®

How To: Import a Point Cloud

1. Either start a new model or open the model you want to import the point cloud into.
2. Open the Data Sources explorer using the In Canvas tools by clicking (Build, manage, and analyze your infrastructure model)> (Create and manage your model)> (Data Sources).
3. In the Data Sources panel, expand (Add file data source) and select the **Point Cloud** file format, as shown in Figure 5–2.

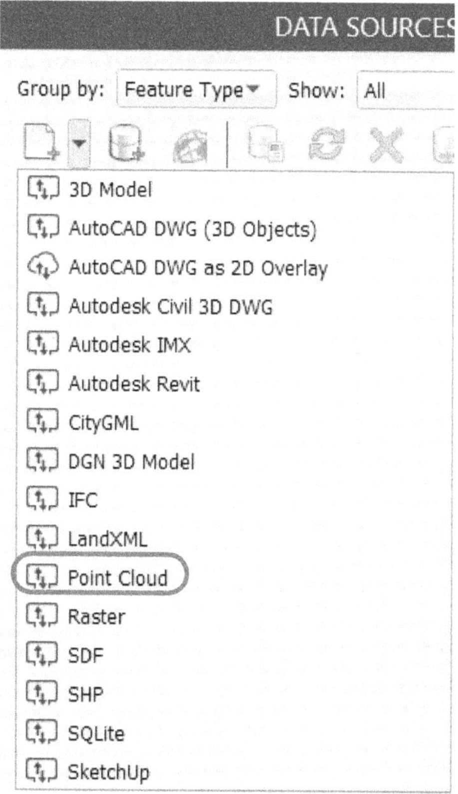

Figure 5–2

Hold <Shift> or <Ctrl> to select multiple files from the directory.

4. Browse to the directory in which the file is located. Select the required file(s) and click **Open**.
5. In the Data Sources palette, double-click on the Point Cloud to configure it.

Point clouds from laser scanners are seldom geo-referenced and need to be positioned manually.

6. In the Data Source Configuration dialog box, set the *Position, Coordinate System* or click **Interactive Placing...**, as shown in Figure 5–3, to correctly position the point cloud in the model.

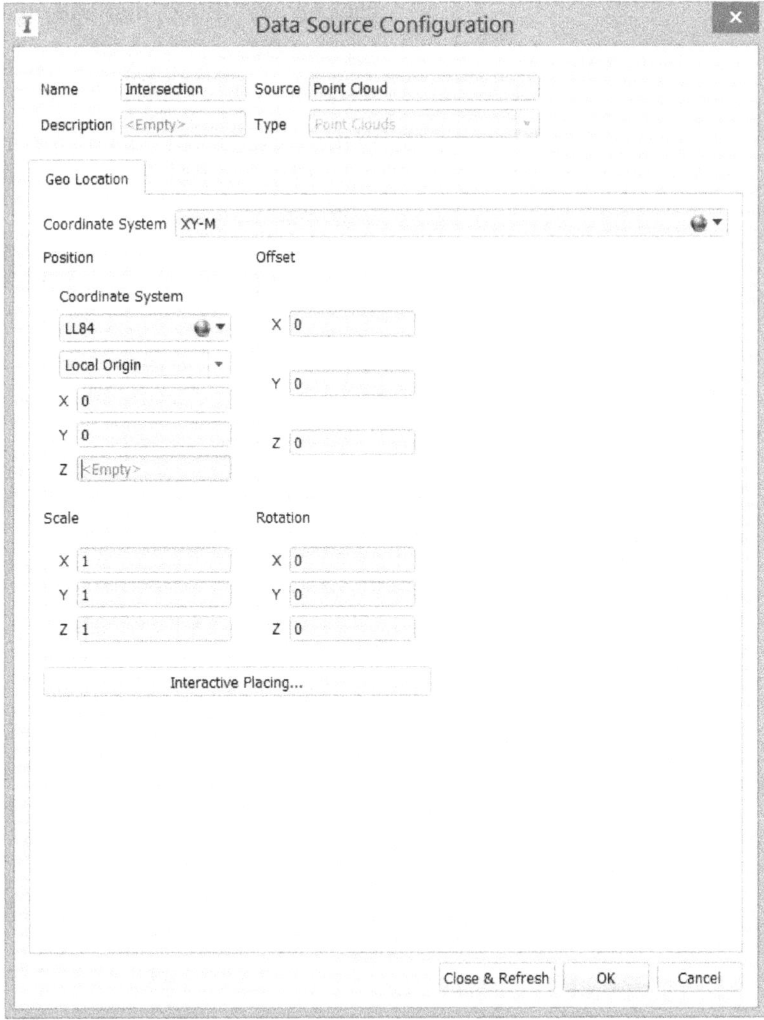

Figure 5–3

7. Click **Close & Refresh**.

© 2019, ASCENT - Center for Technical Knowledge®

Point Cloud Appearance

Theme

Theming a point cloud enables you to view its many points using a range of colors. The colors are based on one of the following analysis types:

Normal *usually refers to the direction in which a surface face is pointing. For points in a point cloud,* ***normal*** *is derived from other points that have a planar relationship with a specific point.*

- **Normal:** Identifies points that are aligned by displaying colors assigned to the X, Y, Z values associated with the direction of the normal for the point. Colors for this type of theme cannot be specified.
- **Elevation:** Similar to the InfraWorks terrain theme by elevation, it colors points according to their Z value or height. The minimum and maximum values are determined automatically, but can be adjusted as required. The color range can be adjusted or a color palette can be set.
- **Single Color:** All points become the same color and no further options are available.
- **Classification:** This option is only available if a point cloud is classified. Points are colored by their classification ID.The color range can be adjusted or a color palette can be set.
- **Intensity:** Normalizes the intensity values of the points.The color range can be adjusted or a color palette can be set.
- **Elevation + Intensity:** Normalizes the intensity values of the points while also considering the elevation. Colors different from an elevation theme are typically uses since saturation is different with the addition of intensity.

Point cloud themes only use the *equal distribution* method for creating ranges.

If you plan to create a surface from the point cloud, it is recommended that you use the *Intensity* options.

© 2019, ASCENT - Center for Technical Knowledge®

How To: Create a Point Cloud Theme

1. In the In Canvas tools, click (Build, manage, and analyze your infrastructure model)> (Analyze your model)> (Point Cloud Themes).
2. In the Point Cloud Themes palette, click (Add a New Theme).
3. In the Theme Properties dialog box (shown in Figure 5–4), define the following settings and click **OK**:
   - **Name:** Type a name for the theme.
   - **Analysis Type:** Select the Analysis type.
   - **Palette Type:** Select the Palette type.
   - **Number of Rules:** If the palette has not already been set, set the number of rules.
   - **Color Range:** Select the color range and transparency. If a Palette Type is selected, the color ranges are set and not editable.

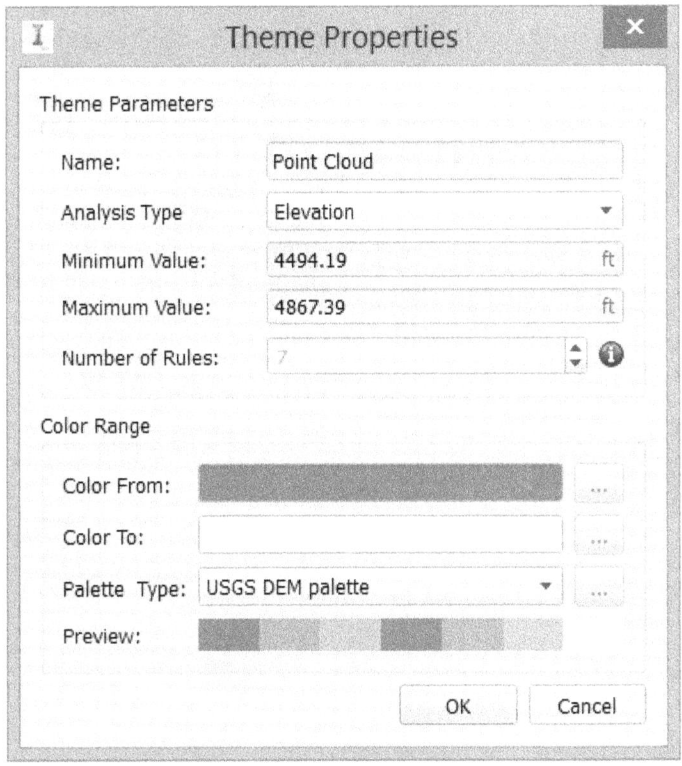

Figure 5–4

© 2019, ASCENT - Center for Technical Knowledge®

Size and Density

In addition to point cloud themes, the application options can be used to change the point cloud appearance. Both the point size and density can be controlled in the Application Options dialog box, under Point Cloud, as shown in Figure 5–5.

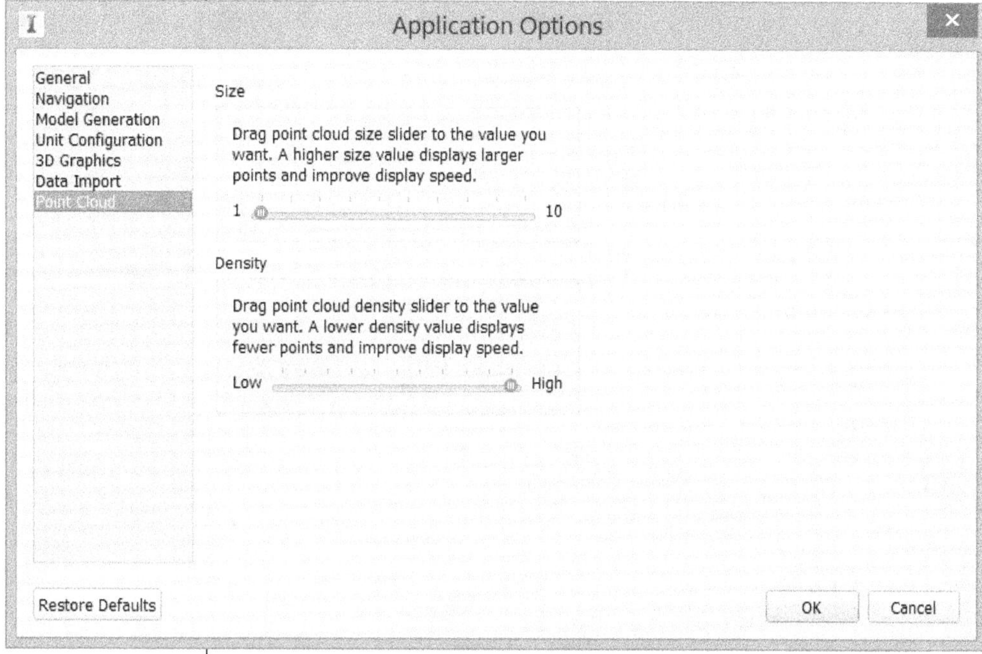

Figure 5–5

Practice 5a Point Cloud Preparation

Practice Objectives

- Import a point cloud.
- Create a point cloud theme.

In this practice, you will create a new model from scratch and then add point cloud data to it. Using the point cloud, you will create a terrain and features for the existing conditions model.

Task 1 - Import a point cloud.

1. In the Home Screen, click **New**.
2. Set the following, as shown in Figure 5–6:
    - *Name*: **Intersection**
    - *Location:* **C:\InfraWorks Design Practice Files**

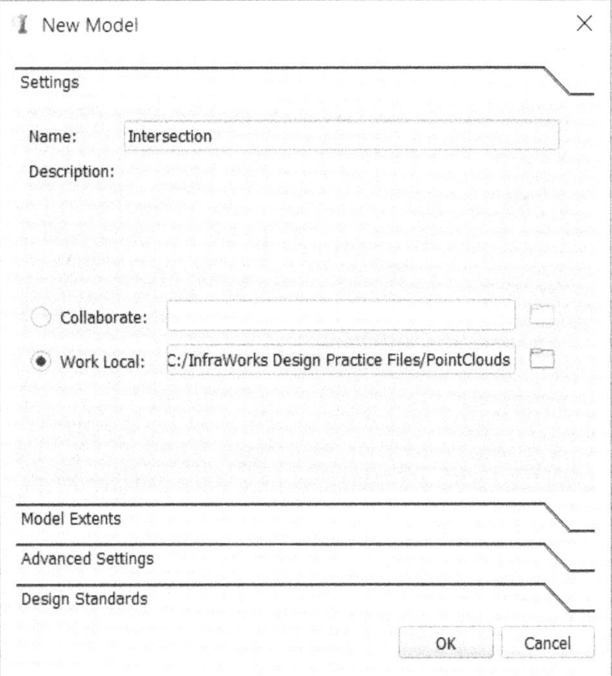

Figure 5–6

3. Click **OK** to create the model.

© 2019, ASCENT - Center for Technical Knowledge®

If the Data Sources palette does not display, in the In Canvas tools, click (Build, manage, and analyze your infrastructure model)> (Create and manage your model> (Data Sources).

4. In the Data Sources palette, expand (Add file data source) and select **Point Cloud**.

5. Browse to *C:\InfraWorks Design Practice Files\PointClouds*, select **Intersection.rcs** and click **Open**.

6. In the Data Sources palette, under *Point Clouds*, double-click on the **Intersection Point cloud** layer to configure it.

7. Note that *Type* is set to **Point Clouds** automatically. In the *Geo Location* tab, ensure that the *Coordinate System* under *Position* is set to **LL84**, then type **0** (zero) in the *X* and *Y* fields, as shown in Figure 5–7. Click **Close & Refresh**.

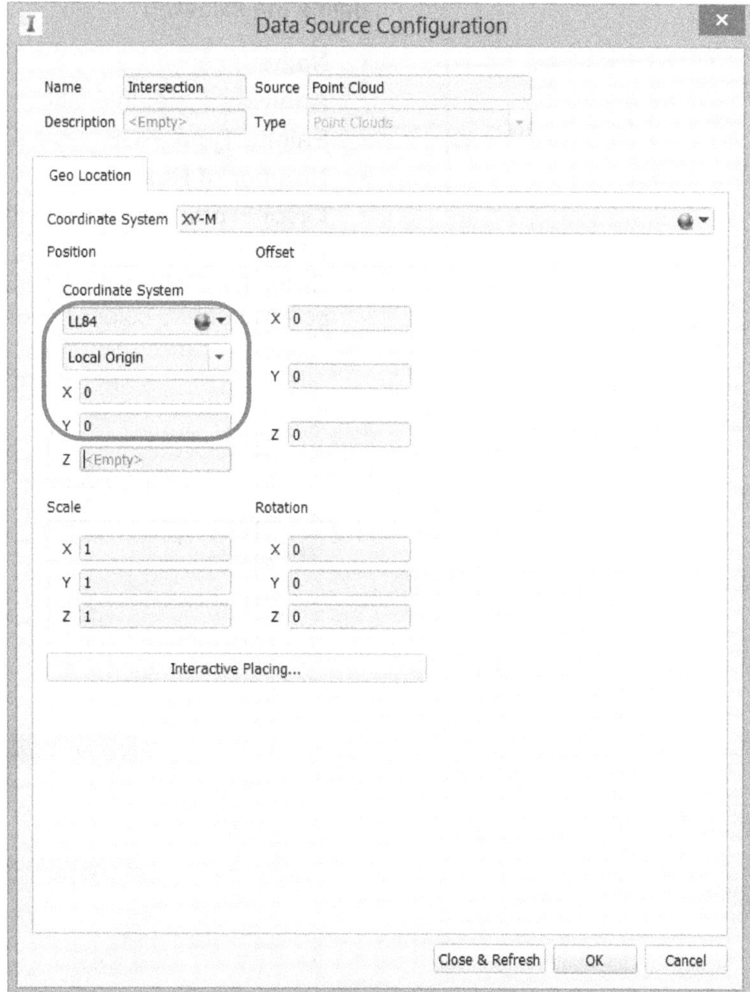

Figure 5–7

Task 2 - Theme a point cloud.

1. In the In Canvas tools, click (Build, manage, and analyze your infrastructure model)> (Analyze your model)> (Point Cloud Themes).

2. In the Point Cloud Themes palette, click (Add a New Theme).

3. In the Theme Properties dialog box (shown in Figure 5–8), define the following:

    - **Name:** Intensity
    - **Analysis Type:** Intensity
    - **Palette Type:** RGB
    - **Number of Rules:** 10
    - **Color From:** Pick on the ellipses (...) and select a color of your choice.
    - **Color To:** Pick on the ellipses (...) and select a complimentary color of your choice.

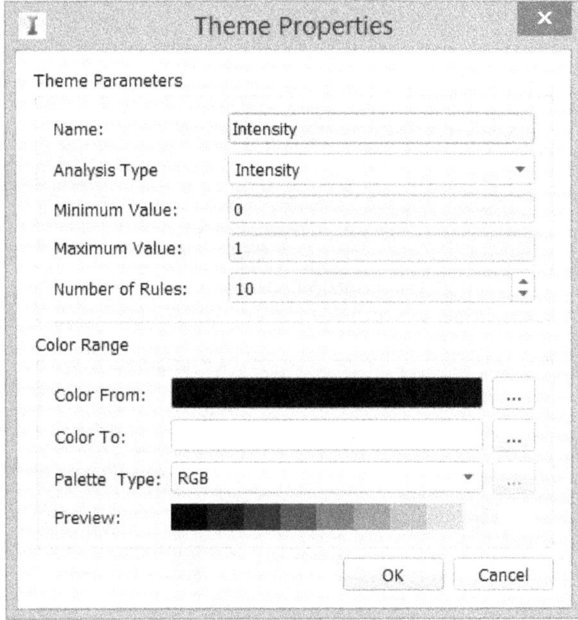

Figure 5–8

© 2019, ASCENT - Center for Technical Knowledge®

- **Palette Type**: Click on the pull-down arrow and select Cyan Ramped Palette, as shown in Figure 5–9.

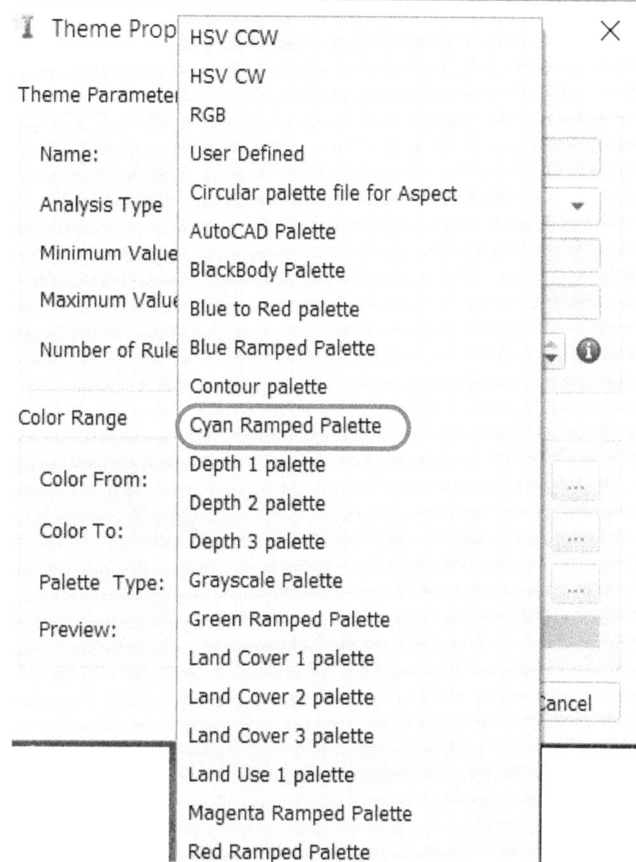

Figure 5–9

- **Color Range**: Note that you can no longer select a different **Color From:** or **Color To:** as they are preset by the color palette.

4. Click **OK**.

5.2 Extract a Point Cloud Terrain

The terrain for the model can be created from one or more point clouds. Simply import the point clouds and use the Point Cloud Terrain tool to process it. During the processing, you can control how the data is analyzed for each of the three feature types:

- **Ground:** Analyzes point groupings that likely fall on the ground to determine the terrain for the model.
- **Linear Feature:** Analyzes linear point groupings to better understand paint stripping and other linear features.
- **Vertical Feature:** Analyzes vertical point groupings to determine where city furniture (signs, benches, etc.) might reside.

Processing Rules determine how much detail within the point cloud to use during the processing. For ground data, you can use the following processing options:

- Less Detail
- Optimum
- More Detail
- Custom

© 2019, ASCENT - Center for Technical Knowledge®

If the **Custom** option is selected, you can set the measurement for the ground detail, the terrain raster resolution, whether or not to fill terrain holes, and the processing window size, as shown in Figure 5–10.

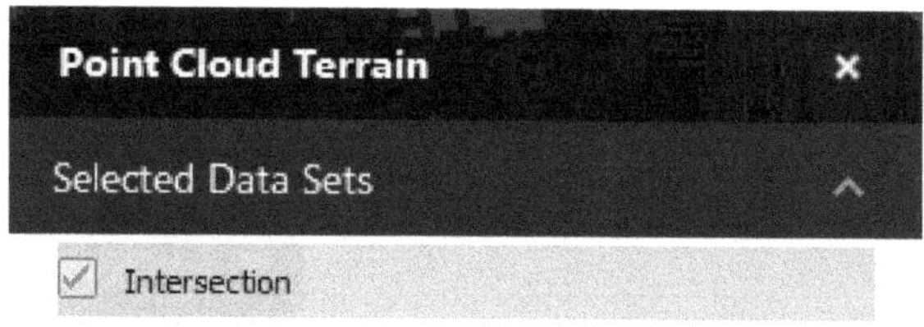

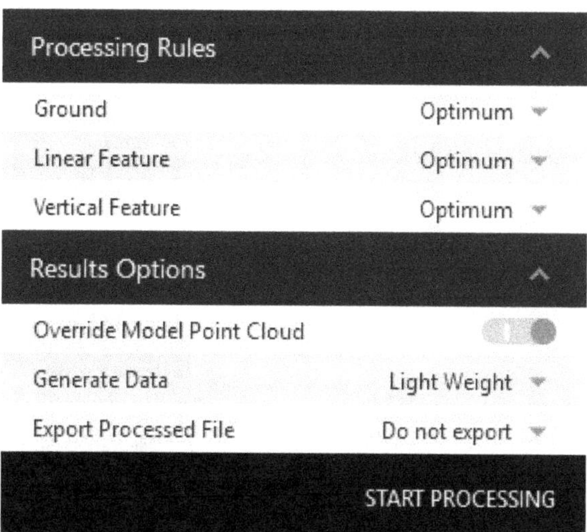

Figure 5–10

How To: Create a Point Cloud Terrain

1. In the In Canvas tools, click (Build, manage, and analyze your infrastructure model)> (Create and manage your model> (Point Cloud Terrain).
2. In the Point Cloud Terrain palette, select which processing rules to use for the ground data, as shown in Figure 5–11.

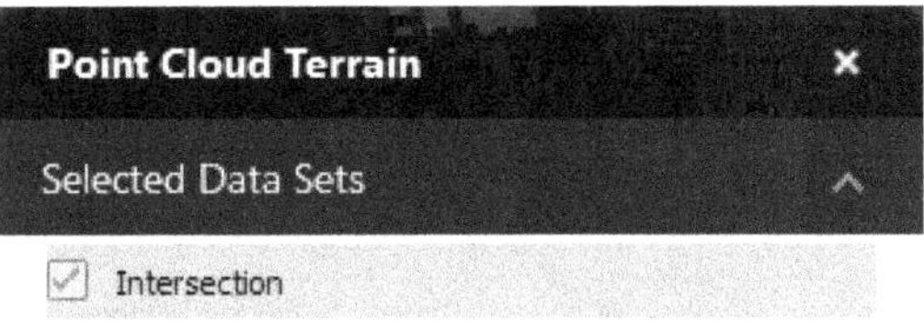

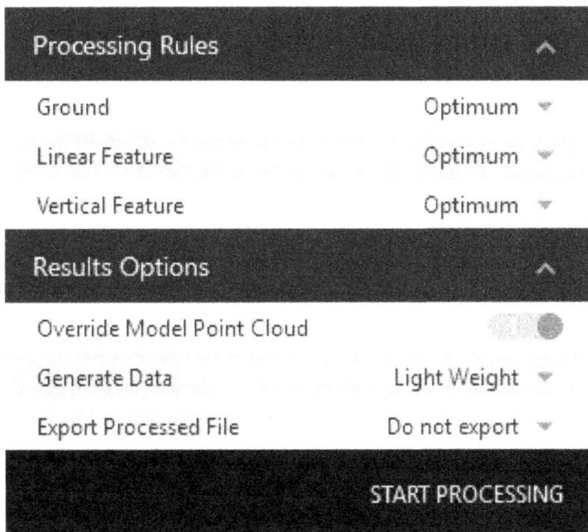

Figure 5–11

3. Click **START PROCESSING**.

© 2019, ASCENT - Center for Technical Knowledge®

5.3 Extract Point Cloud Features

Once the ground data has been extracted, you can also extract additional features. During the Point Cloud Terrain processing, classification ID's are given to points in the point cloud even if they did not exist previously. This can provide more clarity for differentiating features in the model, as shown in Figure 5–12.

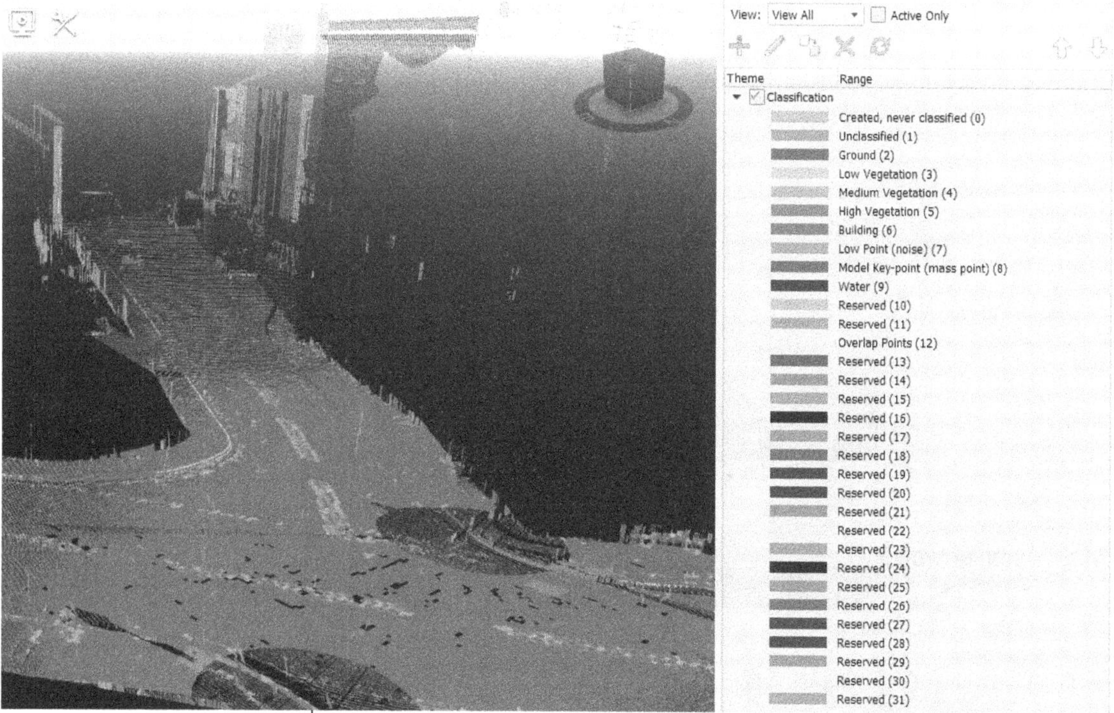

Figure 5–12

Point Cloud Modeling

Point Cloud Modeling analyzes the vertical point groupings to determine where city furniture (signs, street lights, etc.) might reside. Once analyzed, the software automatically zooms to the first feature.

The Point Cloud Modeling palette is used to assign categories to found features. If a feature is automatically assigned an incorrect category, you can change the category in the Point Cloud Modeling palette, as shown in Figure 5–13. Once the category is assigned, the style for the feature can be changed in the feature's asset card, as shown in Figure 5–14.

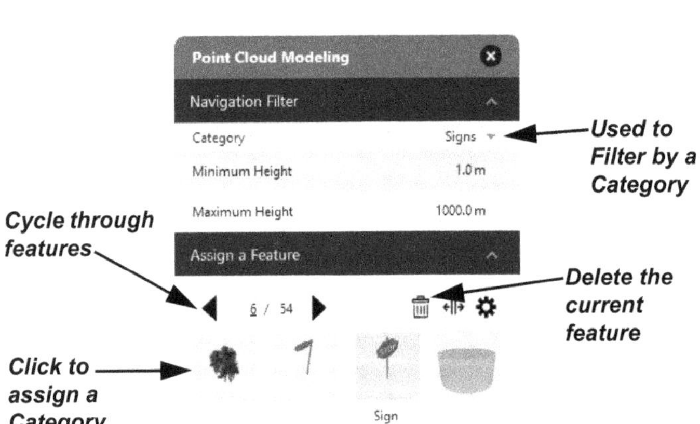

Figure 5–13

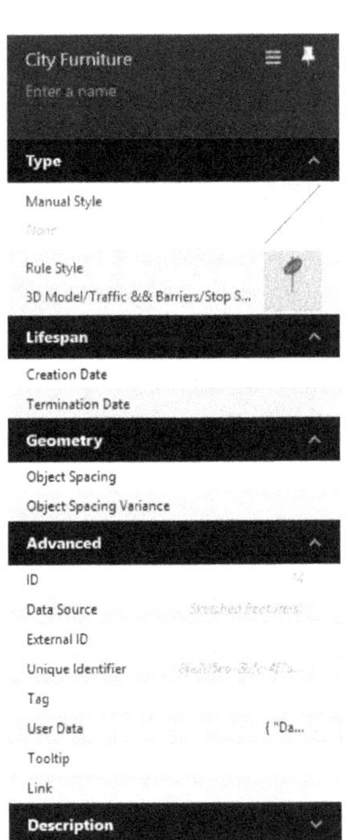

Figure 5–14

How To: Extract Point Cloud Features

1. In the In Canvas tools, click (Build, manage, and analyze your infrastructure model)> (Create and manage your model> (Point Cloud Modeling).

© 2019, ASCENT - Center for Technical Knowledge®

The software automatically zooms in on the first feature found as well as opens that feature's asset card.

2. In the Point Cloud Modeling palette do the following, as shown in Figure 5–15.
   - Select which *Category* you want to filter.
   - Set the *Minimum* and *Maximum Height* values.
   - Under *Assign a Feature*, click on the city furniture to use.

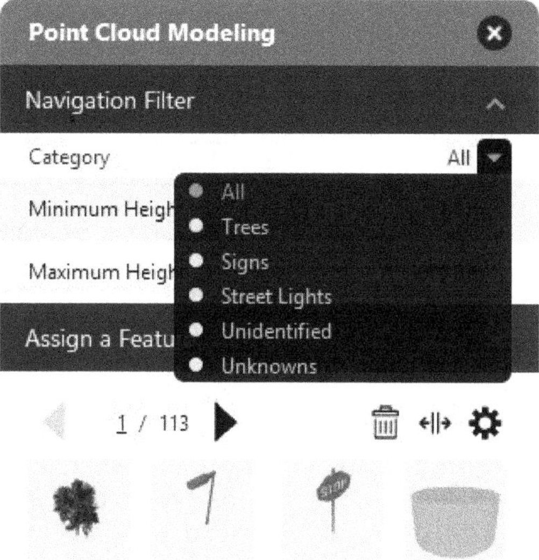

Figure 5–15

3. The generic feature box is turned into the selected category. In the feature palette, select an appropriate style for the feature.
4. Click ▶ (Next) to go to the next found feature.

Practice 5b Point Cloud Modeling

Practice Objectives

- Create a point cloud terrain.
- Create features from point cloud data.

In this practice, you will create a terrain from the point cloud and features for the existing conditions model.

Task 1 - Create a terrain from the point cloud.

1. In the Home Screen, click **Open**.
2. In the *C:\InfraWorks Design Practice Files\RoadwayDesign* folder, select **Modeling.sqlite** and click **Open**.
3. In the Utility Bar, click (Bookmark) and select **Ballard**. Ensure that **B_Task1** is the current proposal.
4. Take some time to navigate around and examine the point cloud.
5. In the In Canvas tools, click (Build, manage, and analyze your infrastructure model)> (Create and manage your model> (Point Cloud Terrain).

© 2019, ASCENT - Center for Technical Knowledge®

6. In the Point Cloud Terrain palette do the following, as shown in Figure 5–16.
   - Select the **Intersection** point cloud to use it. (This is only necessary if you have more than one point cloud in your model.)
   - Leave all the *Processing Rules* set to **Optimum**.
   - Under *Results Options*, set *Generate Data* to **All points**.
   - Click **START PROCESSING**.

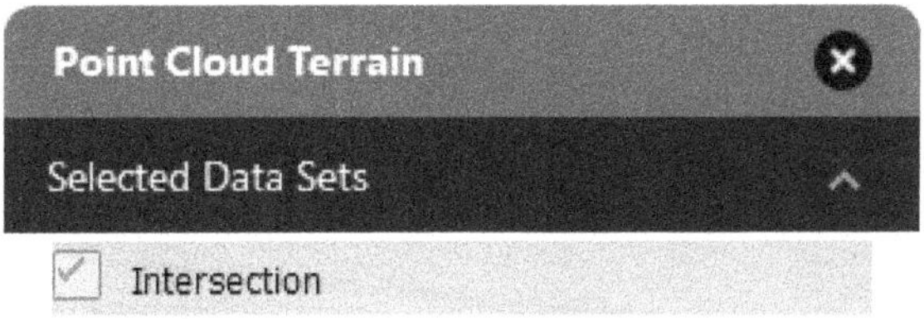

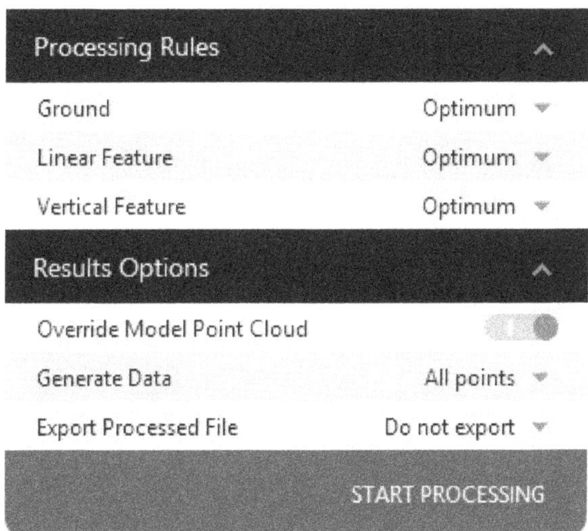

Figure 5–16

7. Review the results.

Task 2 - Classify the point cloud.

1. In the In Canvas tools, click (Build, manage, and analyze your infrastructure model)> (Analyze your model)> (Point Cloud Themes).
2. In the Point Cloud Themes palette, uncheck the *Intensity* theme if it is still selected from the previous task and click (Add a New Theme).
3. In the Theme Properties dialog box, shown in Figure 5–17, define the following:
   - **Name:** Classification
   - **Analysis Type:** Classification
   - **Palette Type:** User Defined
   - **Number of Rules:** Leave the default settings.
   - **Color Range:** Leave the default settings.

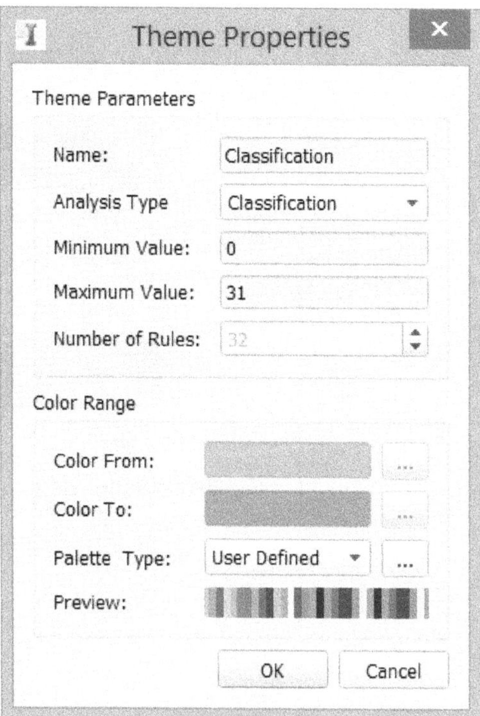

Figure 5–17

4. Click **OK**

© 2019, ASCENT - Center for Technical Knowledge®

Task 3 - Create features from point cloud data.

1. Continue working in the same proposal as the last task. If you did not complete the last task, select **B_Task3** as the current proposal.

2. In the In Canvas tools, click (Build, manage, and analyze your infrastructure model)> (Create and manage your model> (Point Cloud Modeling).

3. The software automatically zooms in on the first feature found as well as opens that feature's asset card. Note that there are *115* features.In the Point Cloud Modeling palette do the following, as shown in Figure 5–18.

Note the reduction in the number of features to assign when Signs is selected.

- Set the *Category* to **Signs**.
- Leave the **Minimum** and **Maximum Height** values as the default heights.
- Under *Assign a Feature*, click on **Signs** as the city furniture to use.

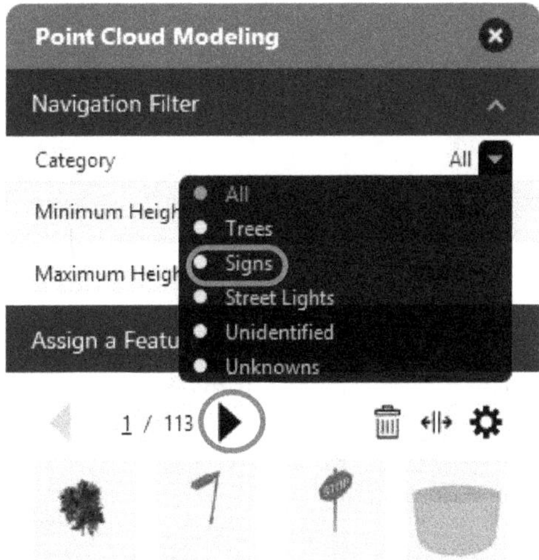

Figure 5–18

4. The generic feature box is turned into the selected style.

5. In the *Assign a Feature* (lower) portion of the Point Cloud Modeling palette, click (Next) to go to the next sign feature.

6. For **Maximum Height,** change the value to **10'**. Note that now 55 objects are found, one less than previous.

7. For **Maximum Height,** change the value to **4'**. Note that now 12 objects are found.

8. Change the **Minimum Height** to **9'** and the **Maximum Height** to **40'**. Now there are only two objects selected and you are zoomed in to the first one, as shown in Figure 5–19.

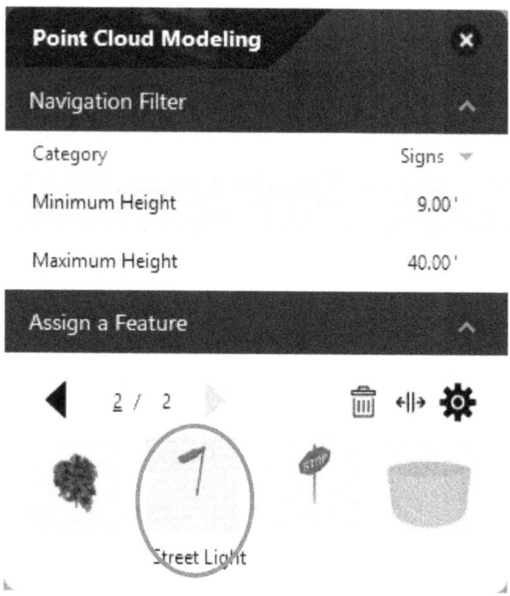

Figure 5–19

9. Assign the two objects to **Street Light**.

10. Continue to choose different heights and select different features as time permits.

© 2019, ASCENT - Center for Technical Knowledge®

Chapter Review Questions

1. Which Point Cloud Theme is recommended if you plan to create a terrain or features from the point cloud?
    a. Normal
    b. Classification
    c. Elevation
    d. Intensity
2. How do you control the size of the points in a point cloud?
    a. In the Point Cloud Modeling palette.
    b. In the Point Cloud Terrain palette.
    c. In the Application Options dialog box.
    d. In the Model Properties dialog box.
3. You can create a Terrain from a point cloud?
    a. True
    b. False
4. How do you change a feature style once it has been assigned a category?
    a. In the Point Cloud Modeling palette.
    b. In the feature asset card.
    c. In the Properties palette.

Command Summary

Button	Command	Location
	Point Cloud Modeling	• **In Canvas Tools:** Build, manage, and analyze your infrastructure model> Create and manage your model
	Point Cloud Terrain	• **In Canvas Tools:** Build, manage, and analyze your infrastructure model> Create and manage your model
	Point Cloud Theme	• **In Canvas Tools:** Build, manage, and analyze your infrastructure model> Create and manage your model

© 2019, ASCENT - Center for Technical Knowledge®

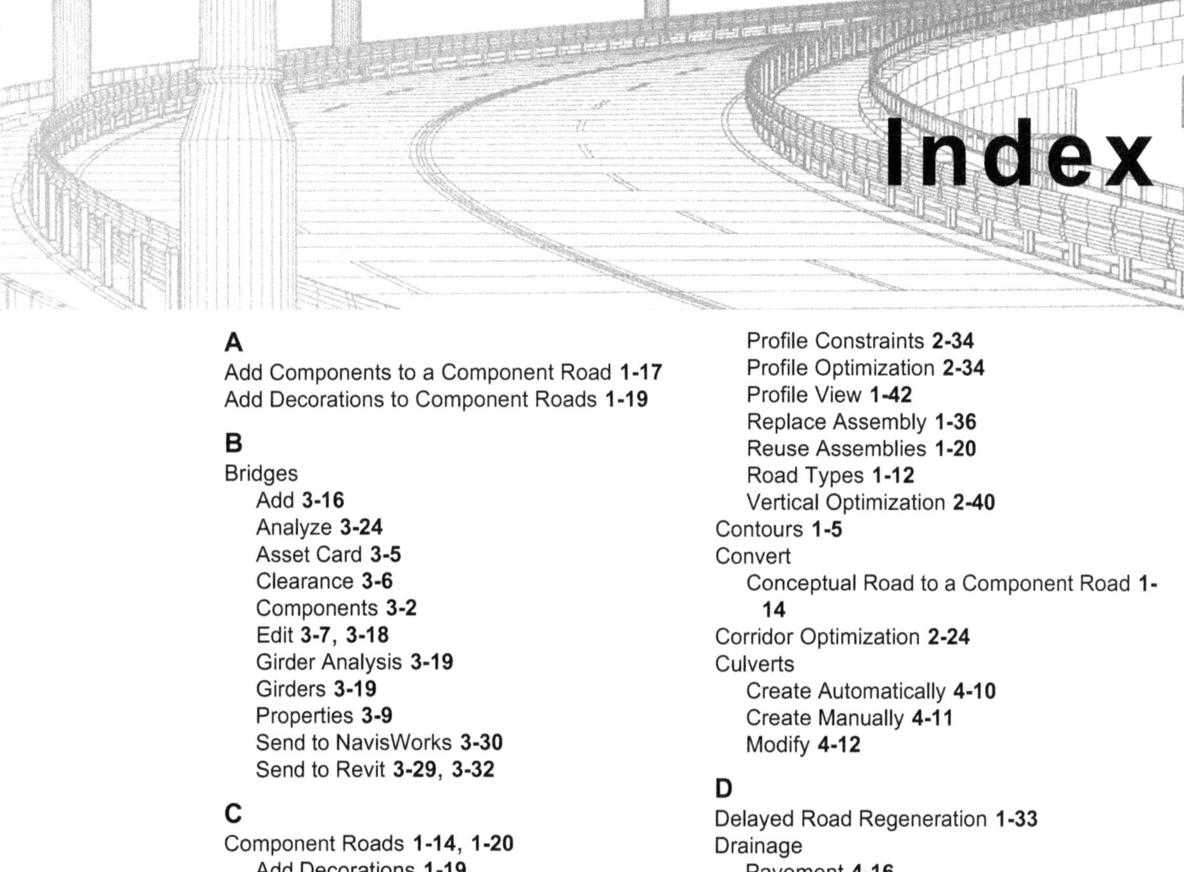

Index

P

Q

R

S

T

W

© 2019, ASCENT - Center for Technical Knowledge®

www.ingramcontent.com/pod-product-compliance
Lightning Source LLC
Chambersburg PA
CBHW061409210326
41598CB00035B/6150

* 9 7 8 1 9 5 1 1 3 9 5 3 7 *